Waking the Dead

George MacDonald
as Philosopher, Mystic & Apologist

Dean Hardy

Waking the Dead
George MacDonald
as Philosopher, Mystic, and Apologist

Copyright © 2020 Dean Hardy

Winged Lion Press
Hamden, CT

All rights reserved. Except in the case of quotations embodied in critical articles or reviews, no part of this book may be reproduced or transmitted in any form or by any means, electronic or mechanical, including photocopying, recording, or by any information storage or retrieval system, without written permission of the publisher. Contact Winged Lion Press www.WingedLionPress.com

Cover portrait of George MacDonald created by Tiffany Hardy

ISBN 13 978-1-935688-21-1

DEDICATION

To my mother
for her encouragement and godly example

ACKNOWLEDGEMENTS

This book, and its previous incarnation as a dissertation, would not have been possible without the help of the communities of Charlotte Christian School, the University of South Africa, and the George MacDonald Society. I would specifically like to thank Ben Ector and Donn Headley for their editing expertise, Robert Trexler and Barbara Amell for their wealth of knowledge and willingness to help with the initial direction of this research, as well as thanks to my dissertation supervisor, Christo Lombaard, for his unending support. Also, I am grateful for John Pennington at *North Wind* for publishing a section of this book while it was still being completed, Kirstin Jeffrey Johnson and John McNeil for their contributions in proofreading and giving valuable input, and Robert Trexler at Winged Lion Press for granting this humble work some exposure to George MacDonald scholars and laypersons alike.

TABLE OF CONTENTS

Introduction ... 1

PART ONE: ... 5
AN EXAMINATION OF GEORGE MACDONALD'S HUMBLE BEGINNINGS AND EXTERNAL INFLUENCES

Chapter 1   George MacDonald: A Brief Biography ... 7
- A Snapshot of the Culture of Nineteenth Century Scotland
- The MacDonald Family
- Other Influences on MacDonald's Thought

PART TWO: ... 23
GEORGE MACDONALD'S PHILOSOPHY AND ITS AFFECT ON HIS MYSTICISM

Chapter 2   MacDonald's Metaphysical Foundations ... 25
- Living in a Shadow World, Examining MacDonald's "Temperamental Platonism"
- *Ex Deo*: Origen, Plotinus and MacDonald's Doctrine of Creation
- "Participation" in the Divine Nature

Chapter 3   Alethiology & Language ... 57
- A Contrast of Propositional Truth with the Embodiment of Truth in Christ
- MacDonald, Augustine, and Swedenborg: Symbols as the Conduit of Divine Truth

Chapter 4   Epistemology and the Attainment of Knowledge ... 75
- Empiricism and Science as the Porch to God's Temple
- The Role of Reason and the Arguments for God's Existence
- Experiential Certainty and Spiritual Logic: A Moral Epistemology

- Samuel Taylor Coleridge, F.D. Maurice, A.J. Scott and MacDonald: the Status and Role of Scripture

Chapter 5   An Outworking of MacDonald's Philosophy and Theology on his Mysticism 113

- Was George MacDonald a "True Mystic?"
- MacDonald's "True Mysticism" and the Doctrine of Becoming

PART THREE: 135
THE APOLOGETICS OF GEORGE MACDONALD

Chapter 6   Modern Implications for George MacDonald's Nineteenth Century Apologetic 137

- An Overview of Apologetic Strategies during the Nineteenth Century
- Was George MacDonald an Apologist?
- An Analysis of MacDonald's Intention, Purpose, and Overall Apologetic Goals
- Rules of Engagement and the Tactful Spirit of the Apologist
- Existential Angst: The Concept of *Sehnsucht* in George MacDonald and C.S. Lewis

Conclusion 189
Bibliography 199
About the Author 211
Index 213
Other Books of Interest 220

INTRODUCTION

Nineteenth century author George MacDonald has influenced some of the greatest writers of the past century. G.K. Chesterton stated, "If we test the matter by strict originality of outlook, George MacDonald was one of the three or four greatest men of 19th century Britain."[1] He even went so far to explain, "I for one can really testify to a book that has made a difference to my whole existence, which helped me to see things in a certain way from the start; a vision of things which even so real a revolution as a change of religious allegiance has substantially only crowned and confirmed. Of all the stories I ever read . . . it remains the most real, the most realistic, in the exact sense of the phrase the most like life. It is called *The Princess and the Goblin*, and is by George MacDonald."[2] *The Oxford Companion to Children's Literature* mentions that MacDonald's *Princess and Goblin* books were some of J.R.R. Tolkien's childhood favorites, and even suggests, "The goblin mines beneath the Misty Mountains in *The Hobbit* owe much to it."[3] C.S. Lewis, on many occasions, identified MacDonald as his literary master and admitted, "I fancy I have never written a book in which I did not quote from him."[4] Oswald Chambers went so far as to write "it is a striking indication of the trend and shallowness of the modern reading public that George MacDonald's books have been so neglected."[5]

While George MacDonald maintained some national and even international success during the later parts of his career, this changed after his death in 1905. Likely due to the peculiarity and complexities of his work, his notoriety wandered off of the edge of the literary map. Chesterton predicted, "Dr. George MacDonald will be discovered some day...until then he will...be neglected, contemned, and quarried

---

1 G.K. Chesterton, "George MacDonald," in *The Daily News* (September 23, 1905).

2 Ibid., 1905.

3 Humphrey Carpenter and Mari Prichard, *The Oxford Companion to Children's Literature* (Oxford: Oxford University Press, 1999), 427.

4 C.S. Lewis, *George MacDonald: An Anthology* (New York: Macmillan, 1947), xxxvii.

5 Oswald Chambers, *Christian Disciplines: Building Strong Christian Character* (Grand Rapids: Discovery House, 1995), 35.

industriously by people who wish to borrow his ideas."[6]

G.K. Chesterton was a prophet. In the last thirty years there has been resurgence in the reading and subsequent scholarly research in the work of George MacDonald. While there seems to be an overwhelming amount of research from critics of the literary as well as the theological persuasion, there is a striking lack of exploration from the mystical, philosophical, and apologetic angle. These aspects of George MacDonald's interior life are usually disregarded.

While many scholars examine MacDonald through the lens of literature or theology, it has yet to be found where a scholar has examined his mysticism in any overt detail. G.K. Chesterton wrote of MacDonald, "When he comes to be more carefully studied as a mystic, as I think he will be when people discover the possibility of collecting jewels scattered in a rather irregular setting, it will be found, I fancy, that he stands for a rather important turning-point in the history of Christendom."[7] It is my contention that Chesterton's suggestion has yet to be fully realized. Whether due to the anti-intellectualism that sometimes is associated with the study of "spirituality," or due to the complex nature of his mysticism[8], the well of his spiritual walk has been seldom tapped.

Even more interestingly, the lack of scholarship in MacDonald's mysticism can only be outdone by the absence of research on his underlying philosophical ideas. This lack of scholarship caused Robert Trexler to write: "Not enough has been written of the theological and political debates of the nineteenth century, especially an exploration of the influence of MacDonald's good friend and mentor, F.D. Maurice, who, after John Henry Newman is probably the most influential and prophetic theologian of the nineteenth century. However, the theological issues of the nineteenth century, as important and under-studied as they have been, *still receive more attention than the philosophical debates upon which they rest.*"[9]

---

6   G.K. Chesterton, "George MacDonald," in *The Daily News* (September 23, 1905).

7   G.K. Chesterton, Introduction to *George MacDonald and His Wife* by Greville MacDonald (Whitehorn: Johannesen, 2005), 13.

8   What Chesterton calls "True Mysticism" in his article, "George MacDonald" in the *Daily News*, 1905.

9   Robert Trexler, "George MacDonald: Merging Myth and Method" in *CSL: The Bulletin of the New York C.S. Lewis Society* Vol. 34, No. 4, July/August 2003, emphasis added.

George MacDonald as Philosopher, Mystic, and Apologist

Thus, the first and foremost focus of this book will be sifting through MacDonald's religious, cultural, and philosophical influences and how these had a direct effect on his personal spirituality and thus, his subsequent writings. Secondarily, the study will focus on establishing MacDonald's philosophical moorings and how these affected his mysticism. Lastly, an emphasis will be placed on modern apologetics and how it contrasts with MacDonald's strategy, as well as an analysis of how MacDonald's approach could be used to influence the new generation of apologists.

Waking the Dead

PART ONE

George MacDonald's Humble Beginnings and External Influences

"My reason for wishing to tell this first portion of my history is, that when I look back upon it, it seems to me not only so pleasant, but so full of meaning, that, if I can only tell it right, it must prove rather pleasant and not quite unmeaning to those who will read it. It will prove a very poor story to such as care only for stirring adventures, and like them all the better for a pretty strong infusion of the impossible; but those to whom their own history is interesting—to whom, young as they may be, it is a pleasant thing to be in the world—will not, I think, find the experience of a boy born in a very different position from that of most of them, yet as much a boy as any of them, wearisome because ordinary."[1]

-George MacDonald

---

1   George MacDonald, *Ranald Bannerman's Boyhood* (Whitehorn: Johannesen, 1999), 9-10.

Waking the Dead

CHAPTER ONE

George MacDonald: A Brief Biography

Introduction

No artist, whether a writer, sculptor, painter, playwright, musician, or architect, operates in a vacuum. To execute due diligence in understanding the work of an artist, one must take into account his environment and influences; this prerequisite is no different in respect to the work of George MacDonald. MacDonald's son-in-law, Edward Troup, writes, "I do not know of any writer the scenes of whose boyhood were so deeply impressed on him, and are so closely associated with his best work."[2] George MacDonald himself wrote in a letter to *The Spectator* in 1867, "Surely it is one of the worst signs of a man to turn his back upon the rock whence he was hewn."[3] Even after a minimal amount of research, a reader can recognize how the Scottish landscapes, the religious severity, and humble living permeate most of MacDonald's work.

While a number of biographies have been written on the life and times of George MacDonald, rewriting a comprehensive memoir will not be my intention here. A brief snapshot of nineteenth century Scotland with a focus on its church history as well as MacDonald's hometown of Huntly should suffice in giving us a scaffolding on which to base our research on his family as well as his religious, philosophical, mystical and literary influences.

A Snapshot of the Culture of Nineteenth Century Scotland

Scotland had been primarily populated by members of the Catholic Church until the work of John Knox in the sixteenth century. This Protestant Reformation changed the religious landscape to predominantly Presbyterianism, and more specifically to the doctrines of John Calvin. Rolland Hein explains that Knox's "convictions, elaborated in the strongly worded Westminster Confession of the mid-seventeenth century, had narrowed and hardened in the people's minds through the centuries of repetition."[4] By the eighteenth century,

---

2   Edward Troup, "George MacDonald's Boyhood in Huntly" reprinted in *North Wind* Vol. 1, 1982, 9.

3   Greville MacDonald, *George MacDonald and His Wife* (Whitehorn: Johannesen, 2005), 38.

4   Rolland Hein, *The Harmony Within: the Spiritual Vision of George*

there were fewer than 30,000 Catholics in all of Scotland and by the time of the birth of George MacDonald in 1824, most religious Scots attended the Church of Scotland, or one of the many churches that seceded from that denomination.[5]

A history of these secessions is not necessary here, and while what was named "The Great Disruption" impacted the later teen years of George MacDonald in 1843, it should be noted that the splintering of the Church of Scotland "had considerably more to do with church government than with doctrine."[6] Thus, while MacDonald was situated in an environment of religious dissension, even rebellion, these squabbles rarely revolved around doctrinal issues.[7] This firm doctrine centered upon "the absolute power, justice, and holiness of God, and the total sinfulness of man" who "can do nothing to contribute to his own salvation."[8] It was the church's dogmatic view of election and man's deserving of eternal punishment, which troubled George MacDonald the most.

The Church of Scotland, better known to Scots as "the Kirk," was an "oppressive, ubiquitous"[9] force in the religious landscape of Scotland. The MacDonalds attended Missionar Kirk in Huntly, which had its grip "firmly on these people."[10] Raeper explains, "The Missionars believed that Christ had died on the cross only for those who had been elected since before the foundation of the world— a limited number chosen capriciously by God with no reference to merit. The thought that people could have a hand in their own salvation was both presumptuous and abhorrent— God chose some and he simply

---

MacDonald (Eureka: Sunrise Books, 1989), 4.

5   John Wolffe, *God and Greater Britain: Religion and National Life in Britain and Ireland* (New York: Routledge, 1994), 31.

6   Rolland Hein, *The Harmony Within*, 4.

7   Greville MacDonald, *George MacDonald and His Wife*, 79. Greville mentions two events of doctrinal consternation during MacDonald's youth: the Church of Scotland dismissed a pastor for his views on atonement in 1831, and in the early 1840s a few churches were disavowed and students dismissed from the Congregational Theological Academy for their adherence to Universal Redemption. It is the latter event of the two that has the strongest effect on MacDonald's theological development.

8   Ibid., 79.

9   Richard H. Reis, *George MacDonald's Fiction: A Twentieth Century View* (Eureka: Sunrise Books, 1989), 20.

10   William Raeper, *George MacDonald* (Batavia: Lion Publishing, 1987), 26.

did not choose others."[11]

This "firm grip" was not merely in the sense of strict Calvinism, but also in the stringent behavioral regulations of day-to-day living. William Raeper continues, "The Missionars were Sabbatarian in the extreme, so much so that the sending out of a child to fetch milk on a Sunday morning was condemned— and while Sunday walking may have been disapproved of by other churches, among the Missionars it was absolutely forbidden. Alcohol…was banned, as was card playing."[12] This influence also extended to the "adventure school" in Huntly that was attended and supported by the Missionars. There the boys learned Latin, Greek and Mathematics, as well as the Shorter Catechism, which by all accounts is "anything but short."[13] MacDonald's teacher was said to be "tyrannical" and if the boys would fail to memorize their text he would keep them "until they could."[14] Later, George MacDonald would use his "adventure school" experience as motivation in *Alec Forbes* where he wrote, "[memorization techniques] made them hate the Catechism, though I am not aware that that was of any great consequence…for my part, I wish the spiritual engineers who constructed it had…glorified God by going no further."[15] While the Missionars were a formidable force in the community, and the youth may have felt squelched by the church's power, they were also, "enthusiastic, exclusive and committed, banding together to protect their morals and worship their God."[16]

Of course, as with any community, Huntly had an undercurrent that flowed in the opposite direction. Raeper notes that in the town, "illicit practices abounded and often burst out into the open."[17] He specifically names the smuggling of duty free goods into the community, the illegal distillation of alcohol, as well as frequent fistfights in the downtown market as examples of this alternate, "godless" subculture.[18] Ironically, while George MacDonald

---

11   Ibid., 26.

12   Ibid., 26.

13   William Raeper, *George MacDonald*, 30.

14   Ibid., 30.

15   George MacDonald, *Alec Forbes of Howglen* (Whitehorn: Johannesen, 2003), 41.

16   William Raeper, *George MacDonald*, 27.

17   Ibid., 27.

18   Ibid., 27.

transferred many of his childhood impressions into his novels, most of the negative elements we find deal not with Huntly's seedy underbelly, but rather with the dogmatism and hypocrisy of the town's religious elite. Just as Jesus of Nazareth focused his spite on the Pharisees of his day, so did MacDonald.

Conversely, MacDonald knew that the poor had a special place in God's heart: "The poor, the beggars in spirit, the humble men of heart, the unambitious, the unselfish…the lowly, who see nothing to admire in themselves, therefore cannot seek to be admired of others; the men who give themselves away— these are the freemen of the kingdom, these are the citizens of the new Jerusalem."[19] Huntly had its share of poor; even the middle class struggled in a hand-to-mouth existence. Raeper explains, "These people had a simple, hard life with little romance in it. Oatmeal was their staple diet. Bread was a luxury. Butcher meat was never on the table except Sunday and then it came with the barley broth in which it was boiled."[20] While the MacDonalds were not rich by any civilization's definition, they were "well off by comparison"[21] to many of the other inhabitants of Huntly. The MacDonalds were generally known as generous to the underprivileged and "held the custom of giving oatmeal to beggars when they came round to beg."[22] George MacDonald's surroundings as a youngster were obviously not a life of privilege, but of "friendship and fights and routine and squalor."[23]

The MacDonald Family

George MacDonald's family was an embodiment of the juxtaposition of security and loss, comfort and pain, life and death. While there were financial constraints on the family due to an uncle's financial mismanagement, these were unnoticed until much later in George's life. In the years of his boyhood, Huntly offered fertile ground for MacDonald's blossoming imagination. Whether it was running in the meadows or playing in the stream that turned the water wheel on his father's mill, or taking a jaunt down to Huntly's castle to relive Scottish history or lore: MacDonald's youth was a world of wonder.

---

19   George MacDonald, *The Hope of the Gospel* (Las Vegas: International Alliance, 2012), "The Heirs of Heaven and Earth," 39.

20   William Raeper, *George MacDonald*, 26.

21   Ibid., 26.

22   Ibid., 28.

23   Ibid., 27.

Greville noted, "To these boys the world was a constant invitation to adventure, for they read into its realistic sweetness and terror the trappings of imaginative romance."[24]

To the other extreme, the MacDonald family struggled with severe health issues. Greville notes that his Grandfather's letters contained anxiety concerning his family's health. Greville himself was "astonished to learn how many of my relatives were thus attacked and yet recovered. When, however, a little later, my Uncles Alec and John suffered from this bleeding, rapid destruction of the lungs ensued."[25] Unfortunately, "the tuberculous disease...destroyed many of them."[26] George himself suffered lung issues all of his life: "George was, however, a delicate boy...he was often kept from school, because of the deep snow or the even more treacherous thaw; his susceptibility to pleurisy, for which he would be bled from the arm, made caution necessary."[27] Of all of these painful reminders of human mortality, the most excruciating was the loss of his mother at the tender age of eight. This obviously had a profound effect on George, but even through this traumatizing event, the family remained stable. Seven years later George's father would marry Margaret McColl. Greville writes, "[t]he new wife took the place of mother in the hearts of both father and boys; indeed my father owed to her everything that the most devoted of mothers can give."[28] He continues to divulge, "[she] revealed a tenderness of heart, a patience in adversity, a penetrating wisdom, together with a power of sympathy..."[29]

The tone of MacDonald's family life centered around one parental figure: his father. George's mother was sickly, then eventually passed away, and his father often had to play both roles as disciplinarian and nurturer. His father was "brave, patient, and generous; finely humorous"[30] and "a man of legendary toughness"[31] as well as having "profound religious convictions."[32] Greville's account

---

24 Greville MacDonald, *George MacDonald and His Wife*, 54.
25 Ibid., 146.
26 Ibid., 54.
27 Ibid., 58.
28 Ibid., 53.
29 Ibid.,53.
30 Ibid., 31.
31 Rolland Hein, *The Harmony Within*, 2.
32 Greville MacDonald, *George MacDonald and His Wife*, 31.

demonstrates his grandfather's humility in strength, as well as the strong bond between George Sr. and his son: "In the care— like woman's rather than man's— with which he tended every human and humbler creature committed to him we behold the strong man. My father knew no fault in him: even as those who are entitled to say it, found no fault in his son."[33]

While death and loss frequently inflicted the MacDonald family, their religious fervor always held fast. They were recognized for their piety, and the Missionar Kirk was attended faithfully each week. It was widely known that George's grandmother had famously thrown a family member's "violin to the flames, lest playing it be detrimental to his faith and that of others."[34] This passion for God, while possibly overzealous, was passed down in a more docile sense to George's father and uncle, who would have prayer meetings at the mill for their workers every week in the evening. Annie Glass, one of their former workers, testified: "They were good Christian men, the MacDonalds."[35]

The MacDonalds' religious fervor is further demonstrated in George's early thoughts of becoming a minister. Greville recounts a humorous story of his father's childhood where a young George "rushed into the kitchen, jumped upon the...table and began a learned discourse, indicating Bell Mavor, the maid, as a reprobate past redemption."[36] After she tried to shoo him away with a towel he responded with, "Ye's no fleg (frighten) awa' the Rev. Geordie MacDonald as gin he war a buzzin' flee (fly)!"[37]

Other Influences on MacDonald's Thought

Tracing the metaphorical "lineage" of George MacDonald's philosophy and theology is crucial in understanding not only the context in which he reasoned, preached and wrote, but also will give us deeper insight about the motivation and influence on his thought. The most obvious way to track MacDonald's influences is to research the books he read, the inferences from the mentioning of philosophers and literary influences in his own writings, and slightly less obviously, the theological viewpoint of the friends he embraced in

---

33   Ibid., 241.
34   Rolland Hein, *The Harmony Within*, 3.
35   William Raeper, *George MacDonald*, 23.
36   Greville MacDonald, *George MacDonald and His Wife*, 59.
37   Ibid., 59.

his inner circle. Demonstration of these facts will be crucial to later arguments in the book. For example, to argue that MacDonald was a "temperamental Platonist" hinges on the fact that MacDonald truly had knowledge of Plato's works, and was at least, whether consciously or subconsciously, influenced by them.

It should be noted that this study will not consult the professors of MacDonald at university, as none stand out as being a particular influence. It should be noted that he did take a course called "Logic and Moral Philosophy" in which Francis Bacon's philosophy of mind and perception was discussed, as well as Natural Theology and the Immorality of the Soul.[38] Beyond this, MacDonald's studies at King's College, Aberdeen, are inconsequential to this research.

A stronger source of influence on MacDonald was his voracious appetite for reading. Later in life, MacDonald revealed his deep, life-long metaphysical affinity toward books:

> Which is the real possessor of a book— the man who has its original and every following edition, and shows, to many an admiring and envying visitor, now this, now that, in binding characteristic, with possessor-pride; yea, from secret shrine is able to draw forth and display the author's manuscript, with the very shapes in which his thoughts came forth to the light of day, —or the man who cherishes one little, hollow-backed, coverless, untitled, bethumbed copy, which he takes with him in his solitary walks and broods over in his silent chamber, always finding in it some beauty or excellence or aid he had not found before— which is to him in truth as a live companion? For what makes the thing a book? Is it not that it has a soul- the mind in it of him who wrote the book?[39]

While the task at hand is crucial, the lineage of MacDonald's reading life is a perplexing enigma. It would be rather uncomplicated if we simply had a listing of MacDonald's library upon death. In 1972, Richard Reis took up this challenge but unfortunately it left him empty-handed: "I have, unfortunately, been quite unable to discover which books were in MacDonald's library; and I presume that it was scattered upon his death."[40] He goes on to elaborate that "Miss Mary MacDonald, Greville MacDonald's adopted daughter, informed

---

38   David S. Robb, *George MacDonald* (Edinburgh: Scottish Academic Press, 1987), 9.

39   George MacDonald, *The Hope of the Gospel*, "The Heirs of Heaven and Earth," 43.

40   Richard H. Reis, *George MacDonald's Fiction*, 33.

me in a private letter of 1958 that the library was, to the best of her knowledge, broken up when George MacDonald died in 1905."[41] Since that time a collection of books from the MacDonald Library have been acquired by the scholars at the Wade Center at Wheaton University. Most of these books were written by MacDonald himself and offer little to no hope of helping in the area of MacDonald's philosophical and literary influences.[42] We are dependent on references to his library in correspondences and Greville's biography, for example, "Law's quarto edition of *Böhme's Complete Works*, and a very early edition of the *Forty Questions* were on his shelves."[43] Beyond this, we will have to infer from MacDonald's own works which books and authors he counted as resources for his own theology and symbolism.

As a youngster, the Bible had a great influence on his thought, but reading fiction was also cherished in the George MacDonald home. Raeper notes that even as a boy MacDonald spent long hours reading books that modern readers would not place into the category of "children's books" such as Klopstock's *Messiah*, Young's *Night Thoughts*, Milton's *Paradise Lost* as well as Bunyan's *Pilgrim's Progress*.[44] Raeper[45] also suggests that these lines from MacDonald's *Ranald Bannerman's Boyhood* were likely autobiographical: "there were very few books to be had in the country, and therefore any mode of literature was precious."[46] In Kirstin Jeffrey Johnson's "Rooted Deep: Relational Inklings of the Mythopoetic Maker, George MacDonald" she makes a point to demonstrate that MacDonald's society may have had more access to literature than once thought, suggesting that it was an "unusually literate environment,"[47] noting the literary scholars of MacDonald's own immediate and distant family as well as the "remarkable" Scottish educational system.

Yet, it was not until his days at King's College, Aberdeen, that MacDonald was granted access to a full library, yet, ironically, the

---

41 Richard H. Reis, *George MacDonald's Fiction*, 147.

42 Wade Center, "George MacDonald Family Library."

43 Greville MacDonald, *George MacDonald and His Wife*, 557.

44 William Raeper, *George MacDonald*, 33.

45 Ibid., 33.

46 George MacDonald, *Ranald Bannerman's Boyhood*, 321.

47 Kirstin Jeffrey Johnson, "Rooted Deep: Relational inklings of the Mythopoetic Maker, George MacDonald" *Informing the Inklings*, Ed. Michael Partridge and Kirstin Jeffrey Johnson (Hamden, CT: Winged Lion Press, 2018), 35.

most influential books were not found on the college campus. The whereabouts of this library has caused much consternation and discussion among MacDonald scholars, for they have not found the location nor the exact contents of the collection. What can be argued succinctly is that in 1842 MacDonald had to forgo a year of college due to financial constraints. While most students would work in the fields during the summer months to earn enough wages to attend school, MacDonald was physically unable to perform such labor and had to look for other employment. He was hired by a family who lived in Northern Scotland who lived in a castle with a large library. Greville remarks that he had "failed to trace" the castle, but "wherever it was, and whatever its scope, added much to the materials upon which his [George MacDonald's] imagination worked in future years."[48] George MacDonald himself writes of the importance of what he discovered therein: "I found in the library…many romances of a very marvelous sort, and plentiful interruption they gave to the formation of the catalogue. I likewise came upon a whole nest of the German classics. I found in these volumes a mine of wealth inexhaustible."[49] William Raeper argues that the library was likely Thurso Castle, of which the owner, George Sinclair, was a German scholar who would likely have had these books in his collection.[50]

Whatever the location, scholars assert that this is where MacDonald was likely "introduced to the strange, yearning, mystic writings of Novalis and the magic of Hoffman. Beyond them he reached to the mystical writings of Swedenborg and Jacob Boehme. The writers he found in the library were the writers who were able to offer MacDonald the key to constructing a theology he could live with and submit to."[51] Many of MacDonald's works are peppered with quotations from these mystics. Most notably, his work *Lilith* ends with Novalis: "Our life is no dream; but it ought to become one, and perhaps will."[52] A little less obvious is MacDonald's connection to Swedenborg, whom he appreciated for his use of symbolism: "Witness some of the writings of the European master of the order—Swedenborg."[53] While these influences altered his theology, these

---

48 Greville MacDonald, *George MacDonald and His Wife*, 71-2.
49 Greville MacDonald, *George MacDonald and His Wife*, 73.
50 William Raeper, *George MacDonald*, 48.
51 Ibid., 49.
52 George MacDonald, *Lilith* (Whitehorn: Johannesen, 2009), 359.
53 George MacDonald, *England's Antiphon* (Whitehorn: Johannesen,

were the same influences that would later cause MacDonald to lose his pastorate, where he was charged with, among other things, being "tainted with German Theology."[54]

MacDonald did not limit his reading to the German Romantics and mystics, but also read the contemporary poets and writers: "He sat and read poetry to the young ladies— Wordsworth and Tennyson and Browning's *Saul* and even his own, but he did not read as an amusement or diversion. Poetry was for him a serious business."[55] One must only look to the table of contents of MacDonald's own *England's Antiphon* to see the dynamic influence of poetry and literature upon the mind of the author. From Spenser to Milton, Lord Bacon to Coleridge, from thirteenth century Miracle Plays to the nineteenth century poets like Browning, MacDonald displays an intimate knowledge of the minds of these writers. MacDonald himself summarized at the end of the book that he had "traced — how slightly! — the course of the religious poetry of England, from simple song, lovingly regardful of sacred story and legend, through the chant of philosophy, to the full-toned lyric of adoration."[56] As a final addition to demonstrate MacDonald's life-long dedication to literature, one only has to look at the table of contents for the *Dish of Orts*; there listed are complete chapters on the work of Shakespeare, Shelley, Wordsworth, and Browning.[57]

While philosophy was not MacDonald's primary reading, it can be established that MacDonald had been exposed to the foundational ideas in ancient and modern philosophy. Kerry Dearborn explains that it was at King's College where MacDonald was exposed to the ancient philosophers, most notably reading the Greek versions of Plato's works.[58] Plato is the most frequently mentioned philosopher in MacDonald's fiction. For example, he had Ethelwin, a character in *Annals of a Quiet Neighbourhood* state: "I took down a volume of Plato to comfort me after the irritation which my nerves had undergone, and sat down in an easy-chair beside the open window of my study."[59]

1996), 232.

54 Greville MacDonald, *George MacDonald and His Wife*, 179.

55 William Raeper, *George MacDonald*, 59.

56 George MacDonald, *England's Antiphon*, 331.

57 George MacDonald, *A Dish of Orts, Chiefly papers on the Imagination, and on Shakespeare* (London: Sampson Low Marston & Co., 1895), iii.

58 Kerry Dearborn, *Baptized Imagination: The Theology of George MacDonald* (Farnham: Ashgate Publishing, 2006), 25.

59 George MacDonald, *Annals of a Quiet Neighbourhood* (Whitehorn:

George MacDonald as Philosopher, Mystic, and Apologist

Plato was also mentioned by Malcolm in *The Marquis of Lossie*, "I can no more do without the truth than Plato. It is as much my needful food and as fully mine to possess as his."[60] Raeper argues that he also focused much of his philosophical reading on "Schelling, the Schlegels, Fichte (whose idealism MacDonald was particularly attracted to), Kant, and Schleiermacher, whose notions of religious experience MacDonald found very attractive."[61] In *Phantastes*, MacDonald quotes from Schleiermacher's *Monologen*: "In still rest, in changeless simplicity, I bear, uninterrupted, the consciousness of the whole of Humanity within me."[62] It also should be mentioned that MacDonald was aware of the rational arguments of the theistic philosophers of his day. Most notably, MacDonald was aware of William Paley, the 18th century clergyman, and the arguments within his *Natural Theology*: "We are not satisfied that the world should be a proof and varying indication of the intellect of God. That was how Paley viewed it. He taught us to believe there is a God from the mechanism of the world."[63]

The information above demonstrates that Ronald MacDonald was right about his father when he wrote that George was:

> ...a great reader, of wide, and, in some subjects, profound erudition. His knowledge of English poetry from Chaucer to Browning surpassed that of any other man whose knowledge I have known. His familiarity with the thought and writings of William Law, Henry More, George Fox, Blake, Swedenborg, Behemen and Jean Paul Richter – and I know not what other mystics . . . He had both the scholar's and the poet's mastery of Milton, Shakespeare, and Dante; he read his Germans, his Frenchmen, and his Italians in their own words; he read the New Testament at least (with which he would always begin his attack upon a new language) in Dutch, modern Greek, and, I think, Spanish.[64]

Not only did he have deep knowledge of these mystics, poets,

Johannesen, 2004), 62.

60 George MacDonald, *The Marquis of Lossie* (Whitehorn: Johannesen, 2004), 90.

61 William Raeper, *George MacDonald*, 242.

62 George MacDonald, *Phantastes* (Whitehorn: Johannesen, 2009), 226.

63 George MacDonald, *A Dish of Orts*, "Wordworth's Poetry," 256.

64 Ronald MacDonald, *From a Northern Window: A Personal Reminiscence of George MacDonald by His Son*, ed. Michael Philips (Eureka: Sunrise Books, 1989), 54.

philosophers and theologians, he was able to use and synthesize their ideas in his own work. For instance in *Seaboard Parish*, MacDonald writes a conversation that discussed the preexistence of the soul, "But you don't agree with Wordsworth, do you, about our having had an existence previous to this?' ... 'Not in the least. But an opinion held by such men as Plato, Origen, and Wordsworth, is not to be laughed at, Mr. Turner."[65] In this one statement MacDonald infers his background knowledge of the ancient philosophers, theologians and early church fathers, as well as contemporary poets.

In review, to say that George MacDonald was a voracious reader of all sorts of literature is an understatement. Kirstin Jeffrey Johnson states: "As a result, while it might appear – even to the Victorian English reader, let alone the reader of today – a little romantic that MacDonald's Scottish farmhands are found out in the field reading Plato and Euclid alongside Burns and Scott (not to mention Dante, Milton, and Klopstock) this is *not* the stuff of fiction: it actually happened."[66] This commitment to literature directly influenced his own work. For instance, Kirstin Jeffrey Johnson researched *David Elginbrod* and found ninety explicit references to other works of literature, and each directly engage the story-line. She concluded that "the clearly evident literary influences upon MacDonald's works alone number in the hundreds, and he is careful to draw explicit attention to many of them."[67]

Last in this series of influences are the friends that MacDonald held dear. George MacDonald was known to be a peer of many of the nineteenth century's most influential writers such as "Alfred Tennyson, Charles Kingsley…Harriet Beecher Stowe, Oliver Wendell Holmes, Samuel Clemens, and H.W. Longfellow."[68] While these were to have an impact on MacDonald, and we have recorded interactions between the authors[69], many of these occurred later in life. These were not

---

65 George MacDonald, *The Seaboard Parish* (Whitehorn: Johannesen, 2004), 314.

66 Kirstin Jeffrey Johnson, *Rooted in All its Story, More is Meant than Meets the Ear* (Ph.D. diss., University of Saint Andrews, 2011), 27.

67 Kirstin Jeffrey Johnson, "Rooted Deep: Relational Inklings of the Mythopoetic Maker, George MacDonald," 42

68 Richard H. Reis, *George MacDonald's Fiction*, 17-8.

69 Greville MacDonald, in his *George MacDonald and his Wife* records a letter from Samuel Clemens to his father (458), as well as a visit to The Retreat in Hammersmith by Tennyson (380).

George MacDonald as Philosopher, Mystic, and Apologist

intimate friendships that affected MacDonald's theological formation. Instead, we will follow the direction of Greville MacDonald who wrote, "I must tell something of A.J. Scott, who takes rank with Greville Matheson, John Ruskin and Frederick Denison Maurice as the choicest friends of my father."[70] While Greville Matheson was the "earliest of brother-like friends"[71] for MacDonald, his influence was more of a literary persuasion; he and MacDonald would spend time critiquing each other's work.[72] While he was a close confidant of MacDonald's, there is little discussion of his influence over MacDonald's theology.

John Ruskin, the art critic and social thinker, was introduced to George MacDonald in 1863; their friendship blossomed to deep intimacy almost immediately.[73] While the initial correspondence usually revolved around Ruskin's relationship with a teenage girl who was twenty-nine years his junior, it later included deep discussion about Ruskin's loss of faith in Christianity and an elaboration of both men's theology. Though the two were "different in temperament and endowment, neither was afraid of speaking plainly in their disagreements . . . Ruskin freely criticized, sometimes scathingly, my father's writings and creed."[74] For instance, Greville documents a letter where Ruskin describes George MacDonald's *Unspoken Sermons* as "unspeakably beautiful" but in the next sentence remarks, "[i]f they were but true."[75] It is here in this correspondence that MacDonald confronts the rational and empirical epistemology of Ruskin, and infuses his own way of knowing and his own particular apologetic.[76]

Upon the death of A.J. Scott, George MacDonald wrote, "He who has left us was the best and greatest of our time...He was—he is—my friend. He understood me, and gave me to understand him."[77] Greville also stated that his father thought him "the greatest intellect he had known."[78] MacDonald thought so much of this man that he

---

70   Greville MacDonald, *George MacDonald and His Wife*, 192.
71   Ibid., 417.
72   William Raeper, *George MacDonald*, 67.
73   Greville MacDonald, *George MacDonald and His Wife*, 328.
74   Greville MacDonald, *George MacDonald and His Wife*, 330.
75   Ibid., 337.
76   This correspondence will be elucidated in Chapter 4.
77   William Raeper, *George MacDonald*, 359.
78   Greville MacDonald, *George MacDonald and His Wife*, 192.

gave his name to his first-born child, Lilia Scott MacDonald.[79] In his mid-twenties, MacDonald began attending Scott's lectures at the Marylebone Institute in London.[80] Scott was invited to become a pastor of a church, but then had to refuse because he could not wholly subscribe to the Westminster Confession of Faith. He disagreed with the statement "none are redeemed by Christ but the elect only."[81] He later would be charged with heresy by the presbytery of Paisley, and his license to preach was seized.[82] He then moved to Manchester to be Principal of Owens College.[83] MacDonald was influenced by Scott's "wider view of salvation, love of literature"[84] as well as his concerns for social issues. It's been suggested by some that Scott introduced MacDonald to the work of Dante, but without a doubt, A.J. Scott became a loyal friend and mentor throughout MacDonald's life.[85] Later in this study, the influence of Scott on MacDonald's view of special revelation will be explored.[86]

While Scott seemed to be one of MacDonald's most intimate confidants, it could be argued that Frederick Denison Maurice had the most profound impact on MacDonald's thinking.[87] Kerry Dearborn argues that MacDonald likely first learned of Maurice while studying for the ministry at Highbury Theological College.[88] In 1853, Maurice's *Theological Essays* was published, and the content therein resulted in Maurice being dismissed from his professorial office at King's College. Ironically, this was the same year in which MacDonald himself was dismissed from his position of ministry. After hearing Maurice's inaugural address at the Working Men's College in 1854, MacDonald soon "became a disciple of his"[89] which resulted in agreement with Maurice on multiple issues such as "the

---

79   Ibid., 159.
80   William Raeper, *George MacDonald*, 67.
81   Ibid., 68.
82   Ibid., 68.
83   Ibid., 97.
84   Ibid., 68.
85   Ibid., 68.
86   This can be found in the last section of Chapter 4.
87   Rolland Hein, *The Harmony Within*, 18.
88   Kerry Dearborn, *Baptized Imagination: The Theology of George MacDonald*, 50.
89   Ibid., 50.

Fatherhood of God and the conviction that Christ is absolutely at one with the Father [affecting his view of the atonement]...rejected the idea that sin would be eternally punished, emphasized the 'Inner Light' with the possibility of revelation to the individual apart from Scripture (but not inharmonious with it)."[90]

Raeper argues, "Maurice's influence on MacDonald cannot be stressed too strongly. MacDonald's son was named after the great man, and where Maurice led with his theological light, MacDonald followed. Maurice, like Coleridge (and MacDonald), looked back to the Cambridge Platonists, to Plato himself and Plotinus, as the wellspring of much of his thinking, stopped off on the way to consult the mystics Swedenborg and Boehme."[91] Greville goes so far as to write that he did not think that doctrinally "there was any sort of difference between F. D. Maurice and George MacDonald."[92]

In conclusion, research has uncovered the extensive cultural, philosophical, literary, and even the social influences on the thought and subsequent writings of George MacDonald. In the following pages, these foundational influences will be quarried and excavated in connection with MacDonald's metaphysic, alethiology, epistemology, mysticism, and finally, his apologetic.

---

90 Rolland Hein, *The Harmony Within*, 18-19.
91 William Raeper, *George MacDonald*, 240.
92 Greville MacDonald, *George MacDonald and His Wife*, 400.

Waking the Dead

PART II

George MacDonald's Philosophy and its Affect on His Mysticism

"Novalis has said: 'Die Philosophie ist eigentlich Heimweh, ein Trieb überall zu Hause zu sein.' (Philosophy is really home-sickness, an impulse to be at home everywhere.) The life of a man here, if life it be, and not the vain image of what might be a life, is a continual attempt to find his place, his centre of recipiency, and active agency…. [But] he is not at home; his soul is astray amid people of a strange speech and a stammering tongue. But the faithful man is led onward; in the stillness that his confidence produces arise the bright images of truth; and visions of God, which are only beheld in solitary places, are granted to his soul."[1]

-George MacDonald

---

1 George MacDonald, *A Dish of Orts*, "Browning's 'Christmas Eve,'" 211-12.

Waking the Dead

CHAPTER TWO

MacDonald's Metaphysical Foundations

Introduction

The fact that the philosophy of MacDonald has rarely been researched is not due to a lack of willing hearts or due to uneducated researchers. It is likely due to the fact that even a tertiary student of MacDonald recognizes that he had a negative attitude toward the discipline. Bruce Hindmarsh stated that the "One thing he [MacDonald] never claimed to be...was a theologian."[2] Hindmarsh is correct, but in addition, MacDonald also ignored the title of "philosopher" for the same reasons. It's possible that the reason for which MacDonald disliked both labels was not due to the disciplines in-and-of themselves, but rather the outworking of these fields of study on the religious culture and the personal spiritual lives of those who lived in the Victorian era. MacDonald's reasons for disregarding these disciplines will be explained, as well as his belief that there is, in fact, a correct theology and philosophy.

MacDonald never publicly placed himself into any theological or philosophical system, and his reasons for doing so were primarily preventative and reactionary. MacDonald himself said in a letter to his father, "I am neither Arminian or Calvinist. To no system could I subscribe"[3] as well as saying "Jesus Christ is my theology, and nothing else."[4] One of the reasons why he never sought to proclaim his systematized theology was that he was worried about being pigeonholed into one system of belief. He writes in his sermon entitled "Light," "But if one happens to utter some individual truth which another man has made into one of the cogs of his system, he is in danger of being supposed to accept all the toothed wheels and their relations in that system."[5] MacDonald was concerned about being

---

2   Douglas Bruce Hindmarsh, "George MacDonald and the Forgotten Father" in *North Wind* Vol. 9, 1991, 55.

3   Beinecke Collection, The George MacDonald Collection at the Beinecke Rare Book and Manuscript Library, 1830-1890, letter dated April 15, 1851.

4   Anonymous, "Dr. MacDonald's Testimony" in *Wingfold: Celebrating the Works of George MacDonald* (Vol. 87, 2012), 31. Originally published in *Christian World,* July 20, 1882.

5   George MacDonald, *Unspoken Sermons,* "Light," (Memphis: Bottom

misconstrued and misinterpreted, and encouraged others to also eschew choosing a system of belief, "Therefore, if only to avoid his worst foes, his admirers, a man should avoid system. The more correct a system the worse will it be misunderstood; its professed admirers will take both its errors and their misconceptions of its truths, and hold them forth as its essence."[6]

Philosophy and theology did much during the Victorian period to divide and dis-unify the church until the body of Christ was barely recognizable. MacDonald contends:

> All those evil doctrines about God that work misery and madness, have their origin in the brains of the wise and prudent, not in the hearts of the children. These wise and prudent, careful to make the words of his messengers rime with their conclusions, interpret the great heart of God, not by their own hearts, but by their miserable intellects; and, postponing the obedience which alone can give power to the understanding, press upon men's minds their wretched interpretations of the will of the Father, instead of the doing of that will upon their hearts. They call their *philosophy* the truth of God, and say men must hold it, or stand outside. They are the slaves of the letter in all its weakness and imperfection, — and will be until the spirit of the Word, the spirit of obedience shall set them free.[7]

MacDonald concluded that to choose and broadcast a specific system or denomination would simply cause more division and detract from the Gospel and the mere Christianity which he advocated. MacDonald argued that, "Division has done more to hide Christ from the view of men, than all the infidelity that has ever been spoken."[8] He specifically pointed out the issue of divisiveness within the church: "The real schismatic is the man who turns away love and justice from the neighbour who holds theories in religious philosophy, or as to church-constitution, different from his own; who denies or avoids his brother because he follows not with him; who calls him

---

of the Hill Publishing, 2012), 250.

6   George MacDonald, *Weighed and Wanting* (Boston: D. Lothrop and Company, 1882), 332.

7   George MacDonald, *The Hope of the Gospel*, "The Yoke of Jesus," 69, emphasis added.

8   George MacDonald, *Paul Faber-Surgeon* (Whitehorn: Johannesen, 2009), 192.

a schismatic because he prefers this or that mode of public worship not his."[9] This concept struck close to MacDonald's heart, for in the middle of the nineteenth century a small schism in his church in Arundel had charged him with heresy that eventually caused him to resign.[10] Rolland Hein summarizes succinctly, "MacDonald, who would ally himself with no system, scorns the sectarian mentality that so vehemently expends its energies in futile clashes with those of opposing opinions."[11] MacDonald was simply concerned that by proclaiming a philosophical or theological system, he would have been throwing fuel on a fire that he longed to extinguish.

Third, MacDonald truly believed that certain theologies, as well as an obsession for theological deliberation, could actually detract from one's relationship with the Father and one's duty to serve him. He argued that men have a habit of spending too much time focusing on their theology, and not enough on loving God and his fellow men: "Zeal for God will never eat them up; why should it? He is not interesting to them: theology may be; to such men religion means theology."[12] MacDonald went so far as to specifically state, "I firmly believe that people have hitherto been a great deal too much taken up about doctrine and far too little about practice."[13]

Not only was MacDonald worried that an infatuation with theology could poorly affect our praxis, but the theology itself could be faulty, and consequently one's view of God could poorly influence our relationship with him. Rolland Hein explains, "In many novels the chief deterrent to a successful journey toward a spiritual maturity is contact with false ideas about God's character and manner of working in the world, particularly those fostered by mean and popular versions of Calvinist doctrines."[14]

George MacDonald did not pull punches when it came to certain theological beliefs; for instance, he goes so far as calling the doctrines of the atonement and eternal torment, "doctrines of devils."[15] In *Robert*

---

9 George MacDonald, *The Hope of the Gospel*, "The Salt and Light of the World," 80.
10 William Raeper, *George MacDonald*, 90.
11 Rolland Hein, *The Harmony Within*, 98.
12 George MacDonald, *The Hope of the Gospel*, "The Yoke of Jesus," 68.
13 Greville MacDonald, *George MacDonald and His Wife*, 155.
14 Rolland Hein, *The Harmony Within*, 120.
15 George MacDonald, *Unspoken Sermons*, "The Truth in Jesus," 179.

Falconer, MacDonald took aim at Federal Calvinism, the creed of his youth: "For now arose within him, not without ultimate good, the evil phantasms of a theology which would explain all God's doings by low conceptions, low I mean for humanity even, of right, and law, and justice, then only taking refuge in the fact of the incapacity of the human understanding when its own inventions are impugned as undivine. In such a system, hell is invariably the deepest truth, and the love of God is not so deep as hell. Hence, as foundations must be laid in the deepest, the system is founded in hell, and the first article in the creed that Robert Falconer learned was, 'I believe in hell.'"[16]

It is also an established fact that MacDonald sought to question the prevailing systems of his day. One of his purposes was to "… deliver the race from the horrors of such falsehoods, which by no means operate only on the vulgar and brutal, for to how many of the most refined and delicate of human beings are not their lives rendered bitter by the evil suggestions of lying systems — I care not what they are called — philosophy, religion, society, I care not! — to deliver men, I say, from such ghouls of the human brain, were indeed to have lived!"[17] He simply believed that strict Calvinism was a barricade to one's relationship with God, even going so far as to write "To have to believe in the God of the Calvinist would drive me to madness or atheism."[18] The following assessment will be helpful in understanding the spirit of MacDonald's stance. This review of one of MacDonald's lectures in London from a direct, albeit anonymous observer, was originally published in *Christian World* in 1882:

> It is the breaking up of old habits of theological thought, or the exercise of a happy liberty in regard to it, that has prepared the way for a preacher who avows himself, as Dr. MacDonald did on Sunday, to be no theologian, but who feels that the truth of God is to be reached in other ways than by a theological key. There ought, indeed, to be nothing startling in this, for it is evident that souls did somehow find the truth of God before Christianity knew anything of scientific theology. That the formulating of the truth of the New Testament into a system has been helpful to some minds, there can be no doubt. But the transposing of 'truth as it is in Jesus' into a system has also

---

16   Greville MacDonald, *George MacDonald and His Wife*, 98.

17   George MacDonad, *Thomas Wingfold, Curate* (Whitehorn: Johannesen, 2002), 38.

18   Rolland Hein, *George MacDonald: Victorian Mythmaker* (Whitehorn: Johannesen, 1999), 497.

hindered some minds from getting at Christ Himself, they having rested in the system, and only comprehend as much of Christ as they could see through the system.[19]

Thus, theological systems could cloud the lenses of one's faith in Christ and MacDonald could help to clean the lens.

While it is obvious that he spoke negatively about these disciplines, and even claimed not to espouse a particular theological system; his claims that he publically dismissed systems didn't mean that he didn't have a systemized theology and philosophy. Just because MacDonald did not like the title of "philosopher" or "theologian" does not mean that he was not one. If we are to take the words of Francis Schaeffer seriously, we should argue that all rational beings are philosophers: "No man can live without a worldview; therefore there is no man who is not a philosopher."[20] The central difficulty with arguing that MacDonald was not a theologian resides in the fact that in order for him to be able to point out the falsity of any system, which he did on many occasions, he must purport to know the truth. MacDonald argued this point himself in his sermon "The Last Farthing": "Any system which tends to persuade men that there is any salvation but that of becoming righteous even as Jesus is righteous; that a man can be made good, as a good dog is good, without his own willed share in the making; that a man is saved by having his sins hidden under a robe of imputed righteousness — *that system, so far as this tendency, is of the devil and not of God.* Thank God, not even error shall injure the true of heart; it is not wickedness. They grow in the truth, and as love casts out fear, so *truth casts out falsehood.*"[21]

This casting out of falsehood was the first step to replacing the erroneous view of God with the truth. The difference between MacDonald and his counterparts is that he would rather the reader seek the truth on his own, rather than have MacDonald force-feed them his own personal views. It is no surprise when he writes, "I know, however, that there were words in it which found their way to my conscience; and, let men of science or philosophy say what they will, the rousing of a man's conscience is the greatest event in his

---

19   Anonymous, "Dr. MacDonald's Testimony," 30-1.

20   Francis A. Schaeffer, *He is There and He is not Silent* (Wheaton, Illinois: Tyndale, 2001), 4.

21   George MacDonald, *Unspoken Sermons*, "The Last Farthing," 125, emphasis added.

existence."²² But for MacDonald himself, his conscience had been raised, and he did, in fact, purport to have a proper philosophical and theological underpinnings. The simplest way of reporting this fact is to recognize when he, in fact, agreed with certain scholars' points of view. He states succinctly in the *Tragedie of Hamlet*, "Note the unity of religion and philosophy in Hamlet: he takes the one true position."²³ Now he does not argue this fact because he merely believes that Shakespeare's Hamlet is correct because he aligns with MacDonald, but even more importantly, he believes that Hamlet aligns with God's own philosophy. MacDonald stated, "Matter, time, space, are all God's, and whatever may become of our philosophies, whatever he does with or in respect of time, place, and what we call matter, his doing must be true in philosophy as well as fact."²⁴ Therefore, God has a philosophy, Hamlet aligned with this philosophy, and MacDonald understands and agrees with this alignment. But in order to make this assessment he must have concluded that he had the correct philosophical and religious position in the first place.

To give another example of MacDonald's affirmation of a philosophical position, take this passage in *England's Antiphon*: "Dr. Henry More was…[c]hiefly known for his mystical philosophy, which he cultivated in retirement at Cambridge, and taught not only in prose, but in an elaborate, occasionally poetic poem…. Whatever may be thought of his theories, they belong at least to the highest order of philosophy; and it will be seen from the poems I give that they must have borne their part in lifting the soul of the man towards a lofty spiritual condition of faith and fearlessness. The mystical philosophy seems to me safe enough in the hands of a poet: with others it may degenerate into dank and dusty materialism."²⁵

In the following pages, we will proceed with the same spirit as MacDonald in his elevation of Dr. More's mystical philosophy. Even while MacDonald occasionally downplayed the role of philosophy, he absolutely asked and discussed questions of a metaphysical nature. Adelheid Kegler goes so far to say that "MacDonald's oeuvre is conceived in a dynamic and dialectic analysis of the central problems

---

22 George MacDonald, *Wilfrid Cumbermede* (Whitehorn: Johannesen, 2009), 173.

23 George MacDonald, *The Tragedie of Hamlet, Prince of Denmarke* (London: Longmans, Green, and Co., 1885), 265.

24 George MacDonald, *Thomas Wingfold, Curate*, 424.

25 George MacDonald, *England's Antiphon*, 223.

of modern philosophy."[26] MacDonald elucidated his philosophical positions on reality, truth, and knowledge, specifically discussed in his *Dish of Orts*, as well as interweaving these ideals in his fantasy works and novels. Richard Reis summarizes, "MacDonald's philosophy is, for one thing, the very foundation upon which his works of fiction are laid. Most writers of fiction, perhaps, are chiefly interested in telling a good story with skill, discipline and art.... But there have been plenty of great writers...to whom their private vision of truth is primary, and who use their art as a means to expression of that end; and MacDonald belongs clearly with this group. Although MacDonald himself never really put forward his ideas as a coherent system, a close examination of his scattered philosophical remarks has convinced me that they all arise from a systematic, consistent set of beliefs."[27]

Living in a Shadow World:
Examining MacDonald's "Temperamental Platonism" —
Under the Shadow of Platonism

It is a habit of many scholars, no matter the field, to take the individual which they are researching and categorize their thought under the auspices of one of the great thinkers of history. This tendency is no different with those who study George MacDonald. Most MacDonald scholars place him under the umbrella of the teachings of Plato. This comes as no surprise, since this is one of the few philosophers that MacDonald ever mentioned in his novels. It is no shock for a reader of MacDonald's to stumble on a passage in which one of the main characters picked up a copy of Plato and read it as a source of truth. For instance, in *Wilfred Cumbermede*, the narrator states that the main character sat "down to my books, and read with tolerable attention my morning portion of Plato."[28] Yet, in the body of his fictional works you will never find mention of Aristotle or Augustine, Plotinus or Schleiermacher, with each of whom he shared similarity and held in high regard.

Most scholars conclude that MacDonald, while he never agreed with Plato's philosophy as a whole, had placed Plato on another plane of authority. Most notably, Stephen Prickett states directly,

---

26 Adelheid Kegler, "Some Aspects of the Oeuvre of George MacDonald in a Curriculum of Philosophy Courses and in the Production of a Play at a German Gymnasium" in *North Wind* Vol. 22, 2003, 19.
27 Richard H. Reis, *George MacDonald's Fiction*, 31.
28 George MacDonald, *Wilfrid Cumbermede*, 232.

"MacDonald is a temperamental Platonist."[29] Colin Manlove wrote, "MacDonald was a Platonist in his thinking...."[30] Frank Riga also contends that "MacDonald's Christianity is also heavily marked by Platonic and neoplatonic elements."[31] MacDonald himself writes, in a footnote in reference to one of John Fletcher's poems, that therein lies "a glimmer of that Platonism of which, happily, we have so much more in the seventeenth century."[32] But is there enough evidence and conformity in the work of MacDonald to argue that he was a true Platonist or even a Neo-Platonist?

To begin our discussion, and to understand MacDonald's frame of reference, it would do the reader well to reconsider Plato's famous cave analogy:

> Plato asks us to imagine an underground cave which has an opening towards the light. In this cave are living human beings, with their legs and necks chained from childhood in such a way that they face the inside wall of the cave and have never seen the light of the sun. Above and behind them, i.e. between the prisoners and the mouth of the cave, is a fire, and between them and the fire is a raised way and a low wall, like a screen. Along this raised way there pass men carrying statues and figures of animals and other objects, in such a manner that the objects they carry appear over the top of the low wall or screen. They see only shadows. These prisoners represent the majority of mankind, that multitude of people who remain all their lives in a state of ignorance beholding only shadows of reality and hearing only echoes of the truth.[33]

Even the casual reader of MacDonald will see some correspondence between Plato's Cave analogy and many of the themes and symbols found in MacDonald's work. Most prominently is MacDonald's unceasing juxtaposition of two realities: eternal and temporal. Simply

---

29   Stephen Prickett, *Victorian Fantasy* (Waco: Baylor University Press, 2005), 170.

30   Colin Manlove, "*The Princess and the Goblin* and *The Princess and Curdie*" in *Northwind* Vol. 27, 2007, 18.

31   Frank Riga, "The Platonic Imagery of George MacDonald and C.S. Lewis" in *For the Childlike: George MacDonald's Fantasies for Children*, ed. Roderick McGillis (Metuchen, NJ: Children's Literature Association, 1992), 112.

32   George MacDonald, *England's Antiphon*, 140.

33   Frederick Copleston, *A History of Philosophy Vol. I: Greece and Rome* (New York: Image Books, 1993), 161.

stated, Kerry Dearborn writes, "MacDonald's belief that the world is the antechamber of the greater reality of the Kingdom of God was redolent of Plato."[34] Stephen Prickett argues that "This world, for him, is not a consistent place, but is the meeting place of two very different kinds of reality."[35] He continues by stating that MacDonald was "only interested in the surface of this world for the news it gives him of another, hidden reality, perceived, as it were, through a glass darkly."[36] MacDonald agreed with Plato that this world was a conduit to a world of a concealed, deeper reality.

MacDonald explains his own position further, "The heavens and the earth are around us that it may be possible for us to speak of the unseen by the seen; for the outermost husk of creation has correspondence with the deepest things of the Creator."[37] Thus this world is part of the intimate revelation of the Father. As will be discussed in the subsequent section, this world is not merely a created entity, but is a revelation of the heart of God. This passage from MacDonald's *Unspoken Sermons* will elucidate his metaphysical position:

> *Things* are given us, this body first of things, that through them we may be trained both to independence and true possession of them. We must possess them; they must not possess us. Their use is to mediate—as shapes and manifestations in lower kind of the things that are unseen, that is, in themselves unseeable, the things that belong, not to the world of speech, but the world of silence, not to the world of showing, *but the world of being*, the world that *cannot be shaken*, and must remain. These things unseen take form in the things of time and space—not that they may exist, for *they exist in and from eternal Godhead*, but that their being may be known to those in training for the eternal; these things unseen the sons and daughters of God must possess. But instead of reaching out after them, they grasp at their forms, reward the things seen as the things to be possessed, *fall in love with the bodies instead of the souls of them*.[38]

---

34   Kerry Dearborn, *Baptized Imagination: The Theology of George MacDonald*, 25.

35   Stephen Prickett, *Victorian Fantasy*, 167.

36   Stephen Prickett, *Victorian Fantasy*, 170.

37   George MacDonald, *Unspoken Sermons*, "The Knowing of the Son," 201.

38   George MacDonald, *Unspoken Sermons*, "The Hardness of the Way,"

Here he delineates between a world of "showing" and a world of "being," one of which is capable of alteration and change, while the other "must remain" and is eternal. MacDonald also makes it clear that things do not come into existence once they are placed in our dimension of time and space, but are already in existence in the eternal mind of God. In another place MacDonald writes, "God began to talk to us ages before we were born: I will not say before we began to be, for, in a sense, that very moment God thought of us we began to exist, for what God thinks of *is*."[39] While it extends beyond appropriate measure to insinuate that scholars agree that Plato held this concept, none would disagree that Neo-Platonists such as Augustine unequivocally held this view.[40] Nevertheless, the parallel can be drawn most distinctly in the last line of the excerpt. While the inhabitants of Plato's cave are continuously enamored by the shadows on the wall of the cave, MacDonald implores his readers not to "fall in love" with the earthly world, but to reach for the unseen as part of the preparation for our eternal destiny.

The fact that MacDonald held to the hypothesis that there is an actual, unseen ideal world is undoubtedly clear as Narve Kragset Nystoyl claims, "one will recognize the Platonic concept of the 'ideas,' or more precisely the division or contrast between our present physical world of senses, and a higher, more real world of ideas, of which our world is merely a shadow."[41] Manlove also concedes that MacDonald believed that "beyond the shifting forms of this world are certain unchanging realities, which no image of them can contain."[42]

MacDonald's metaphysical foundations and the relationship between the realms of the seen and unseen are also made clear in his fiction. It is no secret that George MacDonald often cited Novalis, most famously in the conclusion of *Lilith* where he quoted: "Our life

---

96, emphasis added.

39   George MacDonald, "A Letter to American Boys" in *St. Nicholas Magazine for Boys and Girls*, Vol. 5: No. 3, 202.

40   Thomas Williams, "Augustine and the Platonists." A Lecture given to the Freshman Program of Christ College, the Honors College of Valparaiso University, 2003.

41   Narve Kragset Nystoyl, *Worldviews in George MacDonald's Phantastes and C.S. Lewis' The Chronicles of Narnia* (Master's Thesis: The University of Oslo, 2013), 13.

42   Colin Manlove, "The Princess and the Goblin and The Princess and Curdie," 18.

is no dream; but it ought to become one, and perhaps will."[43] Stephen Prickett notes that upon reading the quotation, as well as the book as a whole, "we are suddenly confronted with a new existential gloss on the traditional Platonic belief that human life is but a dream of a greater reality."[44] MacDonald believed that this world, was in fact, real, but once we reach the world of the unseen, our current world will become as a dream from which we have just awoken. Our cognitive reflection of this world will be reinterpreted by the new world, but this does not devalue our current existence.

David Manley argues "The clearest image in George MacDonald's fiction of how earth whispers of heaven, however, is...*The Golden Key*."[45] While Manley's contention is subjective and potentially worthy of dispute, this passage from MacDonald's tale shows a clear distinction between the world of the seen and the world of the unseen, while also using imagery redolent of Plato's cave:

> It was a sea of shadows. The mass was chiefly made up of the shadows of leaves innumerable, of all lovely and imaginative forms, waving to and fro, floating and quivering in the breath of a breeze whose motion was unfelt, whose sound was unheard... They soon spied the shadows of flowers mingled with those of the leaves, and now and then the shadow of a bird with open beak, and throat distended with song.... For the shadows were not merely lying on the surface of the ground, but heaped up above it like substantial forms of darkness, as if they had been cast upon a thousand different planes of air. Tangle and Mossy often lifted their heads and gazed upwards to descry whence the shadows came; but they could see nothing more than a bright mist spread above them, higher than the tops of the mountains, which stood clear against it.... After a while, they reached more open spaces, where the shadows were thinner; and came even to portions over which shadows only flitted, leaving them clear for such as might follow.... After sitting for a while, each, looking up, saw the other in tears: they were each longing after the country whence the shadows fell. "We *MUST* find the country from which the shadows come," said Mossy. "We must, dear Mossy," responded Tangle. "What if

---

43   George MacDonald, *Lilith*, 359. (also quoted in the subheading of the last chapter of *Phantastes* and *The Portent*.)

44   Stephen Prickett, *Victorian Fantasy*, 199.

45   David Manley, "Shadows that Fall: The Immanence of Heaven in the Fiction of C.S. Lewis and George MacDonald" in *Northwind* Vol. 17, 1998, 45.

your golden key should be the key to *it*?"[46]

Thus, in Tangle and Mossy's travels, as if executing a slow escape from Plato's cave, they begin to transcend the world of shadows and approach the world from which the shadows come. As they travel, the shadows become thinner, and their hope for reaching the unseen world wells up in their hearts, and the prediction that the golden key is, in fact, the key to the door of this other world comes to fruition. Manley concedes that when "they finally come to the threshold of their destination, they know they are approaching the source of those shadows of beauty; they know they will soon 'see face to face.'"[47]

This theme of "two juxtaposed worlds"[48] runs through many of MacDonald's works, including *Lilith*. Mr. Vane, most strikingly, in one of his internal debates after returning from "the other world"[49] questioned, "Had I come to myself out of a vision? —or lost myself by going back to one? Which was the real—what I now saw, or what I had just ceased to see? Could both be real, interpenetrating yet unmingling?"[50] While Vane does not follow this with a direct answer to his own question, it can be assumed from the end of the story, that Vane, and thus MacDonald himself, would answer with a resounding "Yes":

> Strange dim memories, which will not abide identification, often, through misty windows of the past, look out upon me in the broad daylight, but I never dream now. It may be, notwithstanding, that, when most awake, I am only dreaming the more! But when I wake at last into that life which, as a mother her child, carries this life in its bosom, I shall know that I wake, and shall doubt no more. I wait; asleep or awake, I wait.[51]

Both of the realities mentioned above, whether 'asleep or awake,' do not diminish the actuality of either frame of reference. Salvey agrees with this assessment of MacDonald's metaphysic in *Lilith*, "Both worlds are real, although, possibly not equally real,

---

46 George MacDonald, *The Light Princess and Other Fairy Tales* (Whitehorn: Johannesen, 2009), 193-196.

47 David Manley, "Shadows that Fall," 45. (reference to I Cor. 13:12)

48 Stephen Prickett, "The Two Worlds of George MacDonald," 15.

49 George MacDonald, *Lilith*, 131.

50 Ibid., 52.

51 Ibid., 359.

and both worlds are good, although perhaps not equally good."[52] As Salvey suggests, MacDonald held that the unseen world may have heightened reality, a heightened goodness that is clearly evident in this passage from *Lilith*: "We stood for a moment at the gate whence issued roaring the radiant river. I know not whence came the stones that fashioned it, but among them I saw the prototypes of all the gems I had loved on earth — far more beautiful than they, for these were living stones — such in which I saw, not the intent alone, but the intender too; not the idea alone, but the imbodier present, the operant outsender: nothing in this kingdom was dead; nothing was mere; nothing only a thing."[53] The unseen world is not a mere reflection of the divine creator, but, in some sense, exudes an existential presence of the creator that, in some way, transcends what we experience in this physical world. To conclude this argument, this passage from *Unspoken Sermons* demonstrates both MacDonald's concept that the heavens are higher than this world, while goodness still remains in this world: "The true soul sees, or will come to see, that his words, his figures always represent more than they are able to present; for, as the heavens are higher than the earth, so are the heavenly things higher than the earthly signs of them, let the signs be good as ever sign may be."[54]

The research above places MacDonald firmly in the "metaphysical realist" camp, since these realities, whether seen or unseen, do not depend on the mind or the observation of man. Yet the investigation should not stop there. The next inquiry along the metaphysical vein is obvious: "What about the physical world, the world of shadows. In what way is it real?"

Once we question the metaphysical nature of these "shadows," the differences between MacDonald's view and Plato's metaphysics becomes unmistakably clear. To the prisoners in Plato's cave, elucidated in his *Republic*, "the truth would be literally nothing but the shadows of the images."[55] Plato argued that this world was merely a shadow of the real, eternal world of ideals, and the only goodness to be found in these shadows are their usage as epistemic conduits through which we can possibly gain knowledge of the unseen, real world. They are tools

---

52 Courtney Salvey, "Riddled with Evil: Fantasy as Theodicy in George MacDonald's *Phantastes and Lilith*" in *North Wind* Vol. 27, 2008, 25.

53 George MacDonald, *Lilith*, 355-6.

54 George MacDonald, *Unspoken Sermons*, "Self-Denial," 174.

55 Plato, *The Dialogues of Plato* (Chicago: William Benton, 1952), 515.

by which we find reality, but their metaphysical goodness beyond this function is questionable. The shadows are not good in and of themselves; their only good is in the fact that some shadows, or the "shadows of true existence"[56] are useful to gain true knowledge. Our observations in the physical world are only reflections, or "images in the water,"[57] of true reality. Even the cave itself, an analogy of our physical world, is not natural, but is to be broken free from to gain knowledge of the real world.

In contrast, MacDonald's view of the physical world has intrinsic value, apart from its epistemic usefulness. MacDonald "does not reject and devalue the physical, particular embodiment of the ideal after it has been used as a tool for contemplating that ideal."[58] Frank Riga states, "MacDonald's Platonism is impure, not because he misunderstands it or distorts it, but because of his vision of life embraces the flesh and the material world in a way that a pure Platonism would not allow."[59] Simply put, MacDonald's Christian worldview could not accommodate a pure Platonism; instead his "Platonism had to be impure in order to accommodate the essential goodness of the flesh and its ultimate purification and resurrection."[60] Thus, to MacDonald, even the darkness of Plato's cave is not an inherent evil, but instead is "one of the constituent elements of reality."[61] As will be discussed in the next section, God is the creator of this world, and his creation was, and is, inherently good.

The goodness of this world can be most clearly observed in the narrative of Tangle and Mossy in *The Golden Key*. Frank Riga contends, "The quest parallels the journey of Plato's unchained prisoner who seeks the reality beyond the shadows and images of the cave. Unlike the freed prisoner, however, Mossy and Tangle do not discover the intelligible world of perfect form through philosophic meditation; instead they live an ordinary human life, loving the things of the world and yet dimly knowing these prefigure something

---

56 Ibid., 532.

57 Ibid., 532.

58 Courtney Salvey, "Riddled with Evil: Fantasy as Theodicy in George MacDonald's *Phantastes and Lilith*," 20.

59 Frank Riga, "The Platonic Imagery of George MacDonald and C.S. Lewis," 126.

60 Ibid., 112.

61 Ibid., 127.

more pleasing than either can describe."[62] Thus this world is "not an accident of spiritual geography or a psychological quirk, but a part of man's normal condition of existence."[63]

In summary, Narve Kragset Nystoyl contends that "Although MacDonald is frequently deemed a Platonist...others argue that this is a difficult claim to make. At least, calling MacDonald a Platonist definitely stretches the term somewhat, as MacDonald, ever unorthodox, hardly fits the bill in all aspects."[64] In an even more specific condemnation of this labeling of MacDonald's philosophy as Platonic, Robert Trexler argues, "As to MacDonald (or Lewis for that matter) who is sometimes called a Neo-Platonist, I do not see it fitting the truth of the matter. They both use Platonist imagery, shadows/caves, etc. But I think that's just a symbolist use of those images...they are sacramentalist writers, who see nature as reflecting God's truth."[65] While none of the scholars mentioned in this research would put MacDonald's philosophy directly in line with Plato, some, like Robert Trexler, find far more aversion to this labeling than others. But most, like Roderick McGillis, admit "Plato is never too far from MacDonald's thinking."[66]

In *England's Antiphon*, MacDonald spoke of the work of Thomas Heywood thusly: "He had strong Platonic tendencies, interesting himself chiefly however in those questions afterwards pursued by Dr. Henry More...which may be called the shadow of Platonism."[67] As MacDonald spoke of Heywood, I firmly contend that we should also apply this to the work of MacDonald himself. While no MacDonald scholar should argue that he was a thorough Platonist, it has been demonstrated that he lived and operated under "the shadow of Platonism," and that this terminology is an accurate description of MacDonald's metaphysic. Thus, in conclusion, MacDonald was a metaphysical realist who openly acknowledged that he operated under the shadow of Platonism.

---

62   Ibid., 115.

63   Stephen Prickett, "The Two Worlds of George MacDonald" in *North Wind* Vol. 2, 1983, 15.

64   Narve Kragset Nystoyl, *Worldviews in George MacDonald's Phantastes and C.S. Lewis' The Chronicles of Narnia*, 34.

65   Robert Trexler, George MacDonald Society, facebook post, 2014.

66   Roderick McGillis, "Fantasy as Miracle" in *George MacDonald: Literary Heritage and Heirs* (Wayne: Zossima Press, 2008), 203.

67   George MacDonald, *England's Antiphon*, 135.

Ex Deo: Origen, Plotinus, and MacDonald's Doctrine of Creation

A discussion of MacDonald's doctrine of creation may seem out of place immediately following a study of MacDonald's metaphysic; yet, at the end of this section, it will become obvious that an understanding of this doctrine is essential to appreciating the connection between MacDonald's metaphysic and his mystical theology. According to William Raeper, MacDonald believed that "men and women were born out of the heart of God, not *ex nihilo* as traditionally held by the church, and thus MacDonald aligned himself with the Neo-Platonic theories of Plotinus and Origen."[68] Here again, MacDonald operated under the shadow of Plato; thus not only will MacDonald's view be explored, but also be compared and contrasted with the Neo-Platonic doctrines of Plotinus and Origen.

It is believed by most scholars that in the second and third century A.D., Ammonius Saccas of Alexandria taught his students the rudimentary knowledge of what will later be dubbed Neo-Platonism. While not much is known of Ammonius since he has left no extant writings, it is beyond question, simply by an understanding of his students' teachings, that he subscribed to the teachings of Plato, or at least a personal interpretation thereof.[69] This Platonic influence manifested itself in two of his most influential students: Origen and Plotinus.

While Origen did hold to a creation of matter *Ex Nihilo*,[70] one can quickly see the Platonic influence on his view of creation in his *Commentary on the Gospel of John*: "We must ask about this; whether, when the saints were living a blessed life apart from matter and from any body, the dragon, falling from the pure life, became fit to be bound in matter and in a body, so that the Lord could say, speaking through storm and clouds, "This is the beginning of the creation of God, made for His angels to mock at."[71] Similarly to Plato, Origen

---

68   William Raeper, *George MacDonald*, 243.

69   John M. Riddle, *A History of the Middle Ages, 300-1500* (Plymouth: Rowman & Littlefield, 2008), 46.

70   Origen, *De Principiis II.1.5*, from Ante-Nicene Fathers, Vol. 4. ed. by Alexander Roberts, James Donaldson, and A. Cleveland Coxe (Buffalo, NY: Christian Literature Publishing Co., 1885).

71   Origen, *Commentary on the Gospel of John*, from Ante-Nicene Fathers, Vol. 9, ed. by Allan Menzies (Buffalo, NY: Christian Literature Publishing Co., 1896), p.306..

held to a pre-existence of the soul before the placement of that soul into matter. Before this physical world began, we lived in a spiritual realm with God, and originally "He created all whom He made equal and alike."[72] It was only through the free will of these rational creatures that diversity had been caused.[73] It is also likely that Origen believed in an infinite regress of ever-recurring existences, which falls in line with Plato's contention that the world is coeternal with the *Demiurgos*. Origen writes, "we say that not then for the first time did God begin to work when He made this visible world; but as, after its destruction, there will be another world, so also we believe that others existed before the present came into being."[74]

Where Origen's doctrine of creation intrigues the devotees of MacDonald is where he dips his toes into the pool of emanationism. But, unlike Plotinus and MacDonald who chronologically followed him, Origen only suggests creation *Ex Deo* for God alone. John Riddle explains, "Origen's theory of emanation, derived from Plato, provided imagery that could help explain how the Father, Son, and Holy Spirit could be one God in three persons."[75] Origen explains in his *Commentary on the Gospel of John*, "One might assert, and with reason, that God Himself is the beginning of all things, and might go on to say, as is plain, that the Father is the beginning of the Son; and the demiurge the beginning of the works of the demiurge, and that God in a word is the beginning of all that exists.... In the Word one may see the Son, and because He is in the Father He may be said to be in the beginning."[76] Thus, in his view, Jesus emanated from the Father, and the Holy Spirit originated in Christ. Origen explains, "But we for our part are convinced that there are three distinct existents—Father, Son and Holy Spirit—and we do not believe any of these is unbegotten except the Father."[77] Of course, this would more than ruffle a few feathers of third century theologians, especially when Origen argued that the "Holy Spirit was brought into being through

---

72   Origen, *De Principiis*, II.9.6.

73   Ibid., II.9.6.

74   Ibid., III.5.3.

75   John M. Riddle, *A History of the Middle Ages, 300-1500*, 46.

76   Origen, *Commentary on the Gospel of John*, I.17.

77   Maurice Wiles, *Documents in Early Christian Thought* (Cambridge: Cambridge University Press, 2001), 78.

the Word [Christ], and the Word is senior to him."[78] Thus implying that there was a true ontological subordination in the Trinity. Origen's ideas led to heresy in the early church, and therein is a foundation of emanationism. This leads us to another one of Ammonius' students, Plotinus.

Plotinus' concept of emanationism was not limited to the divine, but branched out into all creation. Norman Geisler states categorically, "Plotinus' God created the world *Ex Deo* (out of himself) out of a necessary and emanational unfolding and not *Ex Nihilo* (out of nothing)."[79] In Plotinus' own words: "the One is perfect and…has overflowed, and its exuberance has produced the new."[80] For the uninitiated, many would take Plotinus' ideas to lead directly to pantheism, but this is not the case, especially in the strict sense of the word. He elucidates his position: "The One is all things and no one of them; the source of all things is not all things; all things are its possession— running back, so to speak, to it— or, more correctly, not yet so, they will be."[81] The fact of the matter is that Plotinus' "One," while a complex idea, is an ontologically simple and an utterly inexplicable source. The One produces its effect, but the effect is different from its begetter due to the complexity of the creation, "For the Universe is not a Principle and Source: it springs from a source, and that source cannot be the All or anything belonging to the All, since it is to generate the All, and must be not a plurality but the Source of plurality, since universally a begetting power is less complex than the begotten."[82] Plotinus also states more simply, "the produced thing is deficient by the very addition, by being less simplex, by standing one step away from the Authentic."[83] Brandon Zimmerman explains, "There is an ontological gulf between the One and all modes of being that are derived from him, a gulf which words and concepts cannot bridge. Plotinus often expresses this paradoxically by saying that the One is all things in that they come from him, and is nothing in that he is none of the beings that come from him and has none of

---

78 Ibid., 78.

79 Norman Geisler and Winfried Corduan, *Philosophy of Religion* (Eugene, OR: Wipf and Stock, 2003), 153.

80 Plotinus, *Enneads* (Chicago: Encyclopedia Britannica, 1952), V.2.1.

81 Ibid., V.2.1.

82 Ibid., III.8.9.

83 Ibid., II.6.1.

the limiting characteristics of a being or a substance."[84]

Plotinus did ask himself, "from such a unity as we have declared The One to be, how does anything at all come into substantial existence, any multiplicity, dyad, or number?"[85] In common terms, 'How did the One create?" It becomes clear in his fifth *Ennead* that the One produces the Divine Mind, or the Intellectual-Principle or *Nous*, which he stated, "stands as the image of The One."[86] Then this mind, since it is not devoid of creativity like the One, produces the soul. Plotinus explains, "what is left is the phase of the soul which we have declared to be an image of the Divine Intellect, retaining some light from that sun, while it pours downward upon the sphere of magnitudes (that is, of Matter) the light playing about itself which is generated from its own nature."[87] So, to use the two analogies that Plotinus often utilized, the *Nous* is the image of the One, and the soul the image of the *Nous;* or the *Nous* is like a ray of sun from the One, and the soul is sunlight of the *Nous*.

In Origen, the substance by which God creates, in relation to the two other persons of the Trinity, is *Ex Deo*. The Father begets Jesus, and then the Holy Spirit is thus created, all out of his own eternal substance. In Plotinus, the One emanates the *Nous*, then the *Nous* creates the soul, and the lesser realm of matter, in its own image or reflection. Yet how does MacDonald compare?

Dale Nelson states categorically, "MacDonald and Boehme believe God dwells in nature, and that nature proceeds from God, rather than being created out of nothing."[88] Rolland Hein explains how MacDonald rejects the traditional view of creation: "Man in his subconscious being, therefore, does not exist independently from God. God made man out of himself...and man lives and moves and has his being in God.... Thus MacDonald repudiates the doctrine of creation *Ex Nihilo* which Augustine taught, and which many orthodox theologians have believed."[89]

---

84 Brandon Zimmerman, *Sight Becomes Seeing: Plotinian Emanation as a Dynamic of Procession and Return* (Master's Thesis: Catholic University of America, 2009), 15-16.

85 Plotinus, *Enneads*, V.1.6.

86 Ibid., V.1.7.

87 Ibid., V.3.9.

88 Dale J. Nelson, "MacDonald and Jacob Boehme" in *North Wind* Vol. 8, 1989, 28.

89 Rolland Hein, *The Harmony Within*, 47.

Waking the Dead

In MacDonald's *The Castle: A Parable*, one of his characters prays, "We thank thee that we have a father, and not a maker; that thou hast begotten us, and not moulded us as images of clay; that we have come forth of thy heart, and have not been fashioned by thy hands. It *must* be so. Only the heart of a father is able to create. We rejoice in it, and bless thee that we know it. We thank thee for thyself. Be what thou art — our root and life, our beginning and end, our all in all."[90] While it seems like MacDonald's doctrine of creation stands in stark contrast to the biblical account of Genesis 2:7 and 3:19, he argues that his view of creation *Ex Deo* is biblically-based. We find an explication of MacDonald's theory of creation in his commentary of Romans 8:19 where the Scripture reads "For the creation waits with eager longing for the revealing of the sons of God." MacDonald comments on the biblical passage, "I am inclined to believe the apostle regarded the whole visible creation as, in far differing degrees of consciousness, a live outcome from the heart of the living one, who is all in all."[91] In *A Dish of Orts* MacDonald explains, "In the New Testament there is a higher form used to express the relation in which we stand to him— 'we are his offspring;' not the work of his hand, but the children that came forth from his heart."[92]

In survey of MacDonald's doctrine of creation, it would appear as though he believed that the entire physical world was *Ex Deo*, "Our own poet Goldsmith, with the high instinct of genius, speaks of God having 'loved us into being.' Now I think this is not only true with regard to man, but true likewise with regard to the world in which we live. [It is] not merely a thing which God hath made…but is an expression of the thought, the feeling, the heart of God himself."[93] But in other areas he suggests that his doctrine may be more limited: "Perhaps the precious things of the earth, the coal and the diamonds, the iron and clay and gold, may be said to have come from his hands; but the live things come from his heart— from near the same region whence ourselves we came."[94] It is possible that he still continued to hold the entire world as a creation out of the heart of God but simply

---

90 George MacDonald, *The Portent and Other Stories* (Whitehorn: Johannesen, 1999), 233.

91 George MacDonald, *The Hope of the Gospel*, "The Hope of the Universe," 90.

92 George MacDonald, *A Dish of Orts*, "Wordsworth's Poetry," 246.

93 Ibid., "Wordsworth's Poetry," 246.

94 George MacDonald, *Unspoken Sermons*, "The Inheritance," 278.

would not argue the point. Yet the concept that living beings were *Ex Deo* was worthy of dispute. So again, in his commentary on Romans 8:19: "Such view, at the same time, I do not care to insist upon; I only care to argue that the word *creature* or *creation* must include everything in creation that has sentient life."[95]

In further examination, it appears as though, for MacDonald, there is no third option: Either God created out of himself or there is no God. For God must either exist, and we are created out of Him, or he does not exist at all, and we have spontaneously come into existence out of nothingness, "If we came out of nothing, we could not invent the idea of a God — could we, Robert? Nothing would be our God. If we come from God, nothing is more natural, nothing so natural, as to want him, and when we haven't got him, to try to find him. — What if he should be in us after all, and working in us this way? just this very way of crying out after him?."[96] And again he explains, "Only, if man and Nature came both out of nothing, why should they not be nothing to each other? Why should not man be nothing to himself?"[97] MacDonald saw creation out of nothing as an illogical phrase: "There is a false phrase used, that we were made out of nothing. It is a mere logical contradiction."[98] If there was truly "nothing," God would not exist, thus God would not be there to create. To consider these ideas more deeply, consider this extended passage from *A Dish of Orts* in an entry entitled "The Imagination":

> *Poet* means *maker*. We must not forget, however, that between creator and poet lies the one unpassable gulf which distinguishes—far be it from us to say *divides*—all that is God's from all that is man's; a gulf teeming with infinite revelations, but a gulf over which no man can pass to find out God, although God needs not to pass over it to find man; the gulf between that which calls, and that which is thus called into being; between that which makes in its own image and that which is made in that image. It is better to keep the word *creation* for that **calling out of nothing** which is the imagination of God; except it be as an occasional symbolic

---

95 George MacDonald, *The Hope of the Gospel*, "The Hope of the Universe," 90.

96 George MacDonald, *Robert Falconer*, 277.

97 George MacDonald, *There and Back* (Philadelphia: David McKay, 1891), 418.

98 George MacDonald, *George MacDonald in the Pulpit* (Whitehorn: Johannesen, 2009), "The Only Freedom," 121.

expression, whose daring is fully recognized, of the likeness of man's work to the work of his maker. The necessary unlikeness between the creator and the created holds within it the equally necessary likeness of the thing made to him who makes it, and so of the work of the made to the work of the maker. When therefore, refusing to employ the word *creation* of the work of man, we yet use the word *imagination* of the work of God, we cannot be said to dare at all. It is only to give the name of man's faculty to that power after which and by which it was fashioned. The imagination of man is made in the image of the imagination of God. Everything of man must have been of God first; and it will help much towards our understanding of the imagination and its functions in man if we first succeed in regarding aright the imagination of God, in which the imagination of man lives and moves and has its being.[99]

In the passage above, MacDonald has no qualms stating that when God created, he called us out of nothing. At first understanding, one may find it contentious that here he makes no qualms in using *Ex Nihilo*-style language, yet, it must be firmly denoted that MacDonald qualifies the word "nothing" as the "imagination of God." In MacDonald's view, God created from his imagination. God called his creatures, which did not pre-exist, nor are made of God's own essence, into existence.

One must wonder why MacDonald used the verbiage "He makes them, not out of nothing, but out of Himself" in most of his passages on creation. This idea was not a fleeting concept that arose once in MacDonald's mind, then passed on. MacDonald specifically, and I would argue intentionally, used this wording in many of his books. I contend that this diction was used for two specific reasons: First, MacDonald wanted to demonstrate and remind us that God's creative process is quite different and much more glorious then when man, figuratively, brings things into existence. As MacDonald explained, "better to keep the word *creation* for that calling out of nothing which is the imagination of God; except it be as an occasional symbolic expression."[100] No man creates something out of his heart in the same way that God does. When the poet uses the term "create", it can only be used analogically. As Gisela Kreglinger writes, "He goes out of his way to differentiate clearly between the creative activity of God and

---

99 George MacDonald, *A Dish of Orts*, "The Imagination: Its Function and its Culture," 3, bold italic added by Dean Hardy.
100 Ibid., 3.

human creativity. MacDonald establishes God as the one who created the world out of nothing and mankind as part of God's creation,"[101] and as MacDonald continuously implores, "God thinks you out of himself."[102]

Second, MacDonald often wanted to remind the reader of the direct and intimate relational ties between God and his creation. As will be proposed later, MacDonald was a Christian mystic who accentuated God's immanence and fatherhood. Man is no mere accident of nature, but is the offspring of God. In MacDonald's own words: "For God is the heritage of the soul in the ownness of origin; man is the offspring of his making will, of his life; God himself is his birth-place; God is the self that makes the soul able to say *I too, I myself*. This absolute unspeakable bliss of the creature is that for which the Son died, for which the Father suffered with him. Then only is life itself; then only is it right, is it one; then only is it as designed and necessitated by the eternal life-outgiving Life."[103] David Robb illustrates this intimacy, "His belief that the world is a book, given pattern and significance by a writer-god . . . [suggests] the nearness and intimacy which MacDonald sought for in his understanding of God."[104]

Last, it must be noted that some casual readers of MacDonald falsely conclude that being created "out of God's own heart" indicates that he was a pantheist. While the following section will focus on that specific assertion, it can be stated here that MacDonald categorically did not indicate in any of his works that creation *Ex Deo* was a dissemination, or an emanation, of God's essence into his creation. Not even Origen or Plotinus suggests such a strong emanationism, yet MacDonald is sometimes credited with this position, albeit without merit. While it is still legitimate to claim that MacDonald held to creation *Ex Deo*, it cannot be applied in the traditional sense of the term. Like many of his other assessments, his view of creation was not ontological in nature, but rather, MacDonald's *Ex Deo* was focused on the primacy and the complexity of God's creative, imaginative

---

101 Gisela H. Kreglinger, *Storied Revelations: Parables, Imagination and George MacDonald's Christian Fiction*. (Cambridge: Lutterworth, 2014), 84.

102 George MacDonald, *George MacDonald in the Pulpit*, "Alone with God," 106.

103 George MacDonald, *Unspoken Sermons Series II*, "The Truth in Jesus," 189.

104 David S. Robb, *George MacDonald*, 53.

process, as well as the relational implications of creator and his new creation.

"Participation" in the Divine Nature

Any attempt to formally categorize George MacDonald's theological perspective generally results in consternation and even robust dialogue among MacDonald scholars. But an attempt should be made here, not to explicate his entire theological system, but merely to set forth his view of humanity's relation to the divine. Even then, with the focus narrowed to this specific topic, there are reasons for confusion in his readers' opinions. One of the main causes of misunderstanding is a lack of clarity in terminology, and the confusing explanations of these terms in MacDonald's work as well as the work of modern MacDonald scholarship.

First, and most importantly, while George MacDonald knew that the term "pantheism" had heretical implications, he had no problems with categorizing his protagonists as pantheistic. For instance, in MacDonald's *What's Mine's Mine*, one of the characters considers the idea that quite possibly, the protagonist is a pantheist:

> The thought, *Is he a pantheist?* took its place. Had she not surprised him in an act of worship? In that wide outspreading of the lifted arms, was he not worshipping the whole, the Pan? Sky and stars and mountains and sea were his God! She walked aghast, forgetful of a hundred things she had heard him say that might have settled the point. She had, during the last day or two, been reading an article in which *pantheism* was once and again referred to with more horror than definiteness. Recovering herself a little, she ventured approach to the subject ... "There! that is what I was afraid of!" cried Mercy: "you are pantheists!"[105]

The disdain for pantheism rings true in the passage, but the protagonist does something unexpected, he agrees that he is, in fact, a pantheist. But he does so on his own terms, and by his own definition, "'Yes,' answered Ian. 'If to believe that not a lily can grow, not a sparrow fall to the ground without our Father, be pantheism, Alister and I are pantheists. If by pantheism you mean anything that would not fit with that, we are not pantheists.'"[106] What was the point of this manoeuvre? Why use a word that would spark such talk of heresy? It

---
105 George MacDonald, *What's Mine's Mine*, 215.
106 Ibid., 215.

would seem that MacDonald merely wanted to champion the love of nature, and to lessen the disdain for those secularists who participated in that love. MacDonald lectured at one point, "The feeling used to be so strong in these northern parts, that if you talked about nature with anything like enthusiasm, you were worshipping a heathen goddess. Friends, it is rank paganism — worse than paganism. The devil did not make the moonlight, nor did God place us here to strive against the lovely influences of sea and land and sky amid which He has set us. The man who *loves nature aright is a good man* — a man of tender heart."[107]

Another complication of the issue is that George MacDonald often used pantheistic language, and was a lover of nature himself. Greville MacDonald records one of George's letters where he contends that "The beautiful things round about you are the expression of God's face, or, as in Faust, the garment whereby we see the deity. Is God's sun more beautiful than God himself? Has he not left it to us as a symbol of his own life-giving light?"[108] In one instance, MacDonald even goes so far as personifying nature as "she": "we talk even of the world which is but [God's] living garment, as if that were a person; and we call it '*she*' as if it were a woman, because so many of God's loveliest influences come to us through her. She always seems to me a beautiful old grandmother."[109] But due to these personifications of nature and use of poetic, pantheistic terminology, MacDonald's words could be easily taken out of context and twisted into something that the author did not mean. For instance, in an *Unspoken Sermon*, MacDonald wrote that for the Christian, "the life of the Father and the Son flows through him; he is a part of the divine organism."[110] In his "A Sketch of Individual Development," MacDonald contends that, "Oneness with God is the sole truth of humanity."[111] In one letter, he plainly writes of the future final consumation, "we know in ourselves that we are one with God."[112] But if the reader does not read the context or attempt to understand what MacDonald meant by being a part of

---

107 Favour James Gregs, *William Wordsworth* (London: Forgotten Books), 290-1, emphasis added.

108 Greville MacDonald, *George MacDonald and His Wife*, 122.

109 George MacDonald, *What's Mine's Mine*, 212.

110 George MacDonald, *Unspoken Sermons*, "The Creation in Christ," 197.

111 George MacDonald, *A Dish of Orts*, "A Sketch of Individual Development," 74.

112 Greville MacDonald, *George MacDonald and His Wife*, 432.

the 'divine organism' or in what sense can we attain 'oneness' with God, then the reader could falsely conclude that MacDonald was a thoroughgoing pantheist.

This pantheistic vocabulary and decontextualization does not affect just MacDonald, but his scholars as well. Rolland Hein writes in his *The Harmony Within*, "Humanity, when it realizes its highest spiritual potential, will differ in nowise from divinity."[113] If the reader had not read previous pages which included Hein's discussion on human individuality and uniqueness and had read this passage as a mere sound-bite, pantheism could have been concluded. William Raeper says that MacDonald's religion "involves the soul seeking a union with God— a union of substances in fact...a union in which the individuality is retained."[114] Raeper's commentary is unique, especially since he explains that this union between God and man to be substantial. It would seem that he is unquestionably suggesting that MacDonald was a pantheist, but in the next paragraph he writes that "MacDonald believed in a union in which the individuality was retained."[115] While Raeper's explanation of the unifying principle is nonexistent in this text, for it was not the overall point Raeper was making, our point is clear: Due to MacDonald's own use of pantheistic language, as well as his disciples, some have falsely attributed pantheism to our subject.

Lastly, and likely most importantly, MacDonald championed, on numerous occasions, the title "Christian pantheist." It should be noted that this designation should not be unique merely because of the baggage that comes with this terminology, but simply due to the fact that it was rare to have MacDonald advocate any label at all. He was infamous for intentionally avoiding labeling his theological and doctrinal perspective, as he is oft-quoted, "Jesus Christ is my theology, and nothing else."[116] But here, he uses a theological title without hesitation.

Most of MacDonald's significant explanations on Christian Pantheism are contained within his discussions on Wordsworth. Note the positive light in which MacDonald casts this idea: "This Christian pantheism, this belief that God is in everything, and showing himself in everything, has been much brought to the light

---

113   Rolland Hein, *The Harmony Within*, 71.

114   William Raeper, *George MacDonald*, 257.

115   Ibid., 257.

116   Anonymous, "Dr. MacDonald's Testimony," 31.

by the poets of the past generation, and has its influence still, I hope, upon the poets of the present."[117] As was defined in *What's Mine's Mine*,[118] MacDonald defined his Christian pantheism as a theology where God is overwhelmingly immanent. Greville reiterates this concept: "Take *Lessons for a Child* as expressing his *pantheism*: a word I use in Wordsworthian sense, and antithetic to any crude theory that, admitting God's manifestation in natural phenomena, denies His personality and transcendent, creating presence— and there an end of it. George MacDonald's *pantheism was faith in the Father of all life, whose living word perpetually creates, inspires and redeems the whole world.*"[119] While Greville uses the term "pantheism," he strictly points out that this is no "crude theory" which "denies his personality." So, how was this term to be interpreted?

While the term "pantheist" brings its own import into the minds of the reader, it is clear that MacDonald did not mean to use the term in the normative sense, indicating this alteration with the prefix "Christian." Kerry Dearborn explains, "MacDonald identified Wordsworth's orientation as 'Christian Pantheism,' but cautions that it does not follow that he was an apostle of nature who identified nature with God. Rather, nature was seen as "the word of God in his own handwriting" or "the expression of the face of God" which has a "moulding" and formative effect. Because nature was considered part of the overflow of God's love, it could draw one back to a more vibrant perspective on all of life and offer a corrective to mechanistic ways of approaching relationships, theology, and life."[120] In his own words, MacDonald explains why the love of nature should be applauded: "When we understand the Word of God, then we understand the works of God; when we know the nature of an artist, we know his pictures; when we have known and talked with the poet, we understand his poetry far better. To the man of God, all nature will be but changeful reflections of the face of God."[121] MacDonald did argue, as stated by Paul in Ephesians 2:23 and 4:10, that "If there be a God, he is all in all, and filleth all things, and all is well."[122] But

---

117 George MacDonald, *A Dish of Orts*, "Wordsworth's Poetry," 246.

118 George MacDonald, *What's Mine's Mine*, 211.

119 Greville MacDonald, *George MacDonald and His Wife*, 278-9.

120 Kerry Dearborn, *Baptized Imagination: The Theology of George MacDonald*, 36-37.

121 George MacDonald, *A Dish of Orts*, "Wordsworth's Poetry," 256.

122 George MacDonald, *Warlock o' Glenwarlock: A Homely Romance*

Waking the Dead

MacDonald did not fully equate God and the world. For instance, in a letter to Lady Byron on the topic of Arthurian legend he wrote, "*But finding God in Christ, he found God in all things—as certainly, though not so fully manifest.*"[123] He made the distinction between the God-man, and nature itself, showing that MacDonald must exert a substantial distinction between nature and God.

In addition to a separation between God and nature, MacDonald was clear that God and man were quite distinct. Kerry Dearborn explains, "MacDonald was careful to acknowledge a radical difference between God and humanity. He held firmly to belief in God's sovereignty and freedom. In this way he averted the Romantic inclination toward pantheism."[124]

In his own words, he explains without equivocation: "[God] only is the true, original good; I am true because I seek nothing but his will. He only is all in all; I am not all in all, but he is my father, and I am the son in whom his heart of love is satisfied."[125] For clarity and emphasis, MacDonald specifically stated above "I am not all in all." He realizes that he cannot be God— he is not all-in-all— but there still can be oneness, in a sense.

While MacDonald was not a pantheist in the normative sense, it is obvious that he argued that there was a deep connection between God and his creation. Kerry Dearborn concedes that "MacDonald also affirmed an innate connection between God the Creator and human creatures, for humans are created in God's image." [126] This depth of connection was often, in MacDonald's writings, called "oneness," which may cause some to assume pantheism. Yet the following will make clear that while there can be "oneness" this concept of oneness cannot happen without multiplicity. In an *Unspoken Sermon*, MacDonald contends that "the final end of the separation is not individuality; that is but a means to it; the final end is oneness—an impossibility without it. For there can be no unity, no delight of love, no harmony, no good in being, where there is but one. Two at least are needed for oneness; and the greater the number

---

(Boston, Lothrop, Lee & Shepard Co., 1881), 310.

123 Greville MacDonald, *George MacDonald and His Wife*, 311.

124 Kerry Dearborn, *Baptized Imagination: The Theology of George MacDonald*, 79.

125 George MacDonald, *Unspoken Sermons*, "The Creation in Christ," 195.

126 Kerry Dearborn, *Baptized Imagination: The Theology of George MacDonald*, 79.

of individuals, the greater, the lovelier, the richer, the diviner is the possible unity."[127] Thus, it is not divine simplicity, or monism, that MacDonald is suggesting with his terminology, but rather of harmony between distinct individuals.

The next pertinent question revolves around MacDonald's concept of "oneness" and how one can be, as Peter put it in 2 Peter 2:4, a 'partaker of the divine nature'. MacDonald writes, "we must choose to be divine, to be of God, to be one with God, loving and living as he loves and lives, and so be partakers of the divine nature, or we perish."[128] Thus, MacDonald does not argue that to be of the divine nature is, in fact, a part of our nature. In other words, it is not a metaphysical unity; it is a volitional one. Humanity can only choose to be unified with God. This concept in MacDonald's work recurs so consistently it may not be an exaggeration to state that he thought it one of his most important ideas to teach his readers. First, in contrast to the strong Calvinistic determinism during MacDonald's time, he regarded the will of man to be the pinnacle of his personhood, "For the highest creation of God in man is his will, and until the highest in man meets the highest in God, their true relation is not a spiritual fact."[129] Thus, when this will is unified with God's will, the man becomes a partaker of the divine:

> The highest in man is neither his intellect nor his imagination nor his reason; all are inferior to his will, and indeed, in a grand way, dependent upon it: his will must meet God's—a will *distinct* from God's, else were no *harmony* possible between them. Not the less, therefore, but the more, is all God's. For God creates in the man the power to will His will. It may cost God a suffering man can never know, to bring the man to the point at which he will will His will: but when he is brought to that point, and declares for the truth, that is, for the will of God, he becomes one with God, and the end of God in the man's creation, the end for which Jesus was born and died, is gained.[130]

This concept is echoed in his *Unspoken Sermons* where he explains how man can have a "willed harmony of dual oneness—with the All-in-all. When a man can and does entirely say, 'Not my will, but thine

---

127 George MacDonald, *Unspoken Sermons*, "Life," 140.
128 George MacDonald, *Unspoken Sermons*, "The Creation in Christ," 194.
129 George MacDonald, *The Hope of the Gospel*, "Salvation from Sin," 9-10.
130 Ibid., "Salvation from Sin," 10.

be done'—when he so wills the will of God as to do it, then is he one with God—one, as a true son with a true father."[131] Elsewhere he writes, "We are not and cannot become true sons without our will willing his will, our doing-following his making."[132] There are multiple repetitions of this idea in MacDonald's works, some of which are more controversial, for instance where he suggests that by willing God's will that we can be "part of the divine organism."[133] The wording "divine organism" may cause one to stumble, but there is little question, after reading the foregoing passages, that MacDonald only mean this in an analogical, and not in a metaphysical fashion.

In a different twist, and to be complete in our understanding of contemporary modern scholarship, one MacDonald expert has a unique perspective. Bonnie Gaarden, in her *The Christian Goddess* places MacDonald under the category of "panentheism." She defines this term as "The notion that God is expressed but not contained in nature, is immanent as well as transcendent, is more familiar to modern theologians under the term "panentheism." [It is] spread through the theology of Thomas Aquinas, that the regularities we call the 'laws of nature' are not imposed by God from outside, but are an external manifestation of the divine reason that animates nature." This terminology, similarly to pantheism, carries with it some historical baggage. The panentheism of Alfred Whitehead, for instance, is defined as one where "the universe as we know it requires a basic reality, God, that both grounds and participates in its development."[134] Thus in classical panentheism, God exists, but is in the process of becoming, and thus, changing along with the natural world. But this does not seem to be the modern panentheism utilized by Gaarden, especially since she mentioned Thomas Aquinas as a panentheist, an assertion that is not uttered among Thomistic or Panentheistic scholars.[135] This is likely due to the possibility that Gaarden was not speaking of classical panentheism, but modern panentheism. Yet this modern panentheism appears to be quite similar to what MacDonald entitled "Christian Pantheism." Thus Gaarden is merely exchanging one term with historical baggage with another term with its own set

---

131 George MacDonald, *Unspoken Sermons*, "Life," 145.

132 George MacDonald, *Unspoken Sermons*, "The Creation in Christ," 194.

133 George MacDonald, *Unspoken Sermons*, "The Creation in Christ," 197.

134 John W. Cooper, *Panentheism: The Other God of the Philosophers* (Grand Rapids: Baker Academic, 2006), 165.

135 Ibid., 327.

of subconscious import.

Instead of using a word charged with hints of heresy, this researcher recommends a term which upholds MacDonald's theological orthodoxy, but would highlight the uniqueness of the man's vision. Thus we will adopt the term "sacramentalism" which has been used by such scholars as Robert Trexler, Kirstin Jeffrey Johnson, Rolland Hein, as well as alluded to by MacDonald himself. As already quoted at the beginning of this chapter, Trexler lists MacDonald along with other "sacramentalist writers, who see nature as reflecting God's truth."[136] Kirstin Jeffrey Johnson gives some explanation of how his Scottish upbringing likely had a strong influence on his sacramentalism: "Recorded Highland prayers reveal a people who saw a relational Triune God involved in everything from the weather to their laundry to their husbandry. This conviction of an all-encompassing, all-relating God who loves bodies *and* souls, the world *and* humanity's positive interaction within it, is woven throughout MacDonald's work."[137] Thus, MacDonald's view holds that "The sacramental does not recognize a division between earthly and holy: earthiness is holiness, by definition of the Creator's own act."[138] So, it would be proper to "use the term "sacramental," in a very broad sense, to describe MacDonald's view of God's relation to both the world of nature and the world of event and circumstance."[139]

In MacDonald's own words he offered an analogy to help us understand the relationship of God to his creation in *The Portent*: "The very outside of a book had a charm to me. It was a kind of sacrament—an outward sign of an inward and spiritual grace; as, indeed, what on God's earth is not?"[140] Thus, all of the earth is a sacrament, and is a symbol of God and his characteristics. Again, this terminology removes the possible heretical import, and focuses on the biblical concept of God's immanence and revelatory creation.[141] In even more detail, MacDonald explains,

> ...All about us, in earth and air, wherever eye or ear can reach

---

136 Robert Trexler, George MacDonald Society, facebook post, 2014.

137 Kirstin Jeffrey Johnson, *Rooted in All its Story, More is Meant than Meets the Ear*, 33.

138 Ibid., 239.

139 Rolland Hein, *The Harmony Within*, 44.

140 George MacDonald, *The Portent and Other Stories*, 45.

141 Romans 1:20.

there is a power ever breathing itself forth in signs, now in a daisy, now in a wind-waft, a cloud, a sunset; a power that holds constant and sweetest relation with the dark and silent world within us; that the same God who is in us, and upon whose tree we are the buds, if not yet the flowers, also is all about us — inside, the Spirit; outside, the Word. And the two are ever trying to meet in us; and when they meet, then the sign without, and the longing within, become one in light, and the man no more walketh in darkness, but knoweth whither he goeth.[142]

Thus God is utterly immanent, within us and without, and his Holy Spirit and his Word symbolically connect within us to produce and emanate forth his light.

In conclusion, while MacDonald usually carried an attitude of disdain for philosophy and theology, there is no doubt that the information provided above reveals that he did, in fact, hold to a specific philosophy and doctrine, and was concerned that the public might hold beliefs that were contrary to his own, not due to intellectual arrogance, but because he determined that these beliefs would negatively affect their relationship with God. This train of thought will be more thoroughly elucidated in part three. At this point it can be stated unequivocally that MacDonald was a true metaphysical realist who operated under the shadow of Platonism, who held to his own interpretation of creation *Ex Deo* in regard to God's relational character and imagination and not emanationism, and who believed in a purely theistic God under the tradition of "sacramentalism."

---

142 George MacDonald, *Thomas Wingfold, Curate*, 415-16.

CHAPTER THREE
Alethiology and Language

Introduction

In Walter E. Houghton's *The Victorian Frame of Mind*, the author explains the mindset of the people of that era: "Though the Victorians were certain that truth existed and the mind could discover it, they found themselves involved in two forms of doubt: either what is sometimes called negative skepticism, when the judgment is suspended between alternate conclusions, one of which is considered true; or the affirmation of a belief which they only half believed—and half doubted."[1] In this text Houghton goes into exquisite detail, tracing the shift in attitudes from the early nineteenth to the early twentieth centuries.

Early in the Victorian Era the dialectical method was influential due to the heavy dogmatism on both sides of extreme ideals. This is exemplified in the work of Coleridge, taken directly from Hegel, and passed down to the work of John Stuart Mill and F.D. Maurice.[2] Unfortunately, this method did not stand the test of time, and within a few decades fell in popularity. It was around the 1860s where "men began to accept any convenient compromise, however loose and vague...adopting a broad-minded toleration of all ideas regardless of their intrinsic value."[3] By the 1870s skepticism emerged in the form of "historical relativism," which quickly became a prominent viewpoint. It progressed in such degree that John Morley "charged the younger generation with making intellectual sport of the most serious problems of human existence."[4] By the advent of the 20th century, full-blown skepticism permeated the intellectual life of post-Victorians: "They made a virtue of necessity and boasted [of] having tolerant and undecided minds."[5]

Similarly to his other views, MacDonald's view of truth takes on a life of its own, transcending above the views of those in his cultural and philosophical climate. Due to MacDonald's other controversial

---

1   Walter E. Houghton, *The Victorian Frame of Mind* (New Haven: Yale University Press, 1957), 18.

2   Ibid., 170.

3   Ibid., 179.

4   Ibid., 179.

5   Ibid., 180.

ideas, the influence of German thinkers, and his uplifting of the role of the imagination, the mistake of suggesting that MacDonald was a relativist would be an easy one to make. Josh Withrow, while he acknowledges that MacDonald was not a relativist, does suggest in his "In the Service of Freedom: Postmodernism in the Writing of George MacDonald" that "MacDonald's view…more closely adheres to a postmodern narrative…than the empirical views of reason in the Victorian Age."[6] Thus the question must be asked: Was MacDonald a subjectivist or an objectivist, or did he try to unite these following the dialectical tradition? Since "MacDonald was a person dedicated to the pursuit of Truth that he might serve the Truth with his entire being,"[7] the sections below will be dedicated to George MacDonald's view of truth, language, and the symbols he employed in most of his fictional work.

A Contrast of Propositional Truth with the Embodiment of Truth in Christ

To quickly dispense with the notion that George MacDonald held to a subjective view of truth, he states matter-of-factly in his *Unspoken Sermon* entitled, "The Truth": "A thing being so, the word that says it is so, is the truth."[8] This concept aligns most closely to the correspondence view of truth, which simply is the concept that a statement that matches reality can be labeled as "true."

Where MacDonald's view is unique in relation to the normative theory of correspondence is that what most people call "truths" he calls "facts." Basic realities of the world should be deemed "a *fact*, not a truth."[9] He goes so far as to say that water freezing at thirty-two degrees is a fact, but it is not a truth.[10] He simply gave the word "truth" more gravitas; it should not be used to denote elemental facts. He states simply, "the word truth ought to be kept for higher things."[11]

So, the question arises in the reader's mind, how are we to know

---

6   Josh Withrow, "In the Service of Freedom: Postmodernism in the Writing of George MacDonald." in *The Wise Imagination* [blog], 2015.

7   Kerry Dearborn, *Baptized Imagination: The Theology of George MacDonald*, 65.

8   George MacDonald, *Unspoken Sermons*, "The Truth," 210.

9   Ibid., "The Truth," 210.

10 Ibid., "The Truth," 211.

11 Ibid., "The Truth," 211.

when the line is crossed? What must be achieved for a mere fact to then be deemed "truth?" MacDonald asserts that the distinction between fact and truth is when that fact that is "an embodiment of a certain eternal thought...a fact of the being of God, the facts of which alone are truths."[12] He continues his explanation of truths as "a perfect thought from the heart of God—a truth of God!— not an intellectual truth, but a divine fact, a dim revelation, a movement of the creative soul!"[13] Withrow contends, "For MacDonald, truth and faith were an intricate fabric woven together with reason and imagination. To unravel all the knots would destroy the entire tapestry."[14] But in investigating this interwoven tapestry the reader should not automatically assume relativism, "Imaginativeness did not mean relinquishment of objective truth and a collapse into subjective relativism."[15] Dearborn argues that MacDonald's view "prophetically confronts a contemporary postmodern relativism that isolates the individual."[16]

Even while MacDonald focused much of his work through the lens of the imagination, he still believed that truth must be grounded in reality: "Rather than seeking truth in subjective probing or in abstractions, one's thoughts are best informed by the reality of the things around"[17] Dearborn agrees with Manlove, "The imagination cannot wield the sword of truth if it does not correspond with reality as God has created it."[18] Thus, it should be clear that MacDonald did not confuse absolute truth with relativistic opinion: "I do not mean opinion: to treat opinion as if that were truth, is grievously to wrong the truth."[19]

Thus, while MacDonald argued that facts were propositional and not relativistic, he believed that truth was on another plane of

---

12   Ibid., "The Truth," 211.

13   Ibid., "The Truth," 213.

14   Josh Withrow, "In the Service of Freedom: Postmodernism in the Writing of George MacDonald." in *The Wise Imagination* [blog], 2015.

15   Kerry Dearborn, "Bridge over the River Why: The Imagination as a Way to Meaning" in *North Wind* (Vol. 16, 1997), 178.

16   Ibid., 40.

17   Colin Manlove, *Christian Fantasy* (Notre Dame: University of Notre Dame Press, 1992), 165.

18   Kerry Dearborn, *Baptized Imagination: The Theology of George MacDonald*, 77.

19   George MacDonald, *Unspoken Sermons*, "Kingship," 227.

recognition. In fact, it would be best said that truth transcended mere propositions. Rolland Hein argued that MacDonald's view of truth was "incarnational rather than strictly propositional."[20] Dearborn argues that "He was determined as much as possible to avoid mere abstraction, as truth for him was primarily a person, Jesus Christ, who established a condition of truth for people in terms of their entire being and relationships."[21] But of course, the incarnation of truth should not be merely limited to Christ for all have the ability to become true men and women, although, in MacDonald's view, Christ was the most true man who ever lived: "The one originating, living, visible truth, embracing all truths in all relations, is Jesus Christ. He is true. He is the live Truth."[22] The incarnational nature of truth distinctly found in Christ is for what every human can, and should, strive: "The Son came forth to be, before our eyes and in our hearts, that which he had made us for, that we might behold the truth in him, and cry out for the living God, who, in the highest sense of all is The Truth, not as understood, but as understanding, living, and being, doing and creating the truth. 'I am the truth,' said our Lord; and by those who are in some measure like him in being the truth, the Word can be understood. Let us try to understand him."[23]

MacDonald explains, "Truth is truth, whether from the lips of Jesus or Balaam. But, in its deepest sense, *the truth* is a condition of heart, soul, mind, and strength towards God and towards our fellow — not an utterance, not even a *right* form of words; and therefore such truth coming forth in words is, in a sense, the person that speaks."[24] Truth is just as much about the condition of one's soul as it is about the propositional nature of truth. In fact, MacDonald argues that if one's heart is impure, going on a voyage for truth is in vain:

> You know what Christ requires of you is right—much of it at least you believe to be right, and your duty to do, whether he said it or not: do it. If you do not do what you know of the truth, I do not wonder that you seek it intellectually, for that kind of search may well be, as Milton represents it, a solace

---

20   Rolland Hein, *George MacDonald: Victorian Mythmaker*, 7.

21   Kerry Dearborn, *Baptized Imagination: The Theology of George MacDonald*, 4.

22   George MacDonald, *Unspoken Sermons*, "The Truth," 217.

23   George MacDonald, *Unspoken Sermons*, "The Heart with the Treasure," 43.

24   George MacDonald, *Unspoken Sermons*, "The New Name," 38.

even to the fallen angels. But do not call anything that may be so gained, The Truth. How can you, not caring to be true, judge concerning him whose life was to do for very love the things you confess your duty, yet do them not?[25]

More succinctly, MacDonald writes of his innocent, young character Gibbie, "More even than a knowledge of the truth, is a readiness to receive it."[26] Truth must be sought open-heartedly, for this is a necessary condition for the reception and the action of learning and executing the truth. Kerry Dearborn echoes MacDonald's thoughts:

> For MacDonald, the business of the theologian is first to *be* true, that one may be able to speak the truth. A central conviction was that one's vision of the truth becomes clearer as one becomes increasingly true in one's own being. The character of the theologian and the character of theology are thus interdependent. MacDonald exhorts the seeker: "what you call riddles are truths, and seem riddles because you are not true."[27] Much of his own credibility theologically is based on his own *trueness* as a person, and the reality of his life, which, like his theology, was not based on refractions of the truth, but focused primarily on the source of Truth. He was not afraid to admit his doubts because he had found that "doubt is the hammer that breaks the windows clouded with human fancies, and lets in the pure light."[28] [29]

Thus, humans can and must "be true" in order to find "The Truth." But if they are not true, they are going to misinterpret, pervert, misconstrue, or even simply ignore the truth. In this way, MacDonald acknowledges the subjective nature of the reception of truth, most notably instances of individual experience, which will be discussed in a later section of this study.

Walter Houghton held that during the Victorian Era, many thinkers claimed the "love of truth" as their motto. He writes, "But 'love of truth' contains an ambiguity; its meaning depends on which word is emphasized. For Mill and the rational, liberal school the *truth* is paramount. All forms of insincere profession and evasion which put

---

25 George MacDonald, *Unspoken Sermons*, "Justice," 242.

26 George MacDonald, *Sir Gibbie* (Whitehorn: Johannesen, 2000), 216.

27 George MacDonald, *Lilith*, 65.

28 Greville MacDonald, *George MacDonald and His Wife*, 374.

29 Kerry Dearborn, *Baptized Imagination: The Theology of George MacDonald*, 22.

social utility or personal advantage above the supreme obligation to think freely...are anathema. On the other hand, moderns like Carlyle... laid their emphasis on the *love* of truth. What they wanted was a society composed of sincere, truth-loving persons even though what they held were wrong."[30] I would argue that MacDonald attempted to bridge this gap. To answer the question in the introduction related to whether MacDonald was an objectivist or a subjectivist, it can be said that while he thoroughly believed in an objective truth and the horrible damage that could be done for those that held theologically false notions, he also understood the crucial need for transparency, character, open-mindedness and sincerity.

MacDonald, Augustine, and Swedenborg: Symbols as the Conduit of Divine Truth

There is no doubt that one of MacDonald's strongest appeal for scholars of literature is his strong and unique use of symbolism. Stephen Prickett asserts, "MacDonald reasserts the value of myth and symbol, not as a primitive relic nor simply as a literary device, but as a vital medium of human consciousness."[31] Prickett argues that MacDonald's symbolism is not a mere tool, but it reveals, and is inseparably linked to, his deep metaphysic: "MacDonald's philosophy is inseparable from his serious symbolism."[32] Bruce Hindmarsh states, "The line between spiritual and material, symbol and reality, idea and form, is in MacDonald's universe so faint as to be almost invisible. It would perhaps be even better to say that the relationship between these is so intimate as to be, in fact, a union, a co-inherence of reality."[33] This co-inherence of reality will become later realized when MacDonald's symbolism is further explored, and his utilization of Swedenborg's correspondences comes to the forefront.

To usher us into an exploration of MacDonald's use of symbolism, we will consider Augustine's theory of meaning in relation to literature, and most specifically, inspired literature. Although we do not have definitive proof that MacDonald was a student of Augustine, their similarities are strong enough to warrant discussion. Keith Waddle

---

30   Walter E. Houghton, *The Victorian Frame of Mind*, 425-6.

31   Stephen Prickett, "The Two Worlds of George MacDonald," 19.

32   Ibid., 19.

33   Douglas Bruce Hindmarsh, *The Faith of George MacDonald: A Biographical and Critical Examination of the Theology Represented in his Sermons and Letters* (Master's Thesis: Regent University, 1990), 63.

initiates our analysis: "Similarly to Augustine, [MacDonald] believed divine truths can only be conveyed through symbols; therefore it is a mistake to approach Scripture only literally, as if the actual words on the page were self-sufficient articles of truth."[34] MacDonald, as well as Augustine, believed that language could not fully contain the deep meaning for which God was attempting to express in his Holy Scripture. MacDonald writes, "Whatever belonging to the region of thought and feeling is uttered in words, is of necessity uttered imperfectly. For thought and feeling is infinite, and human speech, although far-reaching in scope, and marvelous in delicacy, can embody them after all but approximately and suggestively."[35] Thus, MacDonald did not limit his position on linguistics to Scripture, but asserted that all language is limited in ability to reveal every nuance in meaning from one mind to another.

To return briefly to touch upon the topic of the previous chapter, many find themselves pondering whether MacDonald identified as a linguistic relativist. To be clear, MacDonald believed that distinct literature had specific meaning. For instance, Stephen Prickett argues that this is the exact reason why MacDonald did not appreciate or use the tool of allegory in his work: "An allegory can, by definition, have no more meaning than the author originally put into it. It is, in that sense, a medium entirely under his control. This, for MacDonald, denied it the status of a work of art. It was artifact."[36] So, if a reading has an intended meaning and this meaning is found, then this interpretation corresponds to reality. Yet, MacDonald was not fond of this sort of interpretative method when it came to knowledge about God, especially in words which God was supposed to have inspired. MacDonald explains, "Be sure that, in dealing with any truth, its symbol, however high, must come short of the glorious meaning itself holds. It is the low stupidity of an unspiritual nature that would interpret the Lord's meaning as less than his symbols. The true soul sees, or will come to see, that his words, his figures always represent more than they are able to present; for, as the heavens are higher than the earth, so are the heavenly things higher than the earthly signs of

---

34   Keith Waddle, "George MacDonald and the Homiletics of Religious Imagination," in *North Wind* Vol. 18, 4.

35   George MacDonald, *Unspoken Sermons*, "It Shall Not Be Forgiven," 27.

36   Stephen Prickett, *Victorian Fantasy*, 159.

them."[37] Thus his view of imaginative fiction, as well as Scripture, was that the true man might get a deeper meaning than the uninitiated. He emphatically wrote of the reader's interpretation of his own works of fantasy, "If he [the reader] be a true man, he will imagine true things; what matter whether I meant them or not?"[38] So MacDonald held that the writer's intended meaning may have not been received, yet the interpretation could still be "true." To continue, Augustine's scriptural interpretive method should be explored and compared with MacDonald's.

The fourth century bishop's writings not only enhanced Christian epistemology and theology, but also presented an interesting, metaphorical view of the interpretation of Scripture. Augustine wrote, "All instruction is either about things or about signs; but things are learnt by means of signs."[39] He describes as sign as "a thing which, over and above the impression it makes on the senses, causes something else to come into the mind as a consequence of itself."[40] For example, in that same passage, Augustine argues that a sign could be natural, as in seeing a footprint and knowing a man must have passed by, or more conventional, like soldiers who, at the hearing of the trumpeter's call, hurriedly prepare for battle. But in Scripture, a thing can just be a simple object, but sometimes these "things" can mean more than meets the literalist's eye: "I now use the word 'thing' in a strict sense, to signify that which is never employed as a sign of anything else: for example, wood, stone, cattle, and other things of that kind. Not, however, the wood which we read Moses cast into the bitter waters to make them sweet, nor the stone which Jacob used as a pillow, nor the ram which Abraham offered up instead of his son; for these, though they are things, are also signs of other things."[41] So while he contends that things can potentially be signifying something else, he also argues that not everything in Scripture is a sign, or symbol, pointing to an additional, deeper meaning.

Augustine asserts that there could be multiple meanings to the biblical text, but also argues that there could be multiple, differing

---

37 George MacDonald, *Unspoken Sermons*, "Self-Denial," 174.

38 George MacDonald, *A Dish of Orts*, "The Fantastic Imagination," 320.

39 Augustine of Hippo, *On Christian Doctrine* in the *Nicene and Post-Nicene Fathers*, First Series, Vol. 2. ed. by Philip Schaff, trans. by James Shaw (Buffalo, NY: Christian Literature Publishing, 1887), I.2.

40 Augustine, *On Christian Doctrine*, II.1.

41 Ibid., I.2.

translations of the original language, while changing the meaning somewhat, both translations can hold different, but confirmatory meanings; both can be right.[42] He elucidates this idea, "in that passage of the prophet Isaiah, one translator reads: And do not despise the domestics of your seed; another reads: And do not despise your own flesh. Each of these in turn confirms the other. For the one is explained by the other; because flesh may be taken in its literal sense, so that a man may understand that he is admonished not to despise his own body; and the domestics of your seed may be understood figuratively of Christians, because they are spiritually born of the same seed as ourselves, namely, the Word.... Now which of these is the literal translation cannot be ascertained without reference to the text in the original tongue. And yet to those who read with knowledge, a great truth is to be found in each."[43] So, for Augustine "words might be understood in several senses," and as long as they concur with other biblical text, each can be, in fact, "equally divine."[44] There is not a doubt that MacDonald would wholeheartedly agree with Augustine's assessment. He writes, "A mind that recognizes any of the multitudinous meanings of the revelation of God, in the world of sounds, and forms, and colours, cannot be blind to the higher manifestation of God in common humanity."[45] While the following passage is admittedly directed toward the interpretation of MacDonald's own work, it applies here as well: "It may be better that you should read your meaning into it. That may be a higher operation of your intellect than the mere reading of mine out of it: your meaning may be superior to mine."[46] Thus, while there is meaning in the text, the interpreter may be impressed by the divine light to interpret the text in such a way that the meaning is more significant to the reader than what was originally intended by the author.

But on the other hand, for the uninitiated to read Scripture, as well as MacDonald's own work, only as literal, would be missing important information and personal growth potential. Augustine wrote, "Now it is surely a miserable slavery of the soul to take signs for things, and to be unable to lift the eye of the mind above what is

---

42 Ibid., II.12.

43 Ibid., II.12.

44 Ibid., III.27.

45 George MacDonald, *A Dish of Orts*, "Browning's 'Christmas Eve,'" 198.

46 Ibid., "The Fantastic Imagination," 316-7.

corporeal and created, that it may drink in eternal light."[47] Waddle concludes this line of thought: "Literal language cannot convey adequately the intentions of God. When language is approached in a non-symbolistic fashion it is destructive. MacDonald echoes Saint Augustine's hermeneutic principle that literal interpretation is spiritually deadening."[48] For MacDonald, the simplicity of language could not contain the complete meaning of God's utterance: "The fault of trying to say too much at once, of pouring out stintless the plethora of a soul swelling with life and its thought, through the too narrow neck of human utterance."[49] Thus, Augustine and MacDonald agreed that in Scripture, and in addition for MacDonald— works of fantasy, symbols can hold a deeper meaning than the literal interpretation, and that, depending on the trueness of the reader, can act as a conduit for significant meaning from the divine.

In a similar vein, yet with an even stronger connection to MacDonald than the work of Augustine, is the mysticism and theory of correspondences in the work of Emanuel Swedenborg. MacDonald alluded to this specific concept in his *Malcolm*, "Without having read a word of Swedenborg, he was a believer in the absolute correspondence of the inward and outward."[50] As will be thoroughly discussed below, MacDonald modified Swedenborg's theory of correspondences for his own philosophy. But here it will suffice to have demonstrated that MacDonald was a reader, and it may not be a stretch to say, a proponent of Swedenborg's theory. Kegler stated that MacDonald's "work is penetrated by a significant, partly implicit, partly explicit relationship to Swedenborg's thought—world, and in this too it stands in the context of symbolism"[51] and even goes to far as to state, "the core of MacDonald's symbolic landscapes is based on Swedenborg's teaching."[52] Thus the following research will inquire of Swedenborg's theory of correspondences and how MacDonald modified this theory

---

47 Augustine, *On Christian Doctrine* III.5.

48 Keith Waddle, "George MacDonald and the Homiletics of Religious Imagination," 5.

49 George MacDonald, *Unspoken Sermons*, "The Mirrors of the Lord," 205.

50 George MacDonald, *Malcolm* (Whitehorn: Johannesen, 2004), 35.

51 Adelheid Kegler, "Some Aspects of the Oeuvre of George MacDonald in a Curriculum of Philosophy Courses and in the Production of a Play at a German Gymnasium," 33.

52 Ibid., 32.

in his own writings.

Swedenborg explains the nature of what he means by correspondence: "First, I need to state what correspondence is. The whole natural world is responsive to the spiritual world—the natural world not just in general, but in detail. So whatever arises in the natural world out of the spiritual one is called 'something that corresponds.' It needs to be realized that the natural world arises from and is sustained in being by the spiritual world, exactly the way an effect relates to its efficient cause."[53] So, for Swedenborg, everything in this natural world corresponds to something in the spiritual. He leaves nothing without correspondence. All things great and small have this deeper, symbolic meaning; "In a word, absolutely everything in nature, from the smallest to the greatest, is a correspondence. The reason correspondences occur is that the natural world, including everything in it, arises and is sustained from the spiritual world, and both worlds come from the Divine.[54]

As an example of this concept, here is a discussion on a specific correspondence in which Swedenborg held: he believed that the sun directly corresponded to Jesus Christ: "Heaven's sun is the Lord; light there is the divine truth and warmth the divine good that radiate from the Lord as the sun. Everything that comes into being and manifests itself in the heavens is from this source.... The reason the Lord in heaven appears as the sun is that he is the divine love from which all spiritual things come into being—and, through the agency of our world's sun, all natural things as well. That love is what shines like a sun."[55] Swedenborg even went so far to say that our body parts corresponded to the spiritual realm. For instance the forehead corresponds to heavenly love and our eyes correspond to spiritual discernment[56,] and that our "members, organs, and viscera"[57] all have correspondences.

Swedenborg's position on the Holy Scriptures was that they were written in sheer correspondences: "In order that there might be a union of heaven with humanity, the Word was written in pure

---

53 Emanuel Swedenborg, *Heaven and Hell: the Portable New Century Translation*, trans. by George F. Dole (West Chester, Swedenborg Foundation, 2010), I.89.

54 Ibid., I.106.

55 Ibid., I.117.

56 Ibid., I.145.

57 Ibid., I.100.

correspondences. Absolutely everything in it corresponds. So if we were steeped in a knowledge of correspondences, we would understand the Word in its spiritual meaning and be enabled to know hidden treasures in it that we do not see at all in its literal meaning."[58] Not only did Jesus speak in divine representations and symbolic language,[59] but the whole of the Bible is written, and can be interpreted, according to the law of correspondences. For example, here Swedenborg discusses the Revelation of John, chapter 19, "A knowledge of correspondences tells us the meaning of the white horse and of the one who sat on it, of the eyes that were like a flame of fire, of the gems that were on his head, of the robe dipped in blood, of the white linen worn by the people of his army in heaven, of the angel standing in the sun, of the great supper to which they were coming and gathering, also of the flesh of monarchs and commanders and the many others that they were to eat."[60] This seems similar, with some alterations, to George MacDonald's explication of the white stone found in Revelation 2:17. He explains the meaning behind the white stone in his *Unspoken Sermon* "A New Name," which will be explored more in the following pages. To Swedenborg there is a deep mystical meaning to each of these items found in Revelation as well as the Bible in its entirety; in fact, he saw the union of physical items to a spiritual correspondence as unequivocally necessary. To stress this idea Swedenborg states that "within absolutely everything in the material world there lie more deeply hidden some means and some purpose from the spiritual world, because the things that exist in the material world are the final effects into which prior realities are flowing. It is inner realities that are portrayed and outer ones that do the portraying."[61]

So, how is the reader to know these correspondences? In a word: mystically. The reader's ability to understand correspondences has a direct relation to his connection to the divine. Swedenborg argued that the knowledge of correspondences is not something taught or even a discipline, but rather inferred transcendentally, directly from our Heavenly Father: "So if our efforts to open that meaning come from ourselves and not from the Lord, heaven is closed to us; and once

---

58   Ibid., I.114.

59   Emanuel Swedenborg, *Sacred Scripture /White Horse: the Portable New Century Translation*, trans. By George F. Dole (West Chester, Swedenborg Foundation, 2015), 12.

60   Ibid., 9.

61   Ibid., 12.

it is closed, we either see nothing or lose our spiritual sanity."[62] Thus, like Augustine before him, Swedenborg agreed that interpretation without divine enlightenment is spiritually deadening.

To transition into MacDonald's symbolism, one will not have to look far to find verbiage that is very similar to Swedenborg's: "The heavens and the earth are around us that it may be possible for us to speak of the unseen by the seen; for the outermost husk of creation has correspondence with the deepest things of the Creator."[63] This concept also appeared in his fiction as well; in *The Flight of the Shadow* MacDonald writes, "the useless speculation has only driven me to believe that the relations on the surface of life are but the symbols of far deeper ties, which may exist without those correspondent external ones."[64]

In one of his most revealing discussions on his view of correspondences, MacDonald explains, "What has been called his [the apostle Paul's] mysticism is at one time the exercise of a power of seeing, as by spiritual refraction, truths that had not, perhaps have not yet, risen above the human horizon; at another, the result of a wide-eyed habit of noting the analogies and correspondences between the concentric regions of creation."[65] He describes even further: "For in everything that God has made, there is layer upon layer of ascending significance; also he expresses the same thought in higher and higher kinds of that thought: it is God's things, his embodied thoughts, which alone a man has to use, modified and adapted to his own purposes, for the expression of his thoughts."[66]

Not only does MacDonald note the different regions of creation and the linking of correspondences that is indicative of Swedenborg's thought, he also ends his explanation by noting how there is a metaphysical connection between these regions. It benefits our research on this topic that Greville was quite interested in his father's symbolism. Greville notes that on one occasion he had a deep

---

62 Ibid., 26.

63 George MacDonald, *Unspoken Sermons*, "The Knowing of the Son," 201.

64 George MacDonald, *The Flight of the Shadow* (Whitehorn: Johannesen, 2001), 43.

65 George MacDonald, *Unspoken Sermons*, "The Mirrors of the Lord," 205.

66 George MacDonald, *A Dish of Orts*, "The Fantastic Imagination," 320-1.

conversation with his father on the subject.[67] It is in this portion of Greville's biography of his father where we find the most succinct explanation of his symbolism. Greville explains his father's view: "To him a symbol was far more than an outward and visible sign of an abstract conception: its high virtue lay in a common *substance* with the idea presented."[68] Thus, like Swedenborg, the symbol and the thing being symbolized were not disconnected, but were always in some way metaphysically linked.

But there is a fork in the road where Swedenborg and MacDonald part ways. For Swedenborg, everything in creation corresponds to some spiritual purpose or meaning, but MacDonald did not share this viewpoint. MacDonald held that certain objects in the natural word were endowed with symbolic meaning, and were directly correspondent to something in the spiritual realm, but not all objects had this quality. Greville noted:

> He would allow that the algebraic symbol, which concerns only the three-dimensioned, has no *substantial* relation to the unknown quantity.... But the rose, when it gives some glimmer of the freedom for which a man hungers, does so because of its *substantial* unity with the man, each in degree being a signature of God's immanence.... So may even a gem, giving from its heart reflections of heavenly glory, awaken like memory in ourselves and send our eyes upwards. So also we may find co-substance between the stairs of a cathedral-spire and our own "secret stair" up to the wider vision–the faculty of defying the 'plumb-line of gravity' being the common and imaginative heritage.[69]

Colin Manlove notes this method as well: "Certain images in his experience seemed to him so especially designed to raise a longing for heaven that he believed they were particular manifestations of God. Jewels and flowers did this for him as well as stairs."[70] MacDonald believed that writing while utilizing these types of correspondent symbols was "the highest mode of conveying the deepest truth."[71]

Colin Manlove explains the advantages to using this sort of

---

67   Greville MacDonald, *George MacDonald and His Wife*, 482.

68   Ibid., 481-2.

69   Ibid.

70   Colin Manlove, *Modern Fantasy: Five Studies* (New York: Cambridge University, 1978), 96.

71   George MacDonald, *Unspoken Sermons*, "The New Name," 37.

symbolism as a conduit of truth, "The only theoretic obstacle to the success of the method is the reader's subjectivity (not everyone will respond to a given image of desire): and this MacDonald perhaps circumvents through his use of archetypal rather than 'algebraic' symbolism."[72] In other words, the reader does not need to search for meaning behind every object in his stories, but rather, MacDonald uses a few basic archetypes to rouse the reader's consciousness. Thus, if the reader is a "true man"[73] then he will interpret the deeper truth behind these correspondences, and perhaps "the reader may have a form of religious experience through them."[74]

To help us understand MacDonald's symbolism more deeply, we shall consider how he elucidated and interpreted the symbolism of St. John in the second chapter of Revelation. MacDonald wrote an entire sermon on John's symbols of "the white stone" and "the new name" mentioned in Rev. 2:17 which reads: "Whoever has ears, let them hear what the Spirit says to the churches. To the one who is victorious, I will give some of the hidden manna. I will also give that person a white stone with a new name written on it, known only to the one who receives it." Interestingly enough, MacDonald compared John's symbolism in this passage to Swedenborg's mysticism.[75] He also commented that this passage contained "the essence of religion."[76] Before he interpreted the passage, he interjects his own mystical, relational theology: "See, now, what a significance the symbolism of our text assumes. Each of us is a distinct flower or tree in the spiritual garden of God, —precious, each for his own sake, in the eyes of him who is even now making us, —each of us watered and shone upon and filled with life, for the sake of his flower, his completed being, which will blossom out of him at last to the glory and pleasure of the great gardener. For each has within him a secret of the Divinity; each is growing towards the revelation of that secret to himself, and so to the full reception, according to his measure, of the divine."[77] It is this lens through which MacDonald interprets this passage from John. The culmination of this life is to grow into the flower in which the Father intended each of us to grow. Thus, in reaching the point where we will

---

72 Colin Manlove, *Modern Fantasy: Five Studies*, 97.
73 George MacDonald, *A Dish of Orts*, "The Fantastic Imagination," 320.
74 Colin Manlove, *Modern Fantasy: Five Studies*, 97.
75 George MacDonald, *Unspoken Sermons*, "The New Name," 37.
76 Ibid., 37.
77 Ibid., 40.

receive the "white stone," we have grown to our full potential, and the giving of this object is the culmination of the divine life in which we are partakers.

Upon this foundation, MacDonald interprets thusly: "I think he [John] sees in its whiteness purity, and in its substance indestructibility. But I care chiefly to regard the stone as the vehicle of the name, — as the form whereby the name is represented as passing from God to the man, and what is involved in this communication is what I wish to show."[78] MacDonald thus concludes that the new name will be, "the communication of what God thinks about the man," "the divine judgment," his "soul's picture" and "the personal individual relation of every man to his God."[79] It is through this interpretation, and the knowledge of correspondences and symbolism that underlie this interpretation, that MacDonald believes helps the reader to reach "the deepest things of the Creator."[80] But of course, MacDonald demonstrates his humility by leaving his interpretation up for alteration or rejection altogether: "What his mystic meaning may be, must be taken differently by different minds...."[81] He finishes with, "If my reader will not acknowledge my representation as St. John's meaning, I yet hope so to set it forth that he shall see the representation to be true in itself, and then I shall willingly leave the interpretation to its fate."[82] While he suggests that his interpretation may not be accurate, he believes his words, on their own, actually do correspond to reality and to God's own heart.

Thus, MacDonald's sacramentalist, archetypal symbolism was his common mode of interpretation of biblical Scripture as well as the backbone and mode of operation for many of his fantasies. While MacDonald's novels are often criticized for the narrator's interjection into stories, and, specific to this line of reasoning, his directness; but in his fantasies and fairy tales, the author intentionally spoke less directly, through more obscure, although arguably more potent, correspondences. This will be discussed in more detail in chapter six.

In conclusion, the similarities between Augustine and MacDonald on the limitations of language and the multiplicity of

---

78 Ibid., 38.
79 Ibid., 39.
80 George MacDonald, *Unspoken Sermons*, "The Knowing of the Son," 201.
81 George MacDonald, *Unspoken Sermons*, "The New Name," 38
82 Ibid., 38.

scriptural interpretation are strikingly similar. Also, there is no doubt that Swedenborg's concept of correspondences was the ground upon which MacDonald's symbolic structure rested.

Waking the Dead

CHAPTER FOUR

Epistemology and Attainment of Knowledge

Introduction

The Victorian era had its share of problems: social, industrial, and spiritual, but in addition to these, the minds of the populace swirled with unsettled questions on the topic of empirical grounding and divine revelation. There is little doubt that MacDonald grew up "in a literary age that was still busy reacting to eighteenth-century rationalism"[1] where many Christians of the time found the footing of their epistemology, slipping. They had relied on rationalistic arguments, but when seemingly stronger empirical arguments came along, their faith faltered. Jocelyn Slepyan explains in her study of Ruskin's epistemological struggles: "From 1802 with the publication of Paley's celebrated *Natural Theology* until the middle of the 19th century, many evangelicals relied on nature for proofs of God's existence.... But this reliance on nature became uncomfortable...as nature failed to support literal readings of Scripture , and as advances in geology and biology began to question Scripture -based arguments for the age of the earth and proposed natural selection over a purposeful deity."[2] If this were not problematic enough, not only was philosophical empiricism being undermined, but also divine revelation: "Higher criticism of the Bible also challenged literalist readings with questions of authorship, sources, and the explanation of miracles."[3] In the case of John Ruskin, as well as in many other Victorian evangelicals, the empirical shift ended in a process which Ruskin called "unconversion," mostly due to the fact that the tendency of "Victorian science was to prove man a mechanism."[4] Some scholars consider what happened to Ruskin as "exemplary of what many in his generation experienced."[5] Tanya Ingham writes, "Some evangelicals demonstrated an inability

---

1   Jeff McInnis, *Shadows and Chivalry* (Hamden, CT: Winged Lion Press, 2012), 54-5.

2   Jocelyne Slepyan, "'With all sorts of doubts I am familiar': George MacDonald's Literary Response to John Ruskin's Struggles with Epistemology" in in *Rethinking George MacDonald* (Glasgow: Scottish Literature International, 2013), 37.

3   Jocelyne Slepyan, "With all sorts of doubts I am familiar," 37.

4   Greville MacDonald, *George MacDonald and His Wife*, 338.

5   Jocelyne Slepyan, "With all sorts of doubts I am familiar," 37.

to face the challenges squarely and consequently developed an anti-intellectual reputation. MacDonald's faith was relatively unshaken as he believed that all truth was God's truth. He sustained throughout his life an open and eager disposition towards the advancement of knowledge, which served him well in the wide variety of friendships he maintained."[6]

There is no question that MacDonald was "a part of a revolt against mere rationalism"[7] for those of the Victorian era believed that "all truth must prove itself by the testimony of the senses or by deductive logic."[8] So it is clear that he attempted to "devalue logic and the intellect"[9], but to suggest that MacDonald was anti-reason and anti-science would be to stretch the evidence beyond what is revealed in his work. It is true, as will be observed below, that MacDonald attempted to knock both rationalism and empiricism off of their epistemic pedestals, but to suggest that he placed little value in these other conduits of knowledge would simply be incorrect. There are obvious quotations where reason and science are criticized, but to take these out of context of the whole work, or even his whole opus, would not do justice to MacDonald's epistemological goal.

In modern scholarship, MacDonald's epistemology is a fairly contested issue. While we have those such as Robert Lee Wolff and Bonnie Gaarden who put him on par with the Romantics: "Like other mystics and Romantics, MacDonald valued intuition and feeling over intellect as a means of perceiving ultimate truth"[10]; we also have those who contest this position, including Jeff McInnis: "Identifying MacDonald as closely as [Robert Lee Wolff] does with the Romantics is a mistake [especially in the area of] the Romantic choice of emotion and feeling over the intellect."[11] While there are scholars that hold to extremes, this chapter will argue that, "reason helped sustain

---

6   Tanya Ingham, "George MacDonald: An Original Thinker" in *Knowing and Doing: A Teaching Quarterly for Discipleship of Heart and Mind*. Fall 2009, 12.

7   Jeff McInnis, *Shadows and Chivalry*, 54-5.

8   Jocelyne Slepyan, "With all sorts of doubts I am familiar," 43.

9   Bonnie Gaarden, *The Christian Goddess*. (Lanham: Fairleigh Dickinson University Press, 2011), 8.

10 Bonnie Gaarden, *The Christian Goddess*, 8.

11 Jeff McInnis, *Shadows and Chivalry*, 114.

MacDonald's faith more than one might imagine at first glance."¹² The man who is often cited as siding with the Romantics on being in "favor of feeling and intuition"¹³ as the sole source of knowledge, also leaned, somewhat, on his intellect. MacDonald succinctly stated, "Jesus is the creating and saving lord of our intellects as well as of our more precious hearts."¹⁴ After reflecting on two of his predecessors, the following research will revolve around MacDonald's own brand of moral epistemology, spiritual logic, and experiential certainty. Lastly, as an addendum, this chapter includes a complementary study on MacDonald and his influential contemporaries' attitudes toward the revelation of the Old and New Testaments.

Empiricism and Science as the Porch to God's temple

In an analysis of MacDonald and Charles Kingsley, Colin Manlove wrote, "[MacDonald] acknowledges the problem of doubt in the face of scientific discovery. His answer, as we saw, is simply to dismiss science as an irrelevance. Indeed, he tends as it were to amputate from himself those faculties which are most conscious and outward-looking. Where Kingsley tries to square his intellectual awareness with his faith, MacDonald rather does away with it."[15] Manlove reduces MacDonald's attitude toward the study as "Faith-less science" and that "where Kingsley could entertain a dialogue between science and religion, and consider God Himself as a scientist, for MacDonald there is no real debate for only one side of the 'debate' is real. Ultimately MacDonald's universe is non-dialectical."[16] As was argued in chapter two, and in contrast to Manlove's honorable opinion, MacDonald considered this world as metaphysically "real." But, to digress, the question of MacDonald's opinion of science's validity as an honorable pursuit is an open one. Many scholars may quickly respond with MacDonald's assertion, "I, for my part, protest that rather be a king of science I would be an idiot with a heart"[17] as

---

12   Ibid., 55.

13   Bonnie Gaarden, *The Christian Goddess*, 8.

14   George MacDonald, *Unspoken Sermons*, "Justice," 242.

15   Colin Manlove, "MacDonald and Kingsley: A Victorian Contrast" in *The Gold Thread: Essays on George MacDonald*, ed, William Raeper (Edinburgh: Edinburgh UP, 1990), 151.

16   Colin Manlove, "MacDonald and Kingsley: A Victorian Contrast," 151.

17   George MacDonald, *George MacDonald in the Pulpit*, "Growth in

proof that he dispensed with the study of science as a whole, but this would be an oversimplification of MacDonald's complex view.

It is undeniable that when MacDonald used the phrase "man of science" he meant it as a derogatory term. To him, the "man of science" was an individual with a bloodthirsty appetite for knowledge who operated as if these attained facts were the formal cause and purpose of our existence, and whose conclusions and aspirations are utterly "godless."[18] Thus, MacDonald's "man of science" is his embodiment of the stereotypical, materialistic atheist. Bruce Hindmarsh points out that "MacDonald saw science as knowledge gleaned with our backs to God."[19] In the following paragraphs, MacDonald's disdain for the "man of science" will be revealed, but also, it will also be demonstrated that the fault of scientific study is not its attempt to gain some knowledge via the senses, or rather, its empirical nature, but rather MacDonald condemned it due to the man of science's lack of interest in divine wisdom.

Most specifically, in *The Hope of the Gospel*, MacDonald reveals his contempt: "Such men, so-called of science—let them have the dignity to the fullness of its worth—lust to know as if a man's life lay in knowing, as if it were a vile thing to be ignorant—so vile that, for the sake of his secret hoard of facts, they do right in breaking with torture into the house of the innocent! Surely they shall not thus find the way of understanding! Surely there is a maniac thirst for knowledge, as a maniac thirst for wine or for blood! He who loves knowledge the most genuinely, will with the most patience wait for it until it can be had righteously."[20] Thus, the general quest for knowledge is not to be condemned, but rather, a greedy and purposeless version of science. MacDonald continues, "Alas for the science that will sacrifice the law of righteousness but to behold a law of sequence! The tree of knowledge will never prove to man the tree of life. There is no law says, Thou shalt know; a thousand laws cry out, Thou shalt do right. These men are a law unto themselves—and what a law! It is the old story: the greed of knowing casts out righteousness, and mercy, and faith."[21] The last line forces us to ask the question: can one remove

---

Grace and Knowledge," 144-5.

18   George MacDonald, *A Dish of Orts*, "Individual Development," 60-1.

19   Douglas Bruce Hindmarsh, *The Faith of George MacDonald*, 59.

20   George MacDonald, *The Hope of the Gospel*, "The Hope of the Universe," 102.

21   Ibid., "The Hope of the Universe," 101.

the phrase "the greed of," and the statement still remain true? In consequent paragraphs, and further along in the chapter, this question will be answered. But for now, MacDonald continues to elaborate on the "man of science" in his *Hope of the Gospel*:

> No amount of knowledge or skill in physical science, will make a man the fitter to argue a metaphysical question; and the wisdom of this world, meaning by the term, the philosophy of prudence, self-protection, precaution, specially unfits a man for receiving what the Father has to reveal: in proportion to our care about our own well being, is our incapability of understanding and welcoming the care of the Father. The wise and the prudent, with all their energy of thought, could never see the things of the Father sufficiently to recognize them as true. Their sagacity labours in earthly things, and so fills their minds with their own questions and conclusions, that they cannot see the eternal foundations God has laid in man, or the consequent necessities of their own nature. They are proud of finding out things, but the things they find out are all less than themselves. Because, however, they have discovered them, *they imagine such things the goal of the human intellect*. If they grant there may be things beyond those, they either count them beyond their reach, or declare themselves uninterested in them: for the wise and prudent, they do not exist. They work only to gather by the senses, and deduce from what they have so gathered, the prudential, the probable, the expedient, the protective. They never think of the essential, of what in itself must be. They are cautious, wary, discreet, judicious, circumspect, provident, temporizing. They have no enthusiasm, and are shy of all forms of it—a clever, hard, thin people, who take *things* for the universe, and love of facts for love of truth. They know nothing deeper in man than mere surface mental facts and their relations. They do not perceive, or they turn away from any truth which the intellect cannot formulate. Zeal for God will never eat them up: why should it? he is not interesting to them: theology may be; to such men religion means theology. How should the treasure of the Father be open to such? In their hands his rubies would draw in their fire, and cease to glow. The roses of paradise in their gardens would blow withered. They never go beyond the *porch of the temple*; they are not sure whether there be any *adytum*, and they do not care to go in and see: why indeed should they? it would but be to turn and come out again.[22]

---

22   Ibid., "The Yoke of Jesus," 68-9, emphasis added.

Waking the Dead

MacDonald concludes that the man of science sets knowledge of facts as the "goal of the intellect," even calling scientists "thin people" and persons who confuse mere facts with the much deeper "truth." Note, in this section MacDonald says that the "men of science" are actually, analogously, on the porch of the temple. They are dealing with the workings of the creator, but they do not recognize these as his creations, nor do they care to know. They seek knowledge for its own sake, and not for any deeper revelation.

To begin our transition to a more positive outlook on science, note the difference in how MacDonald contrasts between the "men of science" and the "poet" and, later in the passage, the "children of God":

> Ask a man of mere science, what is the truth of a flower: he will pull it to pieces, show you its parts, explain how they operate, how they minister each to the life of the flower; he will tell you what changes are wrought in it by scientific cultivation; where it lives originally, where it can live; the effects upon it of another climate; what part the insects bear in its varieties—and doubtless many more facts about it. Ask the poet what is the truth of the flower, and he will answer: "Why, the flower itself, the perfect flower, and what it cannot help saying to him who has ears to hear it." The truth of the flower is, not the facts about it, be they correct as ideal science itself, but the shining, glowing, gladdening, patient thing throned on its stalk—the compeller of smile and tear from child and prophet. The man of science laughs at this, because he is only a man of science, and does not know what it means; but the poet and the child care as little for his laughter as the birds of God, as Dante calls the angels, for his treatise on aerostation. The children of God must always be mocked by the children of the world, whether in the church or out of it—children with sharp ears and eyes, but dull hearts. Those that hold love the only good in the world, understand and smile at the world's children, and can do very well without anything they have got to tell them. In the higher state to which their love is leading them, they will speedily outstrip the men of science, for they have that which is at *the root of science*, that for *the revealing of which God's science exists*. What shall it profit a man to know all things, and lose the bliss, the consciousness of well-being, which alone can give value to his knowledge?[23]

---

23 George MacDonald, *Unspoken Sermons*, "The Truth," 212-3.

Observe that to introduce the section MacDonald inserts into his phrase "man of mere science" the qualifier "mere," here, alludes to the earlier targeting of godless scientists whose scientific endeavors are valueless. For a Godly scientist, in MacDonald's mind, is no mere scientist, but is a man of God. It becomes clear further in the paragraph that the poet, and the children of God, "have what is at the root of science" and are spiritually prepared for "the revealing of which God's science exists."[24]

This is one of the few times that MacDonald combined terminology for science and the divine, but it should not surprise the reader that MacDonald found it possible for a man of God to love the study of nature, for there is ample evidence that MacDonald was a budding scientist in his early years, especially in his initial study of chemistry[25], and medicine.[26] One researcher suggested that "MacDonald loved and revered his father, and so an interest in and love of the sciences could have developed from his father's views."[27] No matter the origin of his interest, it did not completely die out but continued into adulthood. His son, Greville, himself a medical doctor, spoke of reading Charles Darwin's *Voyage of the Beagle* and told his father "I think you would enjoy it very much"[28] and he even stated that his father was "as scientific as Ruskin."[29]

The truth of the matter is that, in MacDonald's opinion, the presupposition of God's existence colors all scientific and natural phenomena. For the pure atheistic science, as illustrated in the botanist who finds a primrose, "pulls it to pieces to see its construction, and delights the intellect; but the science itself is dead, and kills what it touches."[30] Even as a college student he realized, "All of the knowledge of this world does seem so incomplete—so spiritless without religion—and I think few minds are more capable of deriving delight from the knowledge of this world's truth than mine. But when

---

24   Ibid., 212-3.

25   William Raeper, George MacDonald, 42-4; and Greville MacDonald, *George MacDonald and His Wife*, 70.

26   Rolland Hein, *George MacDonald: Victorian Mythmaker*, 48.

27   David L. Neuhouser, "Mathematics, Science, and George MacDonald" in *Journal of the Association of Christians in the Mathematical Sciences*, Vol. 1, 2003, 2.

28   Greville MacDonald, *George MacDonald and His Wife*, 93.

29   Ibid., 338.

30   George MacDonald, *A Dish of Orts*, "Wordsworth's Poetry," 257-8.

the light of religion is thrown upon it, it is as if it were a soul to the knowledge which was dead before."[31]

Bruce Hindmarsh writes on MacDonald's thoughts, "To selfishly pursue knowledge is to find that knowledge a dead thing."[32] Even more succinctly, the scientist is "inclined to exalt the intellect at the expense even of the heart."[33] MacDonald sought to undercut the Victorian ideal of this atheistic, scientific man. In MacDonald's mind, the scientist, manifested in the character George Bascombe in *Thomas Wingfold*, should not be our ideal. MacDonald describes the alternative: "Now-a-days, there is such a talk about science, and such a contempt poured forth on the man who thinks to walk without that kind of science for the guide of his life, who has a different goal, a different ambition, whose thoughts stretch further than the things of this life—the things he sees and hears and handles—if there be such a man among us, friends, who does the work of the world, and does it well, but his head is in heaven—that is the kind of thing we ought all to be and to seek."[34]

While he does undercut science, MacDonald argues that the study of nature can be of high value to the true man, the man who seeks out God: "We have already said that the forms of Nature (by which word *forms* we mean any of those conditions of Nature which affect the senses of man) are so many approximate representations of the mental conditions of humanity. The outward, commonly called the material, is *informed* by, or has form in virtue of, the inward or immaterial — in a word, the thought. The forms of Nature are the representations of human thought in virtue of their being the embodiment of God's thought. As such, therefore, they can be read and used to any depth, shallow or profound.... The man, then, who, in harmony with nature, attempts the discovery of more of her meanings, is just searching out the things of God."[35] Even more specifically, "To the man of God, all nature will be but changeful reflections of the face of God."[36]

---

31   Glenn Edward Sadler, *An Expression of Character: the Letters of George MacDonald* (Grand Rapids: Eerdmans, 1994), 20.

32   Douglas Bruce Hindmarsh, *The Faith of George MacDonald*, 59.

33   George MacDonald, *Annals of a Quiet Neighbourhood*, 7.

34   George MacDonald, *George MacDonald in the Pulpit*, "Faith the Proof of the Unseen," 69-70.

35   George MacDonald, *A Dish of Orts*, "The Imagination: Its Function and its Culture," 18.

36   Ibid., "Wordsworth's Poetry," 256.

This falls perfectly in synthesis with our earlier understandings with MacDonald's theory of correspondences observed in the second section of chapter three, "For what thing is there in the world, or what group of things, in which the natural man will not see merely the things of nature, but the spiritual man the things of the spirit."[37] Thus science and the study of nature can be beneficial because "the natural laws reveal the character of God,"[38] and in the right hands, "Nature put into the crucible of a loving heart becomes poetry."[39] The true man will be able to understand these correspondences and their underlying meanings, while the man of science will only deal with facts and lesser truths.

In conclusion, while George MacDonald is well known for rejecting the materialistic, scientific man as an ideal, this should not be taken as an outright rejection of empirical study or rational inquiry. For in fact, MacDonald believed that "The intellect itself is but the scaffolding for the uprearing of the spiritual nature."[40] He also argued, via correspondences, that Nature can inform the poet and even edify our relationship with God. But, as the next chapter will inquire: what was the role of reason in the Christian faith? And can nature inform us concerning the existence of God?

The Role of Reason and the Arguments for God's Existence

Along with the dissension among scholars concerning MacDonald's view of science, the role of reason is also under dispute. Bonnie Gaarden writes that MacDonald ignored rationality in "favor of feeling and intuition."[41] Even when scholars argue that rationality is not outright rejected in MacDonald's opus, it is usually viewed pejoratively: "Certainly the degree to which [C.S.] Lewis believes in reason as a determinant of faith is quite unlike MacDonald, who often regards it as an impertinence."[42] While some dismiss or seek to lessen the role of reason in MacDonald's thought, others suggest that the writer "sought to reestablish a 'rationality' that views the spiritual

---

37 George MacDonald, *The Seaboard Parish*, 248.

38 Ibid., 621.

39 George MacDonald, *A Dish of Orts*, "Wordsworth's Poetry," 257.

40 Ibid., "Wordsworth's Poetry," 257-8.

41 Bonnie Gaarden, *The Christian Goddess*, 8.

42 Colin Manlove, "Parent or Associate? George MacDonald and the Inklings" in *George MacDonald: Literary Heritage and Heirs* (Wayne: Zossima Press, 2008), 232.

not in opposition to the rational and empirical world."[43]

In the normative sense of the word, there is little doubt that MacDonald considered reason as something to be cherished and encouraged. He states unequivocally, "To think well is what everybody ought to be or to become able to do."[44] He also responds to those who may have misinterpreted his warnings of the dangers of materialistic intellectualism: "God forbid I should seem to despise understanding. The New Testament is full of urgings to understand."[45] He even argues that Christ himself "addresses us as reasonable creatures"[46] and that "the Bible urges upon us to search and understand."[47] For MacDonald, the ability to reason is a part of the image of God instilled in humanity: "Do not say [God's truth] is too high for you. God made you in his own image, therefore capable of understanding him."[48]

MacDonald not only argued the value of reason in his oeuvre. Greville even mentions that his father lived out this concept in conversation. While he did not have a passion for debate, when the time arose to interject in conversation, "his keen sense of logic made him shine in controversy."[49] As will be noted in later chapters on MacDonald's apologetic, MacDonald's style was not directly analytical in his approach, but he did have reasons for his belief. McInnis writes that MacDonald "never wrote a chapter attempting to answer logical misgivings by setting out carefully reasoned arguments," but if we "look closely enough,"[50] we can find reasons for his belief therein. No scholar of whom this researcher is aware treats MacDonald as a professor of propositional logic, but to treat MacDonald as an anti-rationalist would swing the pendulum to the other erroneous extreme. While MacDonald did not wholly dispense with rationality, he held

---

43   Gisela H. Kreglinger, "Poets, Dreamers, and Mediators" in *George MacDonald: Literary Heritage and Heirs.* Wayne: Zossima Press, 2008), 30.

44   George MacDonald, *The Wise Woman/Gutta Percha Willie* (Whitehorn: Johannesen, 1998), 213.

45   George MacDonald, *The Hope of the Gospel*, "Salvation from Sin," 11.

46   George MacDonald, *David Elginbrod* (Whitehorn: Johannesen, 1995), 349.

47   George MacDonald, *Annals of a Quiet Neighbourhood*, 442.

48   George MacDonald, *The Seaboard Parish*, 152.

49   Greville MacDonald, *George MacDonald and His Wife*, 365.

50   Jeff McInnis, *Shadows and Chivalry*, 81.

that mere intellectual reasons for believing in God did not result in faith. But to make this argument, one must first see how MacDonald defined faith, for faith, in his mind, is no mere intellectual assent.

In his sermon "Faith and the Proof of the Unseen" he starts with this definition: "This thing of faith means the whole recognized fellowship of man to God and His fellows; it is the right position of the human soul which is made to understand the truth — the right position of that soul towards the truth; that is faith, partly."[51] Faith, and even knowledge, are much more than merely intellectual: "Truly the relation of the world to its maker cannot primarily be an intellectual one; it must be a relation tremendously deeper."[52] MacDonald continues this argument: "Do you see? Faith in its true sense does not belong to the intellect alone, nor to the intellect first, but to the conscience, to the will, and that man is a faithful man who says 'I cannot prove that there is a God, but, O God, if Thou hearest me anywhere, help me to do Thy will.' There is faith, 'Do this,' and he does it."[53] As will be seen below, MacDonald had low expectations for the efficaciousness of rational arguments for God's existence, but his disdain for these arguments should be always tempered with the understanding that MacDonald did not define faith as intellectual assent, but rather, as a dependent relationship of creature to created and the willingness of the creature to do God's will.

To begin, consider MacDonald's direct reproach of the cognitive superiority of rationalism:

> It is natural that we should doubt, with such cries especially on all sides of us, and the intellect so much more awake than ever it was before, and indeed the conscience not more asleep than before; and with one on this side and one on that side crying out, "I have reached, I have seen, and I have found no God." Settle this with yourselves to begin with. *Not all the intellect or metaphysics of the world could prove that there is no God, and not all the intellect in the world could prove that there is a God.* If you could prove that there is a God, that would imply that you could go all round Him, and buttress up his being with your human argument that He should exist. As soon might a child on his mother's bosom, looking up into his

---

51 George MacDonald, *George MacDonald in the Pulpit*, "Faith the Proof of the Unseen," 66.

52 George MacDonald, *There and Back*, 543.

53 George MacDonald, *George MacDonald in the Pulpit*, "Faith the Proof of the Unseen," 72.

mother's face, write a treatise on what a woman was, and what a mother was.

But do not think that God is angry with you because you find it hard to believe. It is not so; that is not like God; God is all that you can honestly wish Him to be, and infinitely more; He is not angry with you for that. And He knows perfectly well what the scientific man calls truth — although you will observe that he is always constantly, and everywhere changing his theories — that what the scientific man calls truth is simply an impossibility with regard to God; and God knows it. Your brain, the symbol of your intellect, cannot, concerning Him, if He exists, receive that kind of proof which you have when you read a proposition of Euclid. It commends itself to your mind and your understanding. You say, "So it is, and it cannot be otherwise." But you cannot receive that kind of proof; there is no such proof with regard to the Mighty God.[54]

MacDonald's son even remembers a personal encounter with his father in which Greville expected rational proof for God's existence:

"Father," said I, tapping the table with a finger, "can you tell me that you *know* the God exists whom Jesus proclaimed? Can you tell it me with the same certainty that I can vouch for this table I am touching?" A look of spiritual indignation—almost of momentary anger at my stupidity—flashed across his face. "Of course not!" he exclaimed. "Do you think I could believe in a God demonstrated, proved by weight, resistance, inevitability?"[55]

The fact of the matter is that MacDonald thought that intellectual proof, whether effective at producing normative knowledge or not, was not the main avenue by which we should find God.

In another work on the same topic, MacDonald even granted that rationality could possibly give proof of God's existence, but this proof still did not result in faith: "We are not satisfied that the world should be a proof and varying indication of the intellect of God. That was how Paley viewed it. He taught us to believe that there is a God from the mechanism of the world. But, allowing all the argument to be quite correct, what does it prove? A mechanical God, and nothing more."[56] Thus, even if Paley's teleological argument were sound, the

---

54 Ibid., "Faith the Proof of the Unseen," 70-1, emphasis added.
55 Greville MacDonald, *George MacDonald and His Wife*, 336-7.
56 George MacDonald, *A Dish of Orts*, "Browning's 'Christmas Eve,'" 216.

argument results in mere knowledge of a deistic God, a creator and designer, but not a loving, relational father. Just like James illustrated in chapter two of his epistle, the demons know of God's existence, but this knowledge is not faith. For MacDonald, there must be more.

Before inquiring what needs to be added to rationality for faith to come to full fruition, it must be demonstrated that MacDonald argued against intellectualism in the same way that he disputed materialistic scientism: "Our vision is so circumscribed, our theories are so small—the garment of them not large enough to wrap us in; our faith so continually fashions itself to the fit of our dwarf intellect, that there is endless room for rebellion against ourselves: we must not let our poor knowledge limit our not so poor intellect, our intellect limit our faith, our faith limit our divine hope; reason must humbly watch over all-reason, the candle of the Lord."[57] He argues here that the intellect can actually be a detriment to faith, if reason is not tempered by humility. If we are not careful, intellect, as well as other pathways to knowledge, can become a stumbling block: "We become such fools of logic and temper that we lie in the prison-houses of our own fancies, ideas, and experiences, shut the doors and windows against the entrance of the free spirit, and will not inherit the love of the Father."[58] To put MacDonald's position succinctly, and in his own words, he simply despised "valuing the bare assent of the intellect"[59] and firmly stated that, in his mind, there was "no room for that unprofitable thing, bare logic."[60]

From a portion of a *Seabourd Parish*, MacDonald elucidates his position:

> "No man can *prove*," [Dr. Turner] said, "that there is not a being inside a snuff-box, existing in virtue of the harmony of its parts, comfortable when they go well, sick when they go badly, and dying when it is dismembered, or even when it stops."
>
> "No," [Mr. Walton] answered. "No man can prove it. But no man can convince a human being of it. And just as little can anyone convince me that my conscience, making me

---

57 George MacDonald, *Unspoken Sermons*, "Man's Difficulty Concerning Prayer," 120.

58 George MacDonald, *A Dish of Orts*, "A Sermon," 296.

59 George MacDonald, *Unspoken Sermons*, "The Word of Jesus on Prayer," 110.

60 George MacDonald, *George MacDonald in the Pulpit*, "A Sermon," 44.

do sometimes what I *don't* like, comes from the harmonious action of the particles of my brain."[61]

Thus, MacDonald, in one small passage, argues that a change of mind, as well as change of heart, is an internal experience which can be influenced by external factors but is overwhelmingly interior. But this does not completely eradicate the use of reason for in the above passage he is internally rationalizing against materialism. MacDonald cannot explain consciousness from the perspective of scientific materialism. How can these thoughts, his experiences, his imagination, spawn from mere particles of his brain? Note that this comment was not an argument set out to convince the reader, but simply a passing comment allowing his character to give a reason why he holds to a belief in something beyond the physical. Jocelyne Slepyan states that while reason and "nature played a regular role in his writings," it was rarely, if ever, seen "as a communal, empirical proof."[62] She continues, "To eighteenth-century theologians such as Paley, nature was once a stable proof that MacDonald, in contrast, saw as a prompt to spiritual things. Nature may at times bear witness to the reality of the spiritual world, but it just as readily confounds those who want it for a materialistic talisman.... [It] does not resolve questions, but encourages those who are searching and stirs up those ready to begin."[63] Thus, his view of rational arguments could be of use to prompting an individual to search for God; as MacDonald himself states: "But the intellect, *great thing though it be*, is yet but the soil out of which, or rather in which, higher things must grow."[64] Yet MacDonald never treated intellectual arguments as a public proof with epistemic force that could challenge and persuade a person from a different point of view. Instead, these reasons need to be an internal, personal conviction.

The question that MacDonald wished his readers to consider, was what was the purpose of one's arguing intellectual proofs? On the fact of God's existence, as well as the reality of Christ's sonship to the Father, attempts to convince others are fruitless:

> I believe that Jesus is the eternal son of the eternal Father; that in him the ideal humanity sat enthroned from all eternity; that

---

61 George MacDonald, *The Seaboard Parish*, 316.

62 Jocelyne Slepyan, "With all sorts of doubts I am familiar," 48.

63 Ibid., 48.

64 George MacDonald, *Donal Grant* (New York: John W. Lovell, 1900), 311, emphasis added.

as he is the divine man, so is he the human God; that there was no taking of our nature upon himself, but the showing of himself as he really was, and that from evermore: these things, friends, I believe, though never would I be guilty of what in me would be the irreverence of opening my mouth in dispute upon them. Not for a moment would I endeavour by argument to convince another of this, my opinion. If it be true, it is God's work to show it, for *logic cannot*.[65]

Thus MacDonald argued that to twist the arms of his listeners using logic was ineffective. But if the listener himself was seeking, there is a potential to help one see and find Christ. As MacDonald speaks through the mouth of the soutar in *Salted With Fire:* "And what's the guid o' history, or sic metapheesics as is the vera sowl o' history, but to help ye to see Christ?"[66] At first glance these two quotations seem to be in tension, but after reflection, in the first, MacDonald is attempting to convince his listeners, and in the second, the soutar is attempting to convince himself. Again, rational arguments are effective if elicited by internal conviction, but not otherwise.

While logic and science are flawed, and are often misused or even venerated, MacDonald argues that "the separation between God and man, although it had destroyed the beatific vision, was not yet so complete as to make the creature deaf to the voice of his Maker."[67] While the following chapter will do much to elucidate MacDonald's position, it can be argued unequivocally that he stated that man could in fact, know God. But this knowledge is much more than intellectual: "So that you see that the same thing that the intellect does with Euclid, the whole mind, heart, intellect, imagination, conscience, and will does with regard to God when a man sees God and knows Him."[68] What is intriguing in this passage is not merely MacDonald's holistic approach, but also that he mentions the intellect in the midst of his list of human qualities, especially after seemingly belittling reason in some of the passages above. The fact of the matter is that MacDonald recognized that the wholeness of man includes the intellect and that Christ commands his followers to love God with their minds, just as

---

65   George MacDonald, *George MacDonald in the Pulpit*, "A Sermon," 51, emphasis added.

66   George MacDonald, *Salted With Fire* (Whitehorn: Johannesen, 2009), 73.

67   George MacDonald, *A Dish of Orts*, "St. George's Day, 1564," 91.

68   George MacDonald, *George MacDonald in the Pulpit*, "Faith the Proof of the Unseen," 75.

much as their souls and strength.

Experiential Certainty and Spiritual Logic: A Moral Epistemology

Returning to a previous topic to facilitate our discussion, MacDonald argued that faith was much more than assent to a specific set of beliefs. The complexities of his concept of faith and knowledge are outlined here in *Paul Faber*:

> Do you long for the assurance of some sensible sign? Do you ask why no intellectual proof is to be had? I tell you that such would but delay, perhaps altogether impair for you, that better, that best, that only vision, into which at last your world must blossom—such a contact, namely, with the heart of God Himself, such a perception of His being, and His absolute oneness with you, the child of His thought, the individuality softly parted from His spirit, yet living still and only by His presence and love, as, by its own radiance, will sweep doubt away forever. Being then in the light and knowing it, the lack of intellectual proof concerning that which is too high for it, will trouble you no more than would your inability to silence a metaphysician who declared that you had no real existence. It is for the sake of such vision as God would give that you are denied such vision as you would have. The Father of our spirits is not content that we should know Him as we now know each other. There is a better, closer, nearer than any human way of knowing, and to that He is guiding us across all the swamps of our unteachableness, the seas of our faithlessness, the desert of our ignorance.[69]

First, MacDonald points out that intellectual, rational proof could be a detriment to faith. It can drive one away, toward rational independence, when instead the Father seeks the realization that we are utterly dependent on his being, presence, love, and radiance. While this can cause confusion for the rationalist, MacDonald's point is that there is a deeper way of knowing, even more multifaceted than our relationship with other human counterparts. It should be acknowledged that MacDonald is not suggesting that certainty is impossible; he actually argues the opposite, that if we follow the Father's guidance, that doubt can be swept away forever. He continues in the same passage from above: "Being then in the light *and knowing it*, the lack of intellectual proof concerning that which is too high

---

69 George MacDonald, *Paul Faber-Surgeon*, 231.

for it, will trouble you no more than would your inability to silence a metaphysician who declared that you had no real existence."[70]

MacDonald's definition of knowledge was not "clear intellectual comprehension, but intimate personal intercourse effected through imagination, feeling, and, most importantly, the doing of that which we know to be good."[71] So it should come to no surprise that MacDonald dispensed with the arguments of the "new schools of a fragmentary philosophy which acknowledge no source of truth but the testimony of the senses and deductions made there from by the intellect."[72] Bruce Hindmarsh stated that MacDonald "quickly tired of the knowledge which must analyze a thing in a detached way" especially concerning knowledge of the divine; MacDonald's "epistemology is always relational and consistently discerns the Father beyond the thing known."[73]

So, how did MacDonald "know," especially on the topic of divine knowledge? As the title of the subchapter denotes, his epistemology was essentially rooted in morality, but the foliage of his epistemological tree was spiritual experience. MacDonald argues, "The sole assurance worth a man's having, even if the most incontestable evidence were open to him from a thousand other quarters, is that to be gained only from personal experience—that assurance in himself which he can least readily receive from another, and which is least capable of being transmuted into evidence for another."[74] Most classical, and even modern philosophers would scoff at such a statement if uttered in their presence, for how can personal, subjective experience be given as a public justification for one's belief? The fact is, MacDonald understood this critique, and even had a few of his characters discuss this problem in his *Seaboard Parish*:

> "But if you will excuse me, Mr. Walton," said Percivale, "you can hardly expect experience to be of use to any but those who have had it. It seems to me that its influences cannot be imparted."
>
> "That depends on the amount of faith in those to whom its results are offered. Of course, as experience, it can have no

---

70 Ibid., 23, emphasis added.
71 Bonnie Gaarden, *The Christian Goddess*, 59.
72 George MacDonald, *The Seaboard Parish*, 293.
73 Douglas Bruce Hindmarsh, *The Faith of George MacDonald*, 58-59.
74 George MacDonald, *Unspoken Sermons*, "The Word of Jesus on Prayer," 110.

weight with another; for it is no longer experience. One remove, and it ceases. But faith in the person who has experienced can draw over or derive—to use an old Italian word—some of its benefits to him who has the faith. Experience may thus, in a sense, be accumulated, and we may go on to fresh experience of our own."[75]

While he acknowledges its difficulties, he nonetheless argues that this "experiential certainty," coined by Jocelyn Slepyan, allows us to "risk intellectual doubts" and by "testing His word by applying it"[76] to our lives, we can know God and his truth through interior means. MacDonald not only used this argument in his works, but also in discussions with John Ruskin: "MacDonald presented Ruskin and his contemporaries with the faith argument of personal investigation of Christ, and the testimony of an internal response rather than external evidences. MacDonald argued for an individualism within Christian experience that allowed for doubts, but didn't insist upon Ruskin's communal proofs."[77] The truth is that MacDonald was much less concerned with the public justification of 'true belief' than his Victorian counterparts.

Some would argue that since public justification is not needed, this removes the need for logic. The fact of the matter is that "MacDonald brought a phenomenal degree of logic to the subject of faith by an expanded definition of both logic and faith, by an analysis less of physical facts than of spiritual ones."[78] Barbara Amell continues: "MacDonald repeatedly attempted to apply logic to faith throughout much of his vast literary output may not be obvious to the average reader."[79] In MacDonald's own words, he coined the term "spiritual logic" as seen here: "The words of the Lord are not for the logic that deals with words as if they were things; but for the spiritual logic that reasons from divine thought to divine thought, dealing with spiritual facts."[80] This topic coincides with Swedenborg's theory of correspondences, as was presented in the second section of chapter

---

75   George MacDonald, *The Seaboard Parish*, 455.

76   Jocelyne Slepyan, "With all sorts of doubts I am familiar," 44.

77   Ibid., 38.

78   Barbara Amell, "George MacDonald on the Logic of Faith" in *Inklings Forever*, Vol. 2, 1999, 83.

79   Ibid., 82.

80   George MacDonald, *Unspoken Sermons*, "The Knowing of the Son," 201.

three, where the facts may be physical, but the deeper meanings behind such physical facts are found on a different metaphysical plane.

A good example of spiritual logic and MacDonald's interpretation of Swedenborg's correspondences can be found in his *Miracles of our Lord* where he discusses the centurion in Luke chapter seven: "This man was a philosopher: he ascended from that to which he was accustomed to that to which he was not accustomed. Nor did his *divine logic* fail him. He begins with acknowledging his own subjection, and states his own authority; then leaves it to our Lord to understand that he recognizes in him an authority beyond all, expecting the powers of nature to obey their Master, just as his soldiers or his servants obey him. How grandly he must have believed in him!"[81] So to define MacDonald's usage of the phrase "spiritual logic" or "divine logic," it is the ability of man to see what is in nature, in natural and human relations, and to appropriately apply these to our relationship with the Heavenly Father. The average man, of course, cannot accomplish this, but rather only the person MacDonald calls a "true man."[82] As was cited above in the discussion on faith, MacDonald explains that a true man has "the right position of the human soul which is made to understand the truth — the right position of that soul towards the truth; that is faith, partly."[83] The true man takes this position and is able to apply spiritual logic to what he observes. MacDonald finishes his section in *Miracles of our Lord* by stating, "Nature is brimful of symbolic and analogical parallels to the goings and comings, the growth and the changes of the highest nature in man."[84]

But how would one take this position? How is a man to become able to have the "right position of the soul" in order to use this spiritual logic which can be given by God and impressed upon the deepest recesses of man? While MacDonald often operated in ambiguity, and took indirect approaches more often than not, the answer to this question was direct and can be found in most, if not all of his works. The answer to the question above is unequivocally: duty. MacDonald explains, "A man may delight in the vision and glory of a truth, and not himself be true. The man whose vision is weak, but who, as far as

---

81   George MacDonald, *Miracles of Our Lord*, ed. Rolland Hein (Wheaton: Harold Shaw, 1980), 85, emphasis added.

82   George MacDonald, *Unspoken Sermons*, "The Truth," 214.

83   George MacDonald, *George MacDonald in the Pulpit*, "Faith the Proof of the Unseen," 66.

84   George MacDonald, *Miracles of Our Lord*, 92.

he sees, and desirous to see farther, does the thing he sees, is a true man. If a man knows what is, and says it is not, his knowing does not make him less than a liar. The man who recognizes the truth of any human relation, and neglects the duty involved, is not a true man."[85] Thus, in order to truly know, one must be a true man, and to be a true man, one must fulfill his duty.

It may seem odd that in a chapter on epistemology to evoke moral duty, but for MacDonald, virtue is the first step on the path to knowledge. He puts it succinctly, "Obedience is the soul of knowledge,"[86] and again "We must do before we can know."[87] He went on to explain: "As to knowledge, let justice guide thy search and thou wilt know the sooner. Do the will of God, and thou shalt know God, and he will open thine eyes to look into the very heart of knowledge."[88] To know, one must first seek, then do the will of God.

MacDonald's notion that duty is a prerequisite for knowledge is biblical, being most obvious in the biblical account of the initiation of the Abrahamic covenant in Genesis fifteen. There Abraham asks God a deep epistemological question, "O sovereign Lord, by what can I know that I am to possess it?" Abraham wants to know if God's promises are trustworthy. What's interesting about this passage is that immediately after this statement left his lips, God commands him to obtain and sacrifice animals. It was not until after this obedience had taken place that Abraham was offered an answer. Justin D. Barnard explains, "What is significant in this context is the structured relationship that remains between Abraham's initial epistemic query, God's immediate response, Abraham's obedience, and God's assurance of epistemic certainty. Attention to this structure reveals that in Abraham's case, knowledge (or at least religious knowledge) follows obedience."[89] Thus, there is biblical support for MacDonald's "obedience precedes knowledge" epistemological framework.

MacDonald also derived this concept from experience. In his testimonial to Highbury College for his admittance, MacDonald points out the struggles with his faith in his teenage years, then states,

---

85 George MacDonald, *Unspoken Sermons*, "The Truth," 214.

86 George MacDonald, *The Hope of the Gospel*, "Salvation from Sin," 11.

87 George MacDonald, *Robert Falconer*, 482.

88 George MacDonald, *The Hope of the Gospel*, "Hope of the Universe," 102.

89 Justin D. Barnard, "Cartesian Epistemology and Religious Belief" in *Journal of the Union Faculty Forum*, Vol. 35, 2015, 25.

"I could only cry to God to help me...I set myself in some measure to do what was right. I began to see the beauty of religion...the Truth has been slowly dawning on me."[90] For MacDonald himself, he needed to start the process of becoming a "true man" before the divine knowledge was revealed to him.

Bruce Hindmarsh argues, "What MacDonald hoped for in the final triumph of the love of God was an epistemology which worked from the inside out."[91] Hindmarsh argues that, for MacDonald, moral epistemology preceded normative epistemology. To say it concisely, for MacDonald, morality precedes knowledge. "Brothers, let us not linger to ask! let us obey, and, obeying, ask what we will! thus only shall we become all we are capable of being; thus only shall we learn all we are capable of knowing! The pure in heart shall see God; and to see him is to know all things."[92] Barbara Amell explains, "MacDonald believed the path to virtue lay in the doing of what we know to be right, and that the resulting contact with God, far from being an emotional vagary, would be an experience that increased our understanding of the divine."[93] Of course, being a complete and "true man" in MacDonald's opinion was as impossible in this world and should be taken akin to Jesus' command to be as perfect as the Heavenly Father in Matthew 5:48. As MacDonald notes, "Jesus Christ is the only man who ever lived. The others were but fragmentary men."[94] Thus, the sanctification process, ever indefinite in this world, is what makes a man true; he is in a constant process of becoming.

MacDonald is not arguing for mere divine epistemology. Note the end of the passage above where MacDonald states that to see God is to "know all things." He is not contending that once God is known that the believer becomes omniscient, but rather, that God is the ultimate being worthy of knowing, and in knowing Him, it casts light on all other things known. MacDonald stated in his twenties, "But when the light of religion is thrown upon [knowledge], it is as

---

90 Glenn Edward Sadler, *An Expression of Character: the Letters of George MacDonald*, 22-3.

91 Douglas Bruce Hindmarsh, *The Faith of George MacDonald*, 60.

92 George MacDonald, *Salted With Fire*, 290.

93 Barbara Amell, "George MacDonald on the Logic of Faith," 83.

94 Anonymous, "Visit of Dr. George MacDonald" in *Wingfold: Celebrating the Works of George MacDonald*, Vol. 88, 2014, 44. Originally published in *Banffshire Journal*, September 23, 1873.

if it were a soul to the knowledge which was dead before."⁹⁵ This is vaguely reminiscent of C.S. Lewis' famous quotation, "I believe in Christianity as I believe that the sun has risen: not only because I see it, but because by it I see everything else."⁹⁶ It is only through the lens of the Christian religion that the image of knowledge becomes clear.

The change that overcame Hugh in MacDonald's *David Elginbrod* exemplifies this concept. Years after leaving his home and becoming a man, and even more importantly— a true man, he returns to see things differently, not merely differently because things have changed, although they have, but more because he had changed:

> Regarding all about him with quiet, almost passive spirit, he was astonished to find how his eyes opened to see nature in the mass. Before, he had beheld only portions and beauties. When or how the change passed upon him he could not tell. But he no longer looked for a pretty eyebrow or a lovely lip on the face of nature: the soul of nature looked out upon him from the harmony of all, guiding him unsought to the discovery of a thousand separate delights; while from the expanded vision new meanings flashed upon him every day. He beheld in the great All the expression of the thoughts and feelings of the maker of the heavens and the earth and the sea and the fountains of water. The powers of the world to come, that is, the world of unseen truth and ideal reality, were upon him in the presence of the world that now is.⁹⁷

Hugh is the archetype of the common man walking through his journey and becoming more mature and "true," and as a result, is able to use the spiritual logic imparted to him because of his obedience to the duty God placed before him. Hugh is the ideal example of MacDonald's argument that "the universe ultimately will be intelligible to the individual who is spiritually mature."⁹⁸

Another example of this concept made alive in one of MacDonald's works is Curdie's epistemological evolution in the *Princess* books. Curdie starts as "an empiricist, who believes only in what he sees. His common sense and his senses alike tell him that

---

95 Glenn Edward Sadler, *An Expression of Character: the Letters of George MacDonald*, 20.

96 C.S. Lewis "They Asked For A Paper" in *Is Theology Poetry?* (London: Geoffrey Bless, 1962), 164-165.

97 George MacDonald, *David Elginbrod*, 449.

98 Rolland Hein, *George MacDonald: Victorian Mythmaker*, 91.

Irene's great-great grandmother does not exist when according to Irene she is right in front of him in her attic workroom."[99] There is no spiritual maturity in Curdie at the beginning of *The Princess and the Goblin*. He has no spiritual logic to see the deeper truths of the world. He can only observe what is plainly obvious to his senses. But over the course of the work "Curdie is changed from being a materialist to a believer in the invisible truths of the world, and all creatures and men in the book are seen as continually able to alter their inner natures by their actions."[100] While the first of the two books "portrays a process of spiritual evolution in Curdie, whereby he learns to trust beyond his senses, and to believe in the unseen,"[101] by the second book[102], Curdie's spiritual maturity had not only affected his internal state, but also altered his ability to perceive the "trueness" of others. He was granted the ability to be "able to tell by a handshake who is good, who evil."[103] Thus, over the course of these two books, we see the transformation of an empiricist into a true man, who has the ability to use his spiritual logic to look not merely into the unseen world in his own life and in nature, but also in others.

In both of these instances in regard to Hugh and Curdie, there was no instantaneous change, but rather a progression of slow growth that came through experience and obedience. Curdie needed to work the mines, obey his parents, and protect the town and the princess from the Goblins, and over time, began to trust the princess and was able to feel her grandmother's thread. Hugh needed to learn from David, teach his pupils, and protect Euphra; only then was he able to understand Euphra's lack of true beauty, a more realistic manifestation of Curdie's supernatural powers. But unlike the *Princess* books, Euphra evolves spiritually before his eyes through the ministering of Margaret, and Hugh grows to trust the authority of Euphra, whose dreams are now the "thread" that leads to the solution of the story's conflict.

---

99   Colin Manlove, "*The Princess and the Goblin* and *The Princess and Curdie*," 10.

100 Ibid., 13.

101 Colin Manlove, "*The Princess and the Goblin* and *The Princess and Curdie*," 22.

102 George MacDonald, *The Princess and Curdie* (New York: Puffin Books/Penguin Group, 1966).

103 Colin Manlove, "*The Princess and the Goblin* and *The Princess and Curdie*," 12.

In conclusion, while MacDonald rejected the normative views of rationalism and empiricism, he embraced the use of his senses and logic, but not until after one has begun the journey of seeking God through his moral will: "God forbid I should seem to despise understanding. The New Testament is full of urgings to understand.... What I cry out upon is the misunderstanding that comes of a man's endeavor to understand while not obeying."[104] For MacDonald, the key to faith, belief, and knowledge, rested in one's ability to obey, "to hold a thing with the intellect, is not to believe it. A man's real belief is that which he lives by; and that which the man I mean lives by, is the love of God, and obedience to his law, so far as he has recognized it."[105]

Samuel Taylor Coleridge, F.D. Maurice, A.J. Scott and MacDonald: the Status and Role of the Holy Scriptures

The Victorian Era was a tumultuous time of debate over the doctrine of inerrancy. Victorians began to realize that "nature failed to support literal readings of Scripture, and as advances in geology and biology began to question Scripture based arguments for the age of the earth and proposed natural selection over a purposeful deity."[106] Even more specifically, "the scientific revolution associated with the writings of Charles Lyell and Charles Darwin…provided a picture of man and his environment difficult to reconcile with the statements of Scripture if literally understood."[107] As will be observed below, these issues did not ordinarily affect the common layperson, but many elite ministers were confronted with the emergence of these scientific theories and felt obligated to respond.

Although there were rumblings of a change in attitude toward the Bible in the nineteenth century, there is no question among modern scholars that "at the threshold of the Victorian era, the Bible was firmly established in society as the Holy Bible, inspired by God and therefore regarded as authoritative to rule matters of faith and life."[108] Alec

---

104 George MacDonald, *The Hope of the Gospel*, "Salvation from Sin," 11.

105 George MacDonald, *Unspoken Sermons*, "The Truth in Jesus," 179.

106 Jocelyne Slepyan, "With all sorts of doubts I am familiar," 37.

107 Alec Cheyne, "The Bible and Change in the Nineteenth Century" in *The Bible in Scottish Life and Literature*, ed. by David Wright (Edinburgh: The Saint Andrews Press, 1988), 192.

108 Gisela H. Kreglinger, "Reading Scripture in Crisis: The Victorian Crisis of Faith and MacDonald's Response to Coleridge" in *Northwind* Vol.

George MacDonald as Philosopher, Mystic, and Apologist

Cheyne explains that especially Scottish Protestants "regarded the Bible as the supreme rule of faith and life, both personal and national, whose divine authority very few were disposed to question."[109] While academics with their new methodology and higher criticism were emerging, "the average minister and his parishioners were unaffected by them."[110]

An undercurrent was, however, flowing to the contrary. To give evidence of this undercurrent opposing inerrancy during the Victorian Era, we shall consider the influential writings of Samuel Taylor Coleridge, F.D. Maurice, and Alexander J. Scott. MacDonald and James Powell, his father-in-law, discussed the issue of biblical inerrancy: "But the remarks of my illustrious friend, S.T. Coleridge, modified my opinion.... I wish I could give you a tithe of his eloquent words, but his meaning was that in reading the Scriptures, while monotony is avoided, the divine source should never be forgotten, and they should be delivered more as the Oracles of God than the opinions of man..."[111] It is certain among scholars of MacDonald that *Confessions of an Inquiring Spirit*,[112] and even more definitely, Maurice's *The Claims of the Bible and of Science*[113] and Scott's *Revelations*[114] were in MacDonald's frame of reference and were significant in his development, especially on his view of Scripture. Below, Coleridge's work shall be considered, then a consideration of the individuals that MacDonald knew more intimately: F.D. Maurice and Alexander J. Scott.

Coleridge was thoroughly acquainted with the "Biblical criticism coming from Germany" and "was an early voice in England that challenged Fundamentalist approaches to the Bible."[115] Coleridge, a strong influence on MacDonald,[116] made the issue of biblical

---

27, 2008, 79.

109 Alec Cheyne, "The Bible and Change in the Nineteenth Century", 192.

110 Ibid., 192.

111 Greville MacDonald, *George MacDonald and His Wife*, 137-8.

112 Rolland Hein, *The Harmony Within*, 149.

113 Kirstin Jeffrey Johnson, *Rooted in All its Story, More is Meant than Meets the Ear*, 177-8.

114 Ibid., 98.

115 Gisela H. Kreglinger, "Reading Scripture in Crisis: The Victorian Crisis of Faith and MacDonald's Response to Coleridge," 81.

116 Ibid., 81.

authority and inerrancy the theme of his *Confessions of an Inquiring Spirit*, published posthumously in 1840 (manuscript complete in 1824). Coleridge explains therein:

> I have heard Speakers of every denomination, Calvinists and Arminians, Quakers and Methodists, Dissenting Ministers and Clergymen, nay, dignitaries of the Established Church: and still have heard the same doctrine — that the Bible was not to be regarded or reasoned about, in the way that other good books are or may be. That it was different in kind, and stood by itself. By some indeed this doctrine was rather implied than expressed, but yet evidently implied. But by far the greater number of the Speakers, it was asserted in the strongest and most unqualified words that Language could supply. What is more, their principal arguments were grounded on the position, that the Bible *throughout* was dictated by Omniscience, and therefore in all its parts infallibly true & obligatory, (and that) the men, whose names are prefixed to the several Books or Chapters were in fact but as different *Pens* in the hand of one and the same Writer, and the words the Words of God Himself. On this account all notes and comments were superfluous, nay, presumptuous — a profane mixing of human with divine, the notions of fallible creatures with the oracles of Infallibility — as if God's meaning could be so clearly or fitly exprest in man's as in God's own words! But how often you yourself must have heard the same language from the pulpit! What could I reply to this? I could neither deny the fact, or evade the conclusion — namely, that such is at present the popular Belief.[117]

Coleridge acknowledges that the view of the Bible that permeated the churches of his day was a high view of inspiration of Scripture and thus, that it was inerrant. Coleridge did not hold to such doctrine, although he absolutely did "revere these Scriptures; —prize them, love them, revere them, beyond all other books!"[118] While he revered them, he did not see them as without error in word or in interpretation. He was bold enough to ask himself the question "Why should I not believe the Scriptures throughout dictated, in word and thought, by an infallible Intelligence?"[119] While the question was clearly asked,

---

117 Samuel Taylor Coleridge, *Confessions of an Inquiring Spirit* (London: Edward Moxon, 1853), 83-5. Collected Works vol. 11, part 2 edited by Jackson, p.1148.

118 Ibid., 63.

119 Ibid., 67.

Coleridge often answered expressively throughout the work, as only a poet could: "Because the doctrine in question petrifies at once the whole body of Holy Writ with all its harmonies and symmetrical gradations—the flexile and the rigid—the supporting hard and the clothing soft—the blood—which is the life—the intelligencing nerves, and the rudely woven, but soft and springy, cellular substance, in which all are imbedded and lightly bound together."[120] The philosopher and theologian may struggle to find specific reason and logical argument in such an explanation, but a few times in the work, clarity and succinctness broke through. Coleridge argued that language was not suitable for God's Word, in and of itself: "How can infallible truth be infallibly conveyed in defective and fallible expressions?"[121] Thus, in his opinion, no utterance from the divine could be written in any language and thus be inerrant. And again, while he had no problem saying that this book was from God, the language, and the likely imperfect interpretation thereof, could not be inerrant: "Every sentence found in a canonical Book, rightly interpreted, contains the dictum of an infallible Mind; but what the right interpretation is—or whether the very words now extant are corrupt or genuine—must be determined by the industry and understanding of fallible, and alas! more or less prejudiced theologians."[122]

Also, like many of the intellectual Christians of his day, Coleridge struggled with the relationship between science and the Bible: "I challenge these divines and their adherents to establish the compatibility of a belief in the modern astronomy and natural philosophy with their and Wesley's doctrine respecting the inspired Scriptures, without reducing the doctrine itself to a plaything of wax."[123] It is obvious that Coleridge respected the Scriptures that he called "the appointed conservatory, an indispensable criterion, and a continual source and support of true belief,"[124] but he asked his readers to consider whether or not "it is the spirit of the Bible, and not the detached words and sentences, that is infallible and absolute?"[125]

In 1862, Bishop John Colenso, a Bible scholar and missionary, released his *The Pentateuch and the Book of Joshua Critically Examined*

---

120 Ibid., 63-4.
121 Ibid., 53.
122 Ibid., 81.
123 Ibid., 74.
124 Ibid., 79.
125 Ibid., 97-8.

where inerrancy, the authorship of books of the Bible, and certain historical events were questioned: "My own knowledge of some branches of science, of Geology in particular, had been much increased since I left England; and I now know for certain, on geological grounds, a fact, of which I had only had misgivings before, viz. that a Universal Deluge, such as the Bible manifestly speaks of, could not possibly have taken place in the way described in the Book of Genesis."[126] F.D Maurice was sincerely asked by an old friend in a letter, "what is the true relation between Science and Revelation?"[127] These letters from "a layman" were spawned by Bishop Colenso's work and motivated Maurice to write *The Claims of the Bible and of Science*. Therein we find Maurice's view, that God himself did not give "us promise or assurance that there shall be no errors in the letter of the Scriptures."[128] Maurice does not believe that the Bible itself makes the claim that it is inerrant; God never made the declaration, "If He has, let the passage be produced; let us hear something more than mere inferences as to what men suppose must be, —inferences which hold to be profane and irreverent."[129]

In reference to the great deluge, often a point of contention among geologists, Maurice explained, "I would take, then, the history of this Deluge as I find it given in the book of Genesis. If there are passages in it which assume that more of the earth was covered by the Deluge than modern investigations show can have been covered by it, I would say 'Either those passages are mistaken, or I am mistaken in the interpretation of them. Both solutions are possible — both are reasonable.'"[130] Maurice seems to accept the Deluge as a worldwide flood, but acknowledges that he may be mistaken, "God, if we accept the statement of the Bible, has given us assurance that we shall have His Spirit to guide us into truth…But the other alternative is also quite possible."[131]

Maurice agreed that there may be historical problems in

---

126 John William Colenso, *The Pentateuch and the Book of Joshua Critically Examined* (London: Longman's, Green, & Co., 1894), 8.

127 F.D. Maurice, *The Claims of the Bible and of Science: A Correspondence between a layman and the Rev. F.D. Maurice on some questions arising out of the controversy respecting the Pentateuch* (London: MacMillan & Co., 1863), 5.

128 Ibid., 113.

129 Ibid., 113.

130 Ibid., 113.

131 Ibid., 113.

Scripture, but there are also linguistic and interpretive issues. Maurice argued that "There must be a continual waiting for light; a distrust of our own assumptions; a readiness to be detected in error, certain that God's meaning is infinitely larger than ours, and that other men may perceive an aspect of it which we do not perceive."[132] The readers of Scripture also "have made prodigious blunders in our interpretations of Scripture . We have forced it to say things which it has never said, that it may square with our conclusions."[133]

While Maurice dispenses with inerrancy and argues that Christianity's "foundation is not the letter of any book,"[134] he still believes that truth can be found therein; yet it is not Scripture that reveals, for this is the work of God: "I believe that the Bible and the Creeds, the holiest traditions of the Church in all ages, the holiest Greeks, Latins, Protestants in all ages, are agreed in this one testimony: that God has revealed, and does reveal, to men that which they want to know; that He only does, or can, reveal anything."[135] He did not see his position on Scripture as revolutionary, but rather precautionary: "We have worshipped the letter of the Bible till we are unable to read the letter of it. We talk of it and its authority, and its infallibility. He is not in all our thoughts. We do not trust Him, but a theory of our own about the correctness of a document."[136]

It would be amiss not to mention Alexander J. Scott's view of Scripture here as an addendum, if not merely for the fact that MacDonald thought he was "the greatest intellect he had known"[137] as well as calling him his "Master."[138] Scott agrees with Maurice and Coleridge that the purpose of Scripture is to reveal the Father, but he intentionally points to the fact this it is only one of the many ways that revelation occurs, "To reveal God is the end for which the Scriptures are given. Relatively to each individual mind among us, this is the aim of the universe. Thereby God utters His Being to us, as an author makes known his existence and form of mind by his book; and as a

---

132 Ibid., 30.

133 Ibid., 113.

134 Ibid., 140.

135 Ibid., 124.

136 Ibid., 77.

137 Kirstin Jeffrey Johnson, *Rooted in All its Story, More is Meant than Meets the Ear*, 67.

138 Glenn Edward Sadler, *An Expression of Character: the Letters of George MacDonald*, 126.

friend by his letter expresses the state of his heart towards us, and seeks communion with ours. The Scriptures form but one element in this, God's manifold utterance of Himself."[139] So, Scott does not put one form of revelation above another: "the Scripture professes not to exhaust into itself any channel of divine knowledge, so that it might be substituted for that other channel, but to indicate it, to explain its use, and to leave it open for us. This is a vast work, and wonderfully has the Bible, in every age since its completion, affected it. What we have said of all revelation, we say of Scripture, — its end is to bring us to God Himself."[140]

Unlike Maurice and Coleridge, Scott never suggested that Scripture might be untrue, but rather stated that the Bible is "a true history of a pure working of a human soul in fellowship with the Spirit of God."[141] He also specified that "It is an inspired history of divine manifestations,"[142] and that there is a "literal, or historical, understanding of Scripture; and to neglect it, is to despise the wisdom of the Spirit in selecting the matter for the record."[143] While he stood firm on the truth of Scripture, Scott also contends, "in every such manifestation there is a spiritual element, for which the other is merely a vehicle; and to meet which is, for the spirit of the man to meet the Spirit of God."[144] While not as direct as Maurice's and Coleridge, his words could be taken as a word of warning to the reader: "The Lord's complaint of the Jewish people is, that they sought that life in the Bible, which the Bible testified to be not in itself, but in Him. 'Ye search the Scriptures, for in them ye think ye have eternal life; and they are they which testify of me; and ye will not come to me that ye might have life.' In like manner Paul opposes not the ministry of the letter of the New Testament to that of the letter of the old: but altogether the ministry of spirit to the ministry of letter."[145] Thus, while Scott stated that Scripture is historically accurate, there can be negative consequences if one elevates the Bible to a status higher than

---

139 Alexander J. Scott, *Discourses* (London and Cambridge: MacMillan and Co., 1866), 35.
140 Ibid., 53.
141 Ibid., 53.
142 Ibid., 54.
143 Ibid., 54.
144 Ibid., 54.
145 Ibid., 53.

was intended, and especially if the letter is elevated above the spirit therein.

Coleridge, Maurice, and Scott, exemplify the environment in which MacDonald's perspective was cultivated: "The writings of Maurice and of his mentor Coleridge both explore the multiple levels in which Scripture works, of how it is stereoscopic in its function of revelation. They explore how language points beyond itself, and how it acts as both the vehicle and symbol used as history shapes and conditions the way humanity interprets the present. These concepts contributed significantly to MacDonald's own understanding of Story – biblical and otherwise."[146] While there are positives gained from these foundations, some argue that these positions were the result of German criticism of Scripture, and what led to the questioning of biblical inerrancy by nineteenth century Victorians: "Scott... Coleridge, and a few others, asserted that Scripture's authority lay essentially in the spiritual, and thus they laid foundations which could not be disrupted by the inevitable extension of historical and literary criticism into the realm of Scriptural study."[147]

So, was MacDonald influenced by German higher criticism of the Bible? Gisela Kreglinger argues that MacDonald was "well aware of German Higher Criticism," but that "there is little evidence that he engaged with it in any serious degree."[148] So while he took the work of Coleridge, Maurice, and Scott seriously, there is no evidence to think that MacDonald delved into this academic arena. This is not to suggest that MacDonald did not examine his Bible critically. Some evidence for this is the fact that he used "the latest critical edition of the Greek text by Westcott and Hort, published in 1881, in the third volume of *Unspoken Sermons*."[149] MacDonald realized that the "King James version of the Bible of 1611 contained many mistakes which needed rectifying," and that correcting the "New Testament texts was like removing fine scratches from a lens."[150] After reading some verses in one of his sermons he commented that "[this] is the

---

146 Kirstin Jeffrey Johnson, *Rooted in All its Story, More is Meant than Meets the Ear*, 177-8.

147 J. Philip Newell, *A.J. Scott and his Circle* (Dissertation: The University of Edinburgh, 1981), 208.

148 Gisela H. Kreglinger, "Reading Scripture in Crisis: The Victorian Crisis of Faith and MacDonald's Response to Coleridge," 92.

149 Ibid., 92.

150 William Raeper, George MacDonald, 246.

reading of the oldest manuscripts. The rest of the verse is pretty clearly a not-overwise marginal gloss that has crept into the text."[151] These quotations demonstrate that MacDonald recognized that older manuscripts had been found and the Greek had been altered to reflect that, and the changes that had been made in these Scriptures, were justified. He also believed that certain parts of Scripture were authentic, and that, through accidental copyist error or intentional annotation, the original text had been corrupted. Thus, there is no question that MacDonald took a critical approach to Scripture.

Before MacDonald's perspective is explored, it must be noted, similarly to the others mentioned above, that he had an utmost reverence for Scripture. He unequivocally stated, "The Bible is to me the most precious thing in the world, because it tells me his story" and that it "is indeed sent us by God."[152] Thus, like Coleridge, Maurice, and Scott before him, MacDonald cherished the Scriptures.

But does reverence and appreciation stem from a view of inerrancy? While this is logically possible, for MacDonald they did not. MacDonald believed, and even unequivocally stated publicly in lectures, personal letters, and even in his novels, that textual problems arise in the Scriptures. While he did not doubt that these existed, he treated them as mere trivialities compared to the whole: "Even its errors and blunders do not touch the truth, and are the merest trifles—dear as the little spot of earth on the whiteness of the snowdrop."[153]

But that notwithstanding, MacDonald scholars have no question that he believed that the "Bible is a historical document written by fallible men who were quite capable of unwitting distortions and misrepresentations of the words of Jesus."[154] Sometimes these errors were due to manuscript or scribal errors, as seen above, others were due to interpretive errors as he explains here: "You dare to say the apostle is wrong in what he so plainly teaches?' 'By no means; what I do say is, that our English presentation of his teaching is in this point very misleading. It is not for me to judge the learned and good men who have revised the translation of the New Testament—with so much gain to every one whose love of truth is greater than his loving prejudice for accustomed form; —I can only say, I wonder what may have been

---

151 George MacDonald, *George MacDonald in the Pulpit*, "A Sermon," 39.

152 Greville MacDonald, *George MacDonald and His Wife*, 373.

153 Glenn Edward Sadler, *An Expression of Character: the Letters of George MacDonald*, 154.

154 Richard H. Reis, *George MacDonald's Fiction*, 33.

their reasons for retaining this word adoption."[155] At other times, the biblical author himself may have added some commentary that was not historically accurate, "While he accepted that the Apostle John may have put some of his own sentiments into Jesus' mouth, he denied firmly that there was anything in the Gospels which contradicted the character of Christ as revealed there."[156] MacDonald stated that Matthew's account of Jesus' temptation by Satan in Matthew chapter four, "may not be just as the Lord told it, and yet may contain in its mirror as much of the truth as we are able to receive."[157]

MacDonald, in his novel *Salted with Fire*, went so far as to suggest that pastors should discuss this topic with congregations: "The next evening he listened to the best sermon he had yet heard from that pulpit—a summary of the facts bearing on the resurrection of our Lord; — with which sermon, however, a large part of the congregation was anything but pleased; for the minister had admitted the impossibility of reconciling, in every particular, the differing accounts of the doings and seeings of those who bore witness to it."[158] Note that, while fictional, MacDonald puts this public admission and exposition in an extremely positive light. In the *Vicar's Daughter*, MacDonald even uses a pseudepigraphal gospel to make his point:

> "The chapter I read to you," she answered, "is part of a pretended gospel, called, 'The First Gospel of the Infancy of Jesus Christ.' I can't tell you who wrote it, or how it came to be written. All I can say is, that, very early in the history of the church, there were people who indulged themselves in inventing things about Jesus, and seemed to have had no idea of the importance of keeping to facts, or, in other words, of speaking and writing only the truth. All they seemed to have cared about was the gratifying of their own feelings of love and veneration; and so they made up tales about him, in his honor as they supposed, no doubt, just as if he had been a false god of the Greeks or Romans. It is long before some people learn to speak the truth, even after they know it is wicked to lie. Perhaps, however, they did not expect their stories to be received as facts, intending them only as a sort of recognized fiction about him, —amazing presumption at the best."

---

155 George MacDonald, *Unspoken Sermons*, "Abba, Father!" 132.

156 William Raeper, *George MacDonald*, 246.

157 George MacDonald, *Unspoken Sermons*, "The Temptation in the Wilderness," 48.

158 George MacDonald, *Salted With Fire*, 218.

"Did anybody, then, ever believe the likes of that, grannie?" asked Jarvis.

"Yes: what I read to you seems to have been believed within a hundred years after the death of the apostles. There are several such writings, with a great deal of nonsense in them, which were generally accepted by Christian people for many hundreds of years."

"I can't imagine how anybody could go inwentuating [sic] such things!" said the blind man.

"It is hard for us to imagine. They could not have seen how their inventions would, in later times, be judged anything but honoring to him in whose honor they wrote them. Nothing, be it ever so well invented, can be so good as the bare truth. Perhaps, however, no one in particular invented some of them, but the stories grew, just as a report often does amongst yourselves. Although everybody fancies he or she is only telling just what was told to him or her, yet, by degrees, the pin's-point of a fact is covered over with lies upon lies almost everybody adding something, until the report has grown to be a mighty falsehood. Why, you had such a story yourselves, not so very long ago, about one of your best friends! One comfort is, such a story is sure not to be consistent with itself; it is sure to show its own falsehood to any one who is good enough to doubt it, and who will look into it, and examine it well. You don't, for instance, want any other proof than the things themselves to show you that what I have just read to you can't be true."

"But then it puzzles me to think how anybody could believe them," said the blind man.

"Many of the early Christians were so childishly simple that they would believe almost anything that was told them. In a time when such nonsense could be written, it is no great wonder there should be many who could believe it."

"Then, what was their faith worth," said the blind man, "if they believed false and true all the same?"

"Worth no end to them," answered Marion with eagerness; "for all the false things they might believe about him could not destroy the true ones, or prevent them from believing in Jesus himself, and bettering their ways for his sake. And as they grew better and better, by doing what he told them, they would gradually come to disbelieve this and that foolish or bad thing."

"But wouldn't that make them stop believing in him altogether?"

"On the contrary, it would make them hold the firmer to all that they saw to be true about him. There are many people, I presume, in other countries, who believe those stories still; but all the Christians I know have cast aside every one of those writings, and keep only to those we call the Gospels. To throw away what is not true, because it is not true, will always help the heart to be truer; will make it the more anxious to cleave to what it sees must be true. Jesus remonstrated with the Jews that they would not of themselves judge what was right; and the man who lets God teach him is made abler to judge what is right a thousand-fold."[159]

The first and most obvious element in the reading is that MacDonald held the Gospels as a much higher authority than the non-canonical, and even other canonical works. He explained that "the epistles are very different from the Apostles preaching; they are mostly written for a peculiar end and aim, and are not intended as expositions of the central truth."[160] Even in a letter to his own father he suggests: "if I might say so to you— will you think me presumptuous if I say—leave the Epistles & ponder *The Gospel*. The story about Christ."[161] To state it frankly, MacDonald focused on the Gospels. This echoes one of his most famous statements: "Jesus Christ is my theology, and nothing else."[162]

The extended quotation above also reveals MacDonald's response to finding truth when mingled with fiction. The blind man asked "Then, what was their faith worth…if they believed false and true all the same?"[163] The problem with the blind man's position is his underlying assumption, which is often made, in an attempt to understand revelation. In MacDonald's view, the Bible was a source of revelation, but was not a complete revelation in and of itself. MacDonald clearly states, "the common theory of the inspiration of the words, instead of the breathing of God's truth into the hearts and

---

159 George MacDonald, *The Vicar's Daughter* (Whitehorn: Johannesen, 1998), 263-5.

160 Greville MacDonald, *George MacDonald and His Wife*, 184.

161 Glenn Edward Sadler, *An Expression of Character: the Letters of George MacDonald*, 59.

162 Anonymous, "Dr. MacDonald's Testimony," 31.

163 George MacDonald, *The Vicar's Daughter*, 263-5.

souls of those who wrote it, and who then did their best with it, is degrading and evil; and they who hold it are in danger of worshipping the letter instead of living in the Spirit, of being idolaters of the Bible instead of disciples of Jesus... It is Jesus who is the Revelation of God, not the Bible; that is but a means to a mighty eternal end. The book is indeed sent us by God, but it nowhere claims to be his very word. If it were—and it would be no irreverence to say it—it would have been a good deal better written."[164] Thus, not only did MacDonald suggest that the doctrine of inerrancy should be dispensed with, he often warned of making the Bible an idol, often calling inerrantists "Bible-worshiping brothers."[165]

In his position, the Bible "nowhere lays claim to be regarded as *the* Word, *the* Way, *the* Truth. The Bible leads us to Jesus, the inexhaustible, the ever unfolding Revelation of God."[166] This is the reason why MacDonald was not concerned with some error being scattered in the Bible, for "Scripture is not the only revelation of God, and it is God's intent that we discover meanings of Scripture that abundantly surpass the literal words themselves."[167] For MacDonald, "the Bible, though the main channel through which God revealed his character and will, was not the only way of learning about him.... The Bible, though crucial, no longer had the monopoly on revelation."[168] As will be argued more thoroughly in the next section, MacDonald's mysticism led him to believe that followers of Christ could gain "knowledge through inspiration, directly from God, including insights which had been 'left out' of the Bible."[169]

How is one then to dissect the truth from falsehood in Scripture? MacDonald argues, in conjunction with our epistemology section above, that a man must be true to understand God's revelation, whether Scriptural or otherwise. MacDonald assumed the above question and answered here: "But if I do not take the words attributed to him by the evangelists, for the certain, absolute, very words of the Master, how am I to know that they represent his truth? By seeing in them what corresponds to the plainest truth he speaks, and commends

---

164 Greville MacDonald, *George MacDonald and His Wife*, 373.

165 George MacDonald, *Unspoken Sermons*, "The New Name," 37.

166 George MacDonald, *Unspoken Sermons*, "The Higher Faith," 22.

167 Keith Waddle, "George MacDonald and the Homiletics of Religious Imagination," 5.

168 William Raeper, *George MacDonald*, 244.

169 Richard H. Reis, *George MacDonald's Fiction*, 33.

itself to the power that is working in you to make of you a true man; by their appeal to your power of judging what is true; by their rousing of your conscience. If they do not seem to you true, either they are not the words of the Master, or you are not true enough to understand them."[170] Thus, if a man is not true, he cannot understand the fullness of Scripture. MacDonald argues that "until we understand Him, until we have His Spirit, promised so freely to them that ask it—all the Epistles, the words of men who were full of Him, and wrote out of that fullness…of such men are to us a sealed book. Until we love the Lord so as to do what He tells us, we have no right to have an opinion about what one of those men meant."[171]

While there are obvious mystical and spiritual implications here, MacDonald also pointed out that his reasons are practical: "Words for their full meaning depend upon their source, the person who speaks them. An utterance may even seem commonplace, till you are told that thus spoke one whom you know to be always thinking, always feeling, always acting. Recognizing the mind whence the words proceed, you know the scale by which they are to be understood. So the words of God cannot mean just the same as the words of man. 'Can we not, then, understand them?' Yes, we can understand them—we can understand them more than the words of men. Whatever a good word means, as used by a good man, it means just infinitely more as used by God. And the feeling or thought expressed by that word takes higher and higher forms in us as we become capable of understanding him, —that is, as we become like him."[172] Thus, when God is known, and it is assured that God is the source of a specific revelation, this makes the hearer confident of the truth, and interpretation, as well as potentially the promissory content of the revelation.

In conclusion, Gisela Kreglinger states that, for MacDonald, "A comprehensive understanding of reality and the world—physical, metaphysical, moral and spiritual—finds its ultimate answer only in Christ, and particularity in his sacrificial death."[173] She continues, "Truth can only be found in Jesus Christ. Science, language and, as a consequence, the Bible are all limited in their ability to express reality

---

170 George MacDonald, *Unspoken Sermons*, "The Knowing of the Son," 200.

171 George MacDonald, *Annals of a Quiet Neighbourhood*, 128.

172 George MacDonald, *Unspoken Sermons*, "It Shall Not Be Forgiven," 28.

173 Gisela H. Kreglinger, "Reading Scripture in Crisis: The Victorian Crisis of Faith and MacDonald's Response to Coleridge," 96.

comprehensively."[174] Thus, in of all reality, including the words of the Bible, truth, especially revelatory truth, cannot be found without a connection with Christ. Only then can a person be true, and while the person may believe some falsehood, only then through Christ can the process of separating the epistemological wheat from the chaff commence. Yet how does this connection with Christ take place, and how does this mystical revelatory process work? This answer will be discussed in the following section, where the question of how MacDonald's philosophy affected his theology and mysticism shall be considered.

---

174 Ibid., 97.

CHAPTER FIVE

An Outworking of MacDonald's Philosophy and Theology on his Mysticism

Introduction

Some may consider a move from philosophy to mysticism to be a sweeping transition from the abstract to application, and while there is truth to this sentiment, for MacDonald these two fields were, in some sense, linked. As was discussed in the introduction to chapter two, MacDonald believed that a person's philosophy and theology could negatively affect their ability to reach their Heavenly Father. Yet in his intention to caution his readers about idolizing theology, he would often advise, "To know about Him is a means of knowing Him...to know about Him is not enough."[1] Again MacDonald reiterated, "All the metaphysics of the world may be true, but all that they can tell you is *about* God, is *about* Him, but they don't give you God; you cannot get God that way."[2] Thus here, in the following pages, the focus shall turn to what MacDonald would have considered as "the way" to reach God.

Compared to most Victorians, MacDonald took a unique spiritual road. In 1905 Chesterton reflected, "MacDonald had made for himself a sort of spiritual environment, a space and transparency of mystical light, which was quite exceptional in his national and denominational environment."[3] While the uniqueness of his spiritual journey is clear, some even argue that its mystical destination was no surprise: "One who sets out, as George MacDonald did, to challenge, not Calvinism merely, which after all may prove to be an ally, but the facts of life—pain, disease, madness, sin, death — in the strength of a faith in the simply but tremendous affirmation that God is Love, is bound sooner or later to take the road of a mystic."[4] Before continuing on, one must challenge the assumptions suggested above. Was George MacDonald, in fact, a mystic? Is the term even definable? And if both are answered in the positive, how did this manifest itself in his works

---

1   George MacDonald, *George MacDonald in the Pulpit*, "Growth in Grace and Knowledge," 148.

2   Ibid., 321-322.

3   G.K. Chesterton, "George MacDonald."

4   H.J.C. Grierson, "George MacDonald" in Aberdeen University Review, Vol. XII, No. 34, 1924, 8.

and in his view of spiritual progression?

Was George MacDonald a "True Mystic?"

In a point of digression, before continuing, MacDonald created a scene in *Salted with Fire* where the parson was attempting to pigeonhole one of his parishioners. The narration finishes with "the minister went away intent on classifying the soutar by finding out with what sect of the middle-age mystics to place him. At the same time something strange seemed to hover about the man, refusing to be handled in that way."[5] While this cannot be directly demonstrated from the passage above, it would not be beyond comprehension to suggest that MacDonald disliked being categorized as a specific type of mystic in the same way that he did not publicly assent to a specific philosophical or theological school of thought. Nonetheless, while the earlier chapters of this book delved into the former topic with difficulty due to semantic complexities and seemingly intentional obscurity, the question of his mysticism will end more clearly; however, MacDonald continued to persist in his uniqueness and unwillingness to fit into a customary category.

To plunge headlong into the subject of mysticism, one must first acknowledge the complexities of defining the term. Evelyn Underhill, in her *Practical Mysticism*, writes, "Those who are interested in that special attitude towards the universe which is now loosely called 'mystical,' find themselves beset by a multitude of persons who are constantly asking — some with real fervour, some with curiosity, and some with disdain — 'What is mysticism?' When referred to the writings of the mystics themselves, and to other works in which this question appears to be answered, these people reply that such books are wholly incomprehensible to them.... One expert tells him that it is simply 'Catholic piety,' another that Walt Whitman was a typical mystic, a third assures him that all mysticism comes from the East. At the end of a prolonged course of lectures, sermons, tea-parties, and talks with earnest persons, the inquirer is still heard saying — too often in tones of exasperation, 'What IS mysticism?'"[6]

Carl McColman agrees that "Mystic, mystical, and mysticism are difficult and challenging words, with vague, abstract, and sometimes

---

5   George MacDonald, *Salted With Fire*, 74.
6   Evelyn Underhill, *Practical Mysticism* (Columbus: Ariel Press, 1942), 22.

directly contradictory meanings."[7] Ironically, it seems McColman exemplifies this in his *Christian Mystics*. He defines a mystic as "someone who had been initiated into the spiritual mysteries, who had ritually received the secret knowledge or power of whichever god or goddess the particular religion revered."[8] As will be discussed later, McColman argues that MacDonald was a mystic, but also admits that MacDonald did not fit his own definition.[9] He digresses by stating a more pragmatic definition of mystics as those who "teach us how to find God, and a great mystic is someone who has been recognized as doing this particularly well."[10]

Underhill's definition of mysticism carries with it authority; it is one which many modern scholars of mysticism employ.[11] Her definition reads: "Mysticism is the art of union with Reality. The mystic is a person who has attained that union in greater or less degree; or who aims at and believes in such attainment."[12] A first glance, this definition may widen the category beyond the normative view of mysticism, but this may, in fact, be Underhill's intention. She further elucidates her definition, "...mysticism is a philosophy, an illusion, a kind of religion, a disease; that it means having visions, performing conjuring tricks, leading an idle, dreamy, and selfish life, neglecting one's business, wallowing in vague spiritual emotions, and being 'in tune with the infinite.' He will discover that it emancipates him from all dogmas — sometimes from all morality — and at the same time that it is very superstitious."[13]

These definitions and the elucidations above tends to cause one, as Underhill alluded, to read and still question "What *is* mysticism?" Some may argue that the vagueness of our attempts here may parallel the mystic's own mindset, but G.K. Chesterton disagrees. He wrote in his obituary of MacDonald: "True Mysticism will have nothing to do with vagueness. True Mysticism will have nothing to do with

---

7   Carl McColman, *Christian Mystics: 108 Seers, Saints, and Sages* (Charlottesville: Hampton Roads, 2016), xiv.

8   Ibid., xv.

9   Ibid., 8.

10 Ibid., xvii.

11 Dana Greene, "The Mystic and the Church" in *Mysticism, Christian Reflection: A Series in Faith and Ethics*, Vol. 17 (Waco: The Center for Christian Ethics at Baylor University, 2005), 70.

12 Evelyn Underhill, *Practical Mysticism*, 23.

13 Ibid., 22.

twilight. True Mysticism is entirely concerned with absolute things; not with twilight, but with the sacred black darkness and the sacred white sun. For to all good Mystics, from Plato downwards, absolute ideas like those of light and darkness, are the real and interesting things. It must always be remembered that the only person in the world who can be really exact and definite is the Mystic. All sane materialism is avowedly agnostic and relative. The Evolutionist cannot be precise. The Positivist cannot be positive. But the Mystic believes that a rose is red with a fixed and sacred redness, and that a cucumber is green by a thundering decree of Heaven…Actuality is the keynote of Mysticism."[14] Thus, alongside Chesterton's assertions above, consider Robert Wild's definition: "Mysticism describes a rather permanent state in which an unusual touch of God breaks into consciousness and remains in a regular or even permanent fashion."[15] This definition carries with it enough particulars to denote an "exact and definite" mystic as Chesterton mentioned, yet with enough latitude to encompass all of the various categories of mystics and styles of mystical experience.

Since our understanding of mysticism has been established, one can now broach the question: "Was MacDonald, in fact, a mystic?" H.J.C. Grierson answered to the contrary, "Was George MacDonald a mystic? It was along the mystical line that he sought the solution of the enigma of sin and pain and death. But that is not sufficient to make one a mystic. For that one must have passed through the mystical experience. We know those who have so passed because they have no more doubts. They have seen and they believe, or rather know. They are no longer questers, doubting, inquiring, adumbrating the allegorical arguers to the questions they are still really asking themselves. The great mystic proclaims… Compared with them [Blake, Jacob Boehme, St. Paul] George MacDonald is, like so many of his generation, a quester after a mystical solution rather than a mystic."[16] Was Grierson operating under the same definition of mystic with which we are now working? This is difficult to ascertain, since Grierson did not define the word. The crux of his statement seems to be the phrase "one must have passed through the mystical experience." The phrase itself is problematic in the sense that all Christians,

---

14   G.K. Chesterton, "George MacDonald."

15   Robert Wild, *The Tumbler of God: Chesterton as Mystic* (Kettering: Angelico Press, 2013), 38.

16   H.J.C. Grierson, "George MacDonald," 11.

similarly, although not explicitly like the apostles' experience with the Holy Spirit at Pentecost, should have some sort of mystical experience. B.G. Collins suggested this much in his assessment of MacDonald: "George MacDonald was not a mystic except in so far as a 'mystical' element enters into Christian experience."[17] Can more be said than this?

It is asserted by some that MacDonald had, at least on one occasion, felt that he had experienced an "unusual touch of God" as mentioned in our definition.[18] The most powerful testimony of this fact comes from his son Greville, who stated that his father indicated that during the writing of *Lilith*, "He was possessed by a feeling... that it was a mandate direct from God..."[19] While MacDonald never alluded to this personal experience, it seems as though he himself experienced it, since he goes into detail about what sort of possible experience with God is universal to humanity:

> If we will but let our God and Father work his will with us, there can be no limit to his enlargement of our existence, to the flood of life with which he will overflow our consciousness... many can recall some moment in which life seemed richer and fuller than ever before... surely God could at any moment give to a soul, by a word to that soul, by breathing afresh into the secret caves of its being, a sense of life before which the most exultant ecstasy of earthly triumph would pale to ashes! If ever sunlit, sail-crowded sea, under blue heaven flecked with wind-chased white, filled your soul as with a new gift of life, think what sense of existence must be yours, if he whose thought has but fringed its garment with the outburst of such a show, take his abode with you, and while thinking the gladness of a God inside your being, let you know and feel that he is carrying you as a father in his bosom![20]

For MacDonald, this unusual experience, while uncommon, is available to all: "God who has made us can never be far from any man who draws the breath of life— nay, it must be in him; not necessarily in his heart, as we say, but still in him."[21] This experience most resembles Mark's dream in *Weighed and Wanting*:

---

17 B.G. Collins, "George MacDonald" in *The Baptist Quarterly*, Vol 1.4, 1951, 73.

18 Robert Wild, *The Tumbler of God: Chesterton as Mystic*, 38.

19 Greville MacDonald, *George MacDonald and His Wife*, 548.

20 George MacDonald, *Unspoken Sermons*, "Life," 143.

21 George MacDonald, *Unspoken Sermons*, "It Shall Not Be Forgiven," 34.

> There was a stone near me, and I sat down upon it, feeling as if I could sit there without moving to all eternity, so happy was I, and it was because Jesus's father was touching me everywhere; my head felt as if he were counting the hairs of it. And he was not only close to me, but far and far and farther away, and all between. Near and far there was the father! I neither saw nor felt nor heard him, and yet I saw and heard and felt him so near that I could neither see nor hear nor feel him. I am talking very like nonsense, majie, but I can't do it better. It was God, God everywhere, and there was no nowhere anywhere, but all was God, God, God; and my heart was nothing, knew nothing but him; and I felt I could sit there forever, because I was right in the very middle of God's heart.[22]

While it is interesting that MacDonald does not go into detail about what these personal encounters and experiences with the divine entailed, it would not be surprising if they parallel his characters' encounters. Colin Manlove notes that whenever there is a mystical event in MacDonald's fictional works, he "never 'explains' the supernatural or fantastic event. It simply happens, and the protagonist is left to account for it as best he may."[23] Hein suggests that the protagonists' encounters, and especially Curdie in the *Princess* books, exemplify the "tenuous and fleeting nature of the faithful soul's true encounters with deity."[24]

This lack of specificity should not be surprising as it is common among mystics, as Urban T. Holmes states, "The mystic will say to us that they cannot describe what they have experienced."[25] As an example of another protagonist's experience with the divine, as well as the inability of expressing the actual experience, take MacDonald's narrative of *Sir Gibbie*.

> The stillness grew great, and slowly descended upon him. It deepened and deepened. Surely it would deepen to a voice! — it was about to speak! It was as if a great single thought was the substance of the silence, and was all over and around him, and closer to him than his clothes, than his body, than his hands. *I am describing the indescribable, and compelled to*

---

22 George MacDonald, *Weighed and Wanting*, 605.

23 Colin Manlove, "MacDonald and Kingsley: A Victorian Contrast," 152.

24 Rolland Hein, *The Harmony Within*, 38.

25 Urban T. Holmes, *A History of Christian Spirituality* (San Francisco: Harper & Row, 1980), 3.

> *make it too definite for belief.* In colder speech, an experience had come to the child; a link in the chain of his development glided over the windlass of his uplifting; a change passed upon him. In after years, when Gibbie had the idea of God, when he had learned to think about him, to desire his presence, to believe that a will of love enveloped his will, as the brooding hen spreads her wings over her eggs — as often as the thought of God came to him, it came in the shape of the silence on the top of Glashgar. [26]

Not only does this echo the above example of Mark's dream in *Weighed and Wanting*, but also MacDonald admits that attempting to describe Gibbie's encounter is simply impossible, and attempts to do so may even make the reader lean toward incredulity. While this is not definitive evidence, it could offer some evidence for why MacDonald did not explore or narrate his own experiences with the divine.

While MacDonald did not agree with most mystics of his time in theology or praxis, he did agree that the culmination of the "mystic way" is union with the divine, as stated by Evelyn Underhill, among others.[27] There should be no doubt that MacDonald thought this mystical union was not only possible, but was the true end of humanity. One of MacDonald's characters, Mr. Graham, cherished "hopes of a glory of conscious being, divinely better than all my imagination when most daring could invent — a glory springing from absolute unity with my creator."[28] MacDonald again states definitively that the goal for each of us is to "find himself in such conscious as well as vital relation with the source of his being, with a Will by which his own will exists, with a Consciousness by and through which he is conscious, would indeed be the end of all the man's ills!"[29]

Richard Reis argued that MacDonald's "strong infusion of mysticism in his outlook led him to flirt with the uncomfortable but incontrovertible position of the typical mystic that he has received knowledge through inspiration, directly from God."[30] MacDonald himself acknowledged this assertion: "For I never could believe that a man who did not find God in other places as well as in the Bible

---

26 George MacDonald, *Sir Gibbie*, 83, emphasis added.

27 Evelyn Underhill, *Mysticism* (New York: Meridian Books, 1957), 169.

28 George MacDonald, *The Marquis of Lossie*, 255.

29 George MacDonald, *A Dish of Orts*, "A Sketch of Individual Development," 69.

30 Richard H. Reis, *George MacDonald's Fiction*, 33.

ever found Him there at all."[31] For MacDonald, God could, and in fact, did explicitly reveal himself to individuals.[32] Reis continues, "MacDonald's answer to the problem of *how* we are to 'educate' ourselves in this life is that of the typical Christian mystic…[God] has provided us with what we need for our education, if only we will look for it."[33] MacDonald explained further: "Then as to all things that are necessary for our growth in the Divine life, that is, for growing like to him in whose image we are made, he promises to teach us by his spirit everything. Nor even if a man could, which is impossible, know with his understanding the deepest mysteries, would these avail him the least, that would not constitute the knowledge of them after the true fashion: they must be spiritually discerned—in a way that no man can by any possibility to teach his neighbour, but which only the Spirit of God can teach."[34] So how are we supposed to learn how this unity transpires? This will be the focal point of the next section.

To definitively answer our initial question, MacDonald puts it to rest: "If anyone accuses me here of mysticism, I plead guilty with gladness: I only hope it may be of that true mysticism which, inasmuch as he makes constant use of it, St. Paul would understand at once. I leave it, however."[35] Not only does MacDonald claim mysticism here, but he also has hopes and aspirations of making his readers mystics as well: "Am I mystical again, reader? Then I hope you are too, or will be before you have done with this same beautiful mystical life of ours."[36] MacDonald's wish is not to make his readers mere mystics, for he argued that the name could denote a negative condition: "But I am talking what the people who do not understand such things lump all together as mysticism, which is their name for a kind of spiritual ash-pit, whither they consign dust and stones, never asking whether they may not be gold-dust and rubies, all in a heap."[37] Similarly with theology and philosophy, MacDonald argued that one's mysticism could end up clogging our conduit to the divine: "You seem to me to

---

31 George MacDonald, *Annals of a Quiet Neighbourhood*, 183.

32 George MacDonald, *Unspoken Sermons*, "The Knowing of the Son," 199.

33 Richard H. Reis, *George MacDonald's Fiction*, 37.

34 Rolland Hein, *George MacDonald: Victorian Mythmaker*, 495.

35 George MacDonald, *The Seaboard Parish*, 140.

36 Ibid., 141.

37 Ibid., 193.

have taken much interest in unusual forms of theory, and in mystical speculations, to which in themselves I make no objection. But to be content with those, instead of knowing God himself, or to substitute a general amateur friendship towards the race for the love of your neighbour, is a mockery which will always manifest itself to an honest mind like yours in such failure and disappointment in your own character as you are now lamenting, if not indeed in some mode far more alarming..."[38] MacDonald did not wish his readers to be content with mere mysticism, but to pursue the "true mysticism" aligned with Paul and John, and whose ultimate goal was unity with the Father.

MacDonald's "True Mysticism" and the Doctrine of Becoming

First, it would be of benefit to begin this section with an exploration of MacDonald's mode of mysticism. Carl McColman arranges mystics into nine categories including poets, saints, wisdom keepers, heretics, and visionaries. It is this last category in which he places George MacDonald.[39] Here he admits that MacDonald does not quite fit in his definition of mysticism: "MacDonald is not a visionary in the traditional sense of someone who receives extraordinary, ecstatic encounters with the Divine. Rather, his visionary genius manifested in creativity— through his ability to write stories about magical worlds filled with a sense of numinous mystery."[40] Here he also contends that MacDonald's imagination was fuel for his mystical fire: "Is there a relationship between the imagination and mystical vision? I believe so."[41]

While McColman positions MacDonald as a visionary mystic, this does not limit MacDonald to a specific mystical path. In fact, as the reader will soon discover, MacDonald held to different modes of mystical progression, including but not limited to dreams and visions. First, it must be directly stated that MacDonald did not hold to immediate sanctification of believers, but rather, he believed that each is on a progressive path. Rolland Hein explains, in reference to MacDonald's "doctrine of becoming," "He sees no magic whereby men are changed suddenly and easily for the better, as too many views of Christian sanctification lightly suggest. To approach the burnings

---

38 George MacDonald, *Annals of a Quiet Neighbourhood*, 384.
39 Carl McColman, *Christian Mystics: 108 Seers, Saints, and Sages*, xxiv-v.
40 Ibid., 8.
41 Ibid., 9-10.

of divine holiness and be purged for true service is a costly experience to which only men of a certain mettle are beckoned."[42] Richard Reis agrees: "The central concept to be traced throughout MacDonald's fantasies is that of his viewing man's life as a stepwise process of cumulative enlightenment, a sort of spiritual education in which a man passes from one 'grade' to another."[43]

As stated above, MacDonald hopes his readers would consider themselves "mystical" by the end of their lives.[44] Yet how is this to be done? What are the steps to MacDonald's metaphorical staircase that reaches to union with the divine? Reis argues that for MacDonald there are four ways an individual can ascend the mystical staircase: "symbols /correspondences, direct mystical insights, dreams, and by doing one's duty."[45] It is this train of thought that the research should now follow, as well as an addendum that will include an exploration of the role that nature, community, and sorrow play in the soul's ascent to God.

Symbols and Correspondences

As was discussed in chapters two and three, MacDonald's sacramentalism and symbolism set the foundation for his philosophy: his alethiology, epistemology; and now, more practically, his mysticism. This concept not only permeated his theology and epistemology, but also undergirds his entire mystical stairway. It may be appropriate to argue that his view of correspondences and symbols are not a step on the ladder, but the stringer, supporting his entire mystical system.

MacDonald wrote, "A mystical mind is one which, having perceived that the highest expression of which the truth admits, lies in the symbolism of nature and the human customs that result from human necessities, prosecutes thought about truth so embodied by dealing with the symbols themselves after logical forms. This is the highest mode of conveying the deepest truth; and the Lord himself often employed it, as, for instance, in the whole passage ending with the words, 'If therefore the light that is in thee be darkness, how great is the darkness!'"[46] MacDonald contends that that is the "highest mode" of conveying and understanding the deepest of truths. Raeper states

---

42   Rolland Hein, *The Harmony Within*, 41.
43   Richard H. Reis, *George MacDonald's Fiction*, 125.
44   George MacDonald, *The Seaboard Parish*, 141.
45   Richard H. Reis, *George MacDonald's Fiction*, 125-6.
46   George MacDonald, *Unspoken Sermons*, "The New Name," 37.

that in MacDonald's fantastic dream-quests, and most obviously in his *Lilith*, he often outlined an "alchemical correspondence between the things of the spirit and the things of matter."[47] These symbolic correspondences are "the deepest man can utter, will be but the type or symbol of a something deeper yet, of which he can perceive only a doubtful glimmer. This will serve for general remark upon the mystical mode...."[48]

Not only does MacDonald state his affinity for this mode of thinking, he also gives us biblical exemplars of mystical writers:

> Of all writers I know, Paul seems to me the most plainly, the most determinedly practical in his writing. What has been called his mysticism is at one time the exercise of a power of seeing, as by spiritual refraction, truths that had not, perhaps have not yet, risen above the human horizon; at another, the result of a wide-eyed habit of noting the analogies and correspondences between the concentric regions of creation; it is the working of a poetic imagination divinely alive, whose part is to foresee and welcome approaching truth; to discover the same principle in things that look unlike; to embody things discovered, in forms and symbols heretofore unused, and so present to other minds the deeper truths to which those forms and symbols owe their being.[49]

It is no surprise that the sermon from which this passage is taken is entitled "The Mirrors of the Lord" and the heading of the sermon includes Paul's own words from 2 Corinthians 3:18, "And we all, with unveiled faces reflecting the glory of the Lord, are being transformed into the same image from one degree of glory to another, which is from the Lord, who is the Spirit." Even the casual reader of MacDonald would recognize his deep regard for the symbolism he employed in the reflection of a mirror, especially in his *Phantastes*, as researched in Soto's "Mirrors in MacDonald's *Phantastes*: A Reflexive Structure."[50] Second, and in no respect subordinate, MacDonald lists Jesus as another famous purveyor of symbols: "The true soul sees, or will come to see, that his [Christ's]

---

47 William Raeper, *George MacDonald*, 370-371.

48 George MacDonald, *England's Antiphon*, 257.

49 George MacDonald, *Unspoken Sermons*, "The Mirrors of the Lord," 205.

50 Fernando Soto, "Mirrors in MacDonald's *Phantastes*: A Reflexive Structure" in *North Wind: A Journal of George MacDonald Studies*, Vol. 23, 2004.

words, his figures always represent more than they are able to present; for, as the heavens are higher than the earth, so are the heavenly things higher than the earthly signs of them, let the signs be good as ever sign may be."[51] He stated "the Lord himself often employed" symbols, as cited earlier, and mentions Matthew 6:23 as an example, referred to above as well: "If therefore the light that is in thee be darkness, how great is the darkness!'"[52]

While MacDonald offered few practical implications for such a mystical approach, Reis encourages those who are willing to embark on such spiritual education to "study the language of correspondences by which God has given man clues to His meaning; the man skilled in seeing the eternal Idea behind a limited, physical object has the means to understand more than the man who has not yet developed this faculty."[53] While MacDonald speaks little on this subject, there is a broad consensus that MacDonald himself learned these symbols by studying Emmanuel Swedenborg[54] and Jacob Boehme.[55]

Direct Mystical Insights

This category of mystical experience is mostly likely what one expects under the heading of mysticism. In fact, William Raeper defines mysticism as that which "involves knowing God intuitively through the senses without the need of words as a mediator."[56] Thus, scholars occasionally limit the mystical experience to this one category. Yet Reis contends that this is a less common class, which God only "grants to some" and that this "direct perception is not available except at the 'graduate level' – that is, it is a discipline requiring a long preparatory apprenticeship."[57]

While some may still struggle with the term "mystic" being tied to Christianity, note that MacDonald not only had no issue with this label, he also thought that there was a mystical element, a direct connection and revelation between God and man, that was inherent in

---

51   George MacDonald, *Unspoken Sermons*, "Self-Denial," 174.

52   George MacDonald, *Unspoken Sermons*, "The New Name," 37.

53   Richard H. Reis, *George MacDonald's Fiction*, 125.

54   William Raeper, *George MacDonald*, 370; and George MacDonald, *England's Antiphon*, 232.

55   Greville MacDonald, *George MacDonald and His Wife*, 557.

56   William Raeper, *George MacDonald*, 257.

57   Richard H. Reis, *George MacDonald's Fiction*, 125.

Christian belief. In fact, he argued that to teach otherwise was heresy: "The great heresy of the Church of the present day is unbelief in this Spirit. The mass of the Church does not believe that the Spirit has a revelation for every man individually — a revelation as different from the revelation of the Bible, as the food in the moment of passing into living brain and nerve differs from the bread and meat."[58] The style of connection between God and individual men was not universal — God did not connect to each man in the same way. MacDonald explained, "My reader must not mistake my use of the words especial and private, or suppose that I do not believe in an individual relation between every man and God, yes, a peculiar relation differing from the relation between every other man and God! But this very individuality and peculiarity can only be founded on the broadest truths of the Godhood and the manhood."[59] Thus, through introspection and understanding the truths about our individuality, we can come to know some of our relation to our Heavenly Father. MacDonald stated succinctly: "Any true revelation must come out of the unknown in God through the unknown in man."[60] Greville MacDonald understood this teaching when he stated that we each must ascend a "secret stair" up to the wider vision;[61] only the individual and his Heavenly Father know this secret stair.

Again, MacDonald's point of view is closely tied to sacramentalism and his certainty of divine immanence: "The God to whom we pray is nearer to us than the very prayer itself ere it leaves the heart; hence His answers may well come to us through the channel of our own thoughts. But the world too being itself one of his thoughts, He may also well make the least likely of His creatures an angel of His own will to us."[62] In summary, MacDonald believed that God could speak in his own peculiar fashion and according to his particular relationship through the hearts of individual men.

Dreams and Visions

James Ballard writes that "people of the Victorian period were fascinated by dreams and much of the popular press contributed to

---

58   George MacDonald, *Unspoken Sermons*, "The Higher Faith," 23.
59   George MacDonald, *Robert Falconer*, 208.
60   Ibid., 401.
61   Greville MacDonald, *George MacDonald and His Wife*, 482.
62   George MacDonald, *Paul Faber-Surgeon*, 250.

the discourse. The debate centered on whether dreams were a result of communication from God or a phenomenon of our mind."[63] This then begs the question, what did MacDonald think of such dreams? Were they mere subconscious utterings or divine interactions? Ballard argues that "most likely that we would find MacDonald on the 'communication with God' side of the debate, unsurprising given his Christian upbringing and interest in Swedenborg."[64]

While the research will support Ballard's conclusion, there are nuances to this answer. First, in support, Novalis leaned toward this answer: "Naught but dreams might lead to the most sacred place,"[65] and thus one should not be surprised that MacDonald would follow one of his favorite thinkers. MacDonald also used dreams as mystical conduits in many of his works. W.H. Auden stated, "his greatest gift is what one might call his dream realism, his exact and profound knowledge of dream causality, dream logic, dream change, dream morality: when one reads him, the illusion of participating in a real dream is perfect."[66] Rolland Hein elaborates, "God, as MacDonald came to envision him, is a pervading presence, manifesting himself in both nature and dreams to the attentive person."[67]

In both *Lilith* and *At the Back of the North Wind*, "MacDonald raises the issue of the validity of one's good dreams, or imaginative longings."[68] In other words, are dreams, longings, and visions from the mouth and heart of the divine? At first, in *Lilith*, the protagonist, Mr. Vane, seems to lean to the contrary: "What life can there be here but the phantasmagoric—the stuff that dreams are made of? I am indeed walking in a vain show!"[69] Michael Mendelson's analysis concludes, "The obvious pun seems to indicate that this phantasmagoria is a self-generated nightmare projected by the unconscious. And while it has ever been the responsibility of the romance hero to encounter

---

63 James Ballard, "Dreams, Reality, the Soul and the Supernatural in George MacDonald's 'The History of Photogen and Nycteris: A Day and Night Märchen'" (Unpublished manuscript, 2008), 5.

64 Ibid., 6.

65 Novalis, *The Novices of Sais*. Vol. 4, The German Classics, ed. Kuno Francke (Albany, NY: German Publications Society, 1913), 187.

66 W.H. Auden, *The Visionary Novels: Lilith and Phantastes*, ed. Anne Fremantle (New York: Noonday Press, 1962), vii.

67 Rolland Hein, *George MacDonald: Victorian Mythmaker*, 41.

68 Ibid., 282-283.

69 George MacDonald, *Lilith*, 70.

the uncomprehended forces of his own desire, it has also been his prerogative to do so while fully conscious."[70] Thus, it seems that MacDonald leaned toward answering that dreams are mere products of our subconscious.

Yet then again, MacDonald answers to the contrary when North Wind explains to Diamond, "The people who think lies, and do lies, are very likely to dream lies. But the people who love what is true will surely now and then dream true things."[71] Thus, the dream depends on the dreamer, whether or not he is a "true man," as MacDonald commonly implies. How does this answer match with what was cited above in *Lilith*? This is answered clearly when one realizes that Mr. Vane, at this point in his story, was not a true man. At the end of the fantastic tale Mr. Vane explains, "When a man dreams his own dream, he is the sport of his dream; when Another gives it him, that Other is able to fulfill it."[72] When a man is in right standing with God, and the divine chooses to send a true dream, God may, and, according to MacDonald, God does.

Doing One's Duty

As discussed earlier, to do one's duty was paramount in MacDonald's empirical and mystical pursuits. In many, if not all of his works, MacDonald made a point of this deep truth: "To obey him [Jesus Christ] is to ascend the pinnacle of my being."[73] He made it a point to argue that duty is not a final destination, but a stage along the process of becoming: "The doing of things from duty is but a stage on the road to the kingdom of truth and love."[74] Again, later in the same work: "Duty itself is only a stage toward something better. It is but the impulse, God-given I believe, toward a far more vital contact with the truth."[75]

The truth of duty is the crux of MacDonald's *The Wise Woman* as

---

70   Michael Mendelson, "The Fairy Tales of George MacDonald and the Evolution of a Genre" in *For the Childlike: George MacDonald's Fantasies for Children*, ed. Roderick McGillis (Metuchen, NJ: Scarecrow Press, 1985), 203-4.

71   George MacDonald, *At the Back of the North Wind* (Whitehorn: Johannesen, 2002), 370.

72   George MacDonald, *Lilith*, 358.

73   George MacDonald, *Unspoken Sermons*, "Justice," 242.

74   George MacDonald, *Paul Faber-Surgeon*, 24.

75   Ibid., 208.

well as his "Letter to American Boys" where he implores his readers, symbolically, and even directly, to follow in the directives of the divine. In *The Wise Woman*, MacDonald describes the characteristics of an obstinate child in Rosamund, who had been taken from her house of royalty and enclosed in a cottage. While the wise woman simply asks her to "keep the cottage tidy…the hearth swept, and the kettle boiling; no dust on the table or chairs, the windows clear, the floor clean, and the heather in blossom—which last comes of sprinkling it with water three times a day,"[76] the girl initially rejects the wise woman, even going so far as to say that "she wants to fatten and eat me."[77] Over time, and after being placed in a cottage of a shepherd and his wife, the princess improved "by slow degrees."[78] The wise woman gave Rosamund this directive: "You must not do what is wrong, however much you are inclined to do it, and you must do what is right, however much you are disinclined to do it."[79] MacDonald even gives his readers a direct imperative: "Until our duty becomes to us common as breathing, we are poor creatures."[80] Over time, and through many trials, the princess evolves into a young woman who seeks and wants to do the will of the wise woman: "You must not think, because you have seen me once, that therefore you are capable of seeing me at all times. No; there are many things in you yet that must be changed before that can be. Now, however, you will seek me. Every time you feel you want me, that is a sign I am wanting you."[81] In the end, the wise woman puts the princess in charge of her own wayward parents who had been literally, and perhaps figuratively, blinded: "You must be their servant, as I have been yours. Bring them to me, and I will make them welcome."[82]

In "A Letter to American Boys", MacDonald describes a parable where a boy sees a dream in which he sees himself portrayed as a grown man, dirty and defiled, and shackled in a dungeon.[83] He asks the dungeon keeper, "What then am I to do, for the burden of them

---

76   George MacDonald, *The Wise Woman/Gutta Percha Willie*, 45.

77   Ibid., 45.

78   Ibid., 95.

79   Ibid., 124.

80   Ibid., 81.

81   Ibid., 141.

82   Ibid., 156.

83   George MacDonald, "A Letter to American Boys," 202-204.

is intolerable."[84] The keeper responds with "what I will tell thee...for so shall thy chains fall from thee."[85] Unlike Rosamund in *The Wise Woman*, the man immediately listens and obeys. He is asked to clean his cell, to sweep it, to clean his chains, and to carve an image of a man in the wall. He does so and eventually the fetters fall from his wrists and ankles, and one morning the carving of a man in his wall transforms into "an opening in the wall, through which freedom shone!"[86]

Both of these illustrate MacDonald's unwavering dedication in promoting duty as a service to God, which he does not only in his fantastical works, but also his sermons. In the sermon "Eloi" he states succinctly, "Bethink thee of something that thou oughtest to do, and go and do it, if it be but the sweeping of a room, or the preparing of a meal, or a visit to a friend. Heed not thy feelings: do thy work."[87] While in no way is duty merely a novice's task, for it is for all faithful followers, for MacDonald it does signify that one is on the path toward the Father: "He who has begun to recognize duty, and acknowledge the facts of his being, is but a tottering child on the path of life. He is on the path; he is as wise as at the time he can be; the Father's arms are stretched out to receive him," and even more succinctly, "Obedience is the opener of eyes."[88]

The Role of Nature, Fellowship and Community, and Personal Sorrow

In MacDonald's work he often used these three motifs as igniters of mystical living. To continue with our earlier analogy, these may not be steps on the mystical staircase, but possibly the candlelight that allows a person to see that the staircase exists, or possibly even signage directing them upward. In his nonfiction work, he would often compel his readers to meet the person of Jesus in the words of the Gospels,[89] but in his novels MacDonald would take a different tack, likely realizing that his readers were possibly more secular and less spiritually advanced, and would direct his characters to experience

---

84 Ibid., 203.

85 Ibid., 203.

86 Ibid., 204.

87 George MacDonald, *Unspoken Sermons*, "The Eloi," 61.

88 George MacDonald, *Unspoken Sermons*, "The Way," 89.

89 Glenn Edward Sadler, *An Expression of Character: the Letters of George MacDonald*, 59.

nature, other people, or even sorrow to guide them to the mystical staircase.

MacDonald's love of nature is well documented, even in the above information, especially in the treatment of his usage of the term "pantheism" in chapter two. MacDonald held that "...the love of our mother earth is meant to be a beginning."[90] This love of nature is not an end in itself, but a vital step in the right direction; nature is an influence that subtly moves the heart of its charge: "The fact is I was coming in for my share in the spiritual influences of Nature, so largely poured on the heart and mind of my generation.... I was under the same spell as they all. Nature was a power upon me. I was filled with the vague recognition of a present soul in Nature—with a sense of the humanity everywhere diffused through her and operating upon ours."[91]

Rolland Hein explains that for MacDonald, "A mystical life, a spirit from God himself, courses through all nature and strives to communicate with man by using natural objects as symbols."[92] In tandem with our discussion above on sacramentalism, MacDonald held that, "All circumstances and objects that surround a man on any given day of his life are invested by God with the potential to speak to him."[93] So it should not be a surprise that MacDonald often encourages readers to spend time in nature. Most exemplary of this advice is found in *What's Mine's Mine* where Ian prescribes Mercy an exploration of nature:

> "Then what I would have you do," continued Ian, "is—to make yourself alone in one of Nature's withdrawing—rooms, and seat yourself in one of Grannie's own chairs. —I am coming to the point at last! —Upon a day when the weather is fine, go out by yourself. Tell no one where you are going, or that you are going anywhere. Climb a hill. If you cannot get to the top of it, go high on the side of it. No book, mind! nothing to fill your thinking-place from another's! People are always saying 'I think,' when they are not thinking at all, when they are at best only passing the thoughts of others whom they do not even know.
>
> When you have got quite alone, when you do not even know

---

90   George MacDonald, *Malcolm*, 244.
91   George MacDonald, *Wilfrid Cumbermede*, 131-2.
92   Rolland Hein, *The Harmony Within*, 45.
93   Ibid., 45.

the nearest point to anybody, sit down and be lonely. Look out on the loneliness, the wide world round you, and the great vault over you, with the lonely sun in the middle of it; fold your hands in your lap, and be still. Do not try to think anything. Do not try to call up any feeling or sentiment or sensation; just be still. By and by, it may be, you will begin to know something of Nature. I do not know you well enough to be sure about it; but if you tell me afterwards how you fared, I shall then know you a little better, and perhaps be able to tell you whether Nature will soon speak to you, or not until, as Henry Vaughan says, some veil be broken in you."[94]

While this charge is highly encouraged, it also came with a warning: "But even the worship of Nature herself might be an ennobling idolatry, so much is the divine present in her."[95] Thus, he did not want the porch of God's temple, nature and science, to become the object of worship, but rather, a sign, directing one to God's own heart.

Secondly, MacDonald considered community and relationships with one's fellow man as a potential for mystical spark. While it may seem contradictory to stress individuality in a section on community, it would be intellectually dishonest not to begin by stating that MacDonald consistently stressed the individual relation between God, the Father, to man, his child. In fact, he held to the primacy of one's relation with God over and above one's relation to his fellow man. He could possibly be even said to believe that without one's relation to God, a true relationship, a community, or even a true nation, cannot exist: "Only in God can two or many truly meet; only as they recognize their oneness with God can they become one with each other."[96] MacDonald seems to be arguing the simple point that most human interactions are between individuals, not whole entities of individuals: "It is for and by the individuals that the individual lives. A community is the true development of individual relations."[97] The point of these groups of individuals is for the benefit of the individual: "All communities are for the divine sake of individual life, for the sake of the love and truth that is in each heart, and is not cumulative

---

94   George MacDonald, *What's Mine's Mine*, 220.

95   Ibid., 241.

96   George MacDonald, *Miracles of Our Lord*, 62.

97   Ibid., 62.

— cannot be in two as one result."[98] While MacDonald downplayed community as essential and upheld the primacy of the individual, he recognized the need for God's movement in the community of believers to help its constituents. He stated, "In a word, the man, in virtue of standing alone in God, stands with his fellows, and receives from them divine influences without which he cannot be made perfect."[99] Without these relations, *Thomas Wingfold* would not have had the influence of Mr. Polwarth, and would likely have given up the cloth. Without Irene's influence on Curdie in *The Princess and the Goblin* he would have never overcome his skepticism.

To present a specific example, note the relationship between Ian and Christina in *What Mine's Mine*. Ian had saved Christina from a flood and the narrator interjected, "How many of us actually believe in any support we do not immediately feel? In any arms we do not see? But every help is from God; Ian's help was God's help; though to believe in Ian was not to believe in God, it was a step on the road toward believing in God."[100] Again in the same work, Mercy tells Alister, "I was dead until you waked me….."[101] Through Mercy's interactions with nature that had been suggested by the brothers, her love of Alister, and the words of Ian, she was changed from a child to woman.[102]

The last signpost pointing toward the mystical staircase is the most formidable. The idea that sorrow plays a part in God's system is inherent in most, if not all, of MacDonald's fiction. He used sorrow and pain as an instrument to rouse his characters from their dream-like existence: "All who dream life instead of living it require some similar shock. Of the kind is every disappointment, every reverse, every tragedy of life."[103] In some instances MacDonald goes so far as to say that "the only hope of deliverance lies in catastrophe."[104] He even alluded to the fact that sorrow and suffering are often essential and necessary for spiritual progress: "I have all the time been leading you toward the door at which you want to go in. It is not likely, however,

---

98 Ibid., 61.

99 Ibid., 62.

100 George MacDonald, *What's Mine's Mine*, 226.

101 Ibid., 339.

102 Ibid., 339.

103 Ibid., 227.

104 George MacDonald, *Paul Faber-Surgeon*, 283.

that it will open to you at once. I doubt if it will open to you at all except through sorrow."[105]

Dearborn explains: "Through the clarifying power behind suffering, barriers that exist between oneself and God and oneself and one's neighbor may be broken down."[106] While we prefer joy and its comfort, they often cannot lead us to where God wants us to be: "Joy cannot unfold the deepest truths, although truth must be deepest joy. Cometh white-robed Sorrow, stooping and wan, and flingeth wide the doors she may not enter."[107] There is no hesitation in MacDonald's mind that "the Providence of God arranges everything for the best good of the individual."[108] While the "best good" is to be defined in relation to the eternal purposes of God, and there may be disagreement by his followers and detractors alike, MacDonald held that without these negative experiences, one cannot be "fashioned into the perfection of a child of the kingdom."[109]

In conclusion, MacDonald's brand of mysticism has above been defined, and it has been demonstrated that while arguments may still swirl surrounding MacDonald being a mystic; it is unquestionable that he considered himself one, yet under his own unique characterization. It is no surprise that MacDonald's primacy of immanence and sacramentalism affects his mysticism and relationship with the divine, and that his steps of progression and the "doctrine of becoming" would reflect the nearness of God and his theory of correspondences. Lastly, it has been demonstrated what four common directives occurred in his work which encouraged a sort of spiritual education, mystical ascension, or even a "doctrine of becoming." Through symbolism and correspondences, dreams and visions, direct mystical insight, and doing one's duty, MacDonald believed that one could reach unity with God. Beyond those four directives, MacDonald also consistently referenced nature, community, and sorrow to potentially cause a mystical spark in newer initiates, or rekindle connections with God in experienced mystics alike.

---

105 George MacDonald, *What's Mine's Mine*, 216.

106 Kerry Dearborn, *Baptized Imagination: The Theology of George MacDonald*, 157.

107 George MacDonald, *Phantastes*, 126.

108 George MacDonald, *Miracles of Our Lord*, 62.

109 George MacDonald, *David Elginbrod*, 93.

Waking the Dead

PART III

The Apologetics of George MacDonald

"To teach your intellect what has to be learned by your whole being, what cannot be understood without the whole being, what it would do you no good to understand save you understood it in your whole being — if this be the province of any man, it is not mine. Let the dead bury their dead, and the dead teach their dead; for me, I will try to wake them."[1]

-George MacDonald

---

1   George MacDonald, *Unspoken Sermons,* "Righteousness," 268.

Waking the Dead

CHAPTER SIX

Modern Implications for George MacDonald's Nineteenth Century Apologetic

Introduction

To inquire of the famous apologists of the eighteenth and nineteenth centuries, one would likely stumble on a list including, but not limited to, William Paley, Alexander B. Bruce, John Henry Newman and Abraham Kuyper; but one would be hard-pressed to find George MacDonald included in a list of these apologists. Usually the only connection MacDonald finds to the realm of apologetics or philosophy is when he is mentioned in the same breath as C.S. Lewis. Otherwise, MacDonald is regarded for his literary efforts, his practical theology, and the rest is ignored. But is there legitimacy for this dismissal from the realm of apologetics?

First and foremost, let us establish our terminology. From Norman Geisler's perspective, "Apologetics is the discipline that deals with a rational defense of Christian faith."[2] Stephen Cowan agrees that "apologetics has to do with the defending, or making a case for, the truth of the Christian faith."[3] While these two definitions seem to lean toward a conflation of apologetics and rationality, others, like Bernard Ramm, have a more general approach: "Christian apologetics is the strategy of setting forth the truthfulness of the Christian faith and its right to the claim of knowledge of God."[4] He even goes so far as to say, "However, not all Christian apologetics come with a clear label...whatever deals with truth or with knowledge with respect to the Christian faith is apologetically in scope and content."[5] While Ramm goes on to list other genres of books in apologetic nature such as philosophy of religion, philosophical treatises like Kant's *Critiques*, and *Philosophical Theology*, he never mentions works of fiction, but it is possible that he would have been open to that possibility, as long as those works of fiction were involved in "setting forth the truthfulness

---

2   Norman Geisler, *Baker Encyclopedia of Christian Apologetics* (Grand Rapids: Baker Books, 1999), 70.

3   Stephen Cowan, *Five Views on Apologetics*, ed. Stephen Cowan (Grand Rapids: Zondervan, 2000), 8.

4   Bernard Ramm, *Varieties of Christian Apologetics* (Grand Rapids: Baker Book House, 1961), 13.

5   Ibid., 13.

of the Christian faith." Hans Frei even goes further in his generality of apologetics: "I have used the term apologetics to cover (among other things) this appeal to a common ground between analysis of human experience by direct natural thought and by some distinctively Christian thought."⁶

Some automatically unite rationality and apologetics, and this is unequivocally an inappropriate conflation of terms. Dr. Geisler, a foremost popular apologist in this present era, used the term "rational" in his definition. While this fact would have to be conceded, it would be a mistake not to call attention to the fact that in Geisler's own encyclopedia of apologetics he has an entry for "experiential apologetics" which is a "form of defending the faith" that does not rely on rational arguments, but instead, "appeals to Christian experience."⁷ While Geisler is a critic of such an approach, he does not argue that this method is not apologetics at all, but rather, that it is simply not an effective approach. Thus we are going to adopt the definition of James Van Eerden who, in his Master's Thesis entitled *An Inquiry into the Use of Human Experience as an Apologetic Tool*, writes, "The task of the apologist is to defend and advance the central tenets of the Christian faith."⁸ Apologetics is simply the defense of, and an attempt at clearly articulating the central beliefs of Christianity. While, at this point, one may still question such a label applying to George MacDonald, the following research will trace the attitude and approaches to apologetics in MacDonald's historical context, as well as defend MacDonald's placement amongst apologetic scholars of such distinction.

An Overview of Apologetic Strategies during the Nineteenth Century

Apologists "have reasoned their way throughout the centuries, sometimes forcefully and sometimes feebly."⁹ Every era has its

---

6   Hans W. Frei, "Apologetics, Criticism, and the Loss of Narrative Interpretation" in *Why Narrative? : Readings in Narrative Theology*, ed. Stanley Hauerwas and L. Gregory Jones (Grand Rapids: Eerdmans, 1989), 49.

7   Norman Geisler, *Baker Encyclopedia of Christian Apologetic*, 235.

8   James Patrick Van Eerden, *An Inquiry into the Use of Human Experience as an Apologetic Tool: Illustrations from the Writings of George MacDonald, G.K. Chesterton and C.S. Lewis* (Master's Thesis: Grove City College, 1995), 1.

9   Ibid., 1.

apologetic character and epistemic focus, and the eighteenth century was dominated by an appeal to rationalism and the primacy of science and reason. The Christian apologists during this era focused on "two basic theistic proofs: the argument from miracle and prophecy and the argument from design."[10] As will be seen below, this method was "highly scrutinized and came under severe attack by thinkers who were themselves committed to the ideals and scientific methods of the Age of Reason."[11] Even modern philosophical historians have disdain for such an era: "Like the Temple of Reason in Notre Dame de Paris, the popularity of the cult of reason was relatively short-lived."[12]

It would be an easy task simply to paint the nineteenth century apologists as reacting to this rational approach, but the fact of the matter is that this era was a tug-of-war between the traditional rationalist approach on one side and the Romantics and skeptics on the other. Hans Frei points out that this was not an anomaly, but rather, this has happened quite often in the history of apologetics and theology: "Modern mediating theology gives an impression of constantly building, tearing down, rebuilding, and tearing down again the same edifice. Notable instances of this procedure are the revolt of nineteenth-century Christian liberals against the 'evidence'—seeking theology of the eighteenth century, the revolt of the so-called dialectical or neo-orthodox theologians against nineteenth-century liberalism in the 1920s, and contemporary arguments in favor of the meaningfulness of a specific Christian 'language game' among all the other language games people play."[13] To make the point clear, and before we continue into specific apologists and Christian theologians in the nineteenth century, all one would have to do is contrast the work of two prominent thinkers at the turn of the century. Friedrich Schleiermacher believed that theological "truth was now to be found in the symbolic rendering of the experiences of the life of feelings"[14] and was famous for "deemphasizing the fatal falseness of our reasons

---

10 James C. Livingston, *Modern Christian Thought Vol. 1: The Enlightenment and the Nineteenth Century* (Upper Saddle River, NJ: Prentice Hall, 1997), 50.

11 Ibid., 83.

12 Ibid., 400.

13 Hans W. Frei, "Apologetics, Criticism, and the Loss of Narrative Interpretation," 49.

14 James C. Livingston, *Modern Christian Thought*, 105.

and passions."[15] Schleiermacher elevated subjective experience and diminished the cognitive faculties. In contrast, William Paley argued that knowledge of God could be found through our senses and rational faculties. In his *Natural Theology and Tracts* in 1802, he writes:

> The existence, the agency, the wisdom, of the Deity, *could* be testified to his rational creatures. This is the scale by which we ascend to all the knowledge of our Creator which we possess, so far as it depends upon the phenomena, or the works of nature. Take away this, and you take away from us every subject of observation, and ground of reasoning; I mean as our rational faculties are formed at present. Whatever is done, God could have done without the intervention of instruments or means; but it is in the construction of instruments, in the choice and adaptation of means, that a creative intelligence is seen.[16]

During this time period, "religion and science were in mutual support. And such continued to be the prevalent view in the opening years of the nineteenth century, when the writings of William Paley in this country were at the height of their popularity.... The scientific spirit now permeated thought in all its ranges," but as science began to take a larger grip on the minds of the populace, "the appeal to natural phenomena in evidence of the divine existence and attributes began to lose its former cogency."[17] In fact, to some, including those who will be discussed later, Paley's arguments became regarded as "frigid and unpersuasive."[18]

Thus, the apologetic spirit of the nineteenth century was not homogenous, but it was within this conflict and metaphorical tug-of-war where MacDonald's life and work was positioned. Even more specifically, in the midpoint of MacDonald's career, there was heightened conflict in the arena of apologetics: "A clash between religious beliefs and scientific theory was thus inevitable: first, on the question of the Genesis story of the creation, then on

---

15   Nicola Hoggard Creegan, "Schleiermacher as apologist: Reclaiming the Father of Modern Theology" in *Christian Apologetics in the Postmodern World*, ed. by Timothy R. Phillips & Dennis L. Okholm (Downers Grove: InterVarsity Press, 1995), 60.

16   William Paley, *Natural Theology and Tracts* (New York: S. King, 1824), 31.

17   Bernard M.G. Reardon, *Religious Thought in the Victorian Age: A Survey from Coleridge to Gore* (New York: Longman, 1995), 210-211.

18   Ibid., 3.

George MacDonald as Philosopher, Mystic, and Apologist

Darwinism, especially as propounded by T.H. Huxley, whose respect for the susceptibilities of theologians was minimal, and finally on the doctrine of materialism generally, a philosophy destructive of all spiritual values. The issue of science versus religion was most prominent from about 1860 to 1880, when both sides were in the mood for conflict, the theologians from an authoritarian confidence whetted by fear, the scientists (or their publicists) from an exhilaration born of achievements."[19] In the midst of that chaos, MacDonald wrote *Weighed and Wanting* in which he had his protagonist state, "I should be the last to encourage the atheism that is getting so frightfully common, but really it seems to me such extravagant notions about religion as you have been brought up in must have not a little to do with the present sad state of affairs — must in fact go far to make atheists."[20] MacDonald thought that the staunch Calvinism and the rationalistic apologetics that permeated his culture often had ill effect upon the very laymen that they were supposed to be helping. As a prophet's dissonant voice in the wilderness calls for change, so was the voice of François-René de Chateaubriand in 1802.

Chateaubriand's *Le Genie du Christianisme*, or, the *Genius if Christianity* "published in the spring of 1802, marked the beginning of a new style in apologetics. Philosophically null, it disclosed all the same and emotional thirst for religions which only the living imagination could satisfy."[21] He "initiated a new apologetics that looked to the beauty and to the cultural institutions of the past that were, he argued, the achievement of the Catholic genius. The Traditionalists turned away from abstract argument and appealed, rather, to the 'giveness' of a primal divine revelation, passed on over the centuries...."[22] This work marked a turning of the tide in nineteenth century apologetics. He saw the issues in modern apologetics, noted them, and cast them aside to take on a new direction: "The defenders of the Christians fell into an error which had before undone them: they did not perceive that the question was no longer to discuss this or that particular tenet since the very foundation on which these tenets were built was rejected by their opponents. By starting from the mission of Jesus Christ, and descending from one consequence to another, they established the truths of faith on a solid basis; but this mode of reasoning, which

---

19   Ibid., 10.

20   George MacDonald, *Weighed and Wanting*, 481.

21   Bernard M.G. Reardon, *Religious Thought in the Victorian Age*, 7.

22   James C. Livingston, *Modern Christian Thought*, 356.

might have suited the seventeenth century extremely well, when the groundwork was not contested, proved of no use in our days."[23] The following excerpt explains Chateaubriand's commitment to rejecting the old, and embarking on new avenues of demonstration of the truth of the Christian faith:

> It was, therefore, necessary to prove that, on the contrary, the Christian religion, of all the religions that ever existed, is the most humane, the most favorable to liberty and to the arts and sciences; that the modern world is indebted to it for every improvement, from agriculture to the abstract sciences — from the hospitals for the reception of the unfortunate to the temples reared by the Michael Angelo's and embellished by the Raphael's. It was necessary to prove that nothing is more divine than its morality— nothing more lovely and more sublime than its tenets, its doctrine, and its worship; that it encourages genius, corrects the taste, develops the virtuous passions, imparts energy to the ideas, presents noble images to the writer, and perfect models to the artist; that there is no disgrace in being believers with Newton and Bossuet, with Pascal and Racine. In a word, it was necessary to summon all the charms of the imagination, and all the interests of the heart, to the assistance of that religion against which they had been set in array.
>
> The reader may now have clear view of the object of our work. All other kinds of apologies are exhausted, and perhaps they would be useless at the present day. Who would now sit down to read work professedly theological? Possibly few sincere Christians who are already convinced. But, it may be asked, may there not be some danger in considering religion in merely human point of view? Why so? Does our religion shrink from the light? Surely one great proof of its divine origin is, that it will bear the test of the fullest and severest scrutiny of reason. Would you have us always open to the reproach of enveloping our tenets in sacred obscurity, lest their falsehood should be detected? Will Christianity be the less true for appearing the more beautiful? Let us banish our weak apprehensions; let us not, by an excess of religion, leave religion to perish. We no longer live in those times when you might say, 'Believe without inquiring.' People will inquire in spite of us; and our timid silence, in heightening the triumph of the infidel, will

---

23 François-René Chateaubriand, *The Genius of Christianity; or the Spirit and Beauty of the Christian Religion,*. translated by Charles I. White (Philadelphia: John Murphy & Co., 1884), 48.

diminish the number of believers.

> It is time that the world should know to what all those charges of absurdity, vulgarity, and meanness, that are daily alleged against Christianity, may be reduced. It is time to demonstrate, that, instead of debasing the ideas, it encourages the soul to take the most daring flights, and is capable of enchanting the imagination as divinely as the deities of Homer and Virgil. Our arguments will at least have this advantage, that they will be intelligible to the world at large, and will require nothing but common sense to determine their weight and strength. In works of this kind authors neglect, perhaps rather too much, to speak the language of their readers. It is necessary to be scholar with scholar, and poet with poet. The Almighty does not forbid us to tread the flowery path, if it serves to lead the wanderer once more to him; nor is it always by the steep and rugged mountain that the lost sheep finds its way back to the fold.[24]

Chateaubriand started on this journey focused on the positive and beautiful attributes of Christianity, and his insistence on limiting the usage of metaphysical proofs: "Adhering scrupulously to our plan, we shall banish all abstract ideas from our proofs of the existence of God and the immortality of the soul, and shall employ only such arguments as may be derived from poetical and sentimental considerations, or, in other words, from the wonders of nature and the moral feelings."[25] Again, he remarks with specificity: "Without entering too deeply into metaphysical proofs, which we have studiously avoided, we shall nevertheless endeavor to answer certain objections which are incessantly brought forward."[26] As stated in the extended excerpt above, he thought that to expect a non-believer to sit down and read a theological text would be unlikely, and even if this were to take place, it would be unconvincing. But to throw out reason would be to throw out the baby with the bathwater. For Christianity should be able to "bear the test of the fullest and severest scrutiny of reason."[27]

While Livingston states that Chateaubriand "considered the rationalistic arguments of the seventeenth and eighteenth centuries— regarding such matters as revelation, miracles, and God— to be

---

24   François-René Chateaubriand, *The Genius of Christianity; or the Spirit and Beauty of the Christian Religion*, 46-50.

25   Ibid., 138.

26   Ibid., 191.

27   Ibid., 49.

exhausted and useless,"[28] and although there is truth to this claim, it is a slight overstatement. For even while Chateaubriand claimed to repudiate these proofs he stated the following: "To complete what we have said on the existence of God and the immortality of the soul, we shall here present the metaphysical proofs of these truths."[29] After which, Chateaubriand makes an end note and lists metaphysical proofs as an addendum to his work. If these were completely useless, why list them as a supplement? To digress, the sentiment that Chateaubriand sought to reduce the usage of metaphysical proofs, and in order to appeal to the common sense and the beauty in man, still holds. For an example of his style of argument, take his version of the teleological argument, with some suggestion of the anthropic principle:

> We cannot conceive what scene of confusion nature would present if it were abandoned to the sole movements of matter. The clouds, obedient to the laws of gravity, would fall perpendicularly upon the earth, or ascend in pyramids into the air; moment afterward the atmosphere would be too dense or too rarefied for the organs of respiration. The moon, either too near or too distant, would at one time be invisible, at another would appear bloody and covered with enormous spots, or would alone fill the whole celestial concave with her disproportionate orb. Seized, as it were, with strange kind of madness, she would pass from one eclipse to another, or, rolling from side to side, would exhibit that portion of her surface which earth has never yet beheld. The stars would appear to be under the influence of the same capricious power; and nothing would be seen but succession of tremendous conjunctions. One of the summer signs would be speedily overtaken by one of the signs of winter; the Cow-herd would lead the Pleiades, and the Lion would roar in Aquarius; here the stars would dart along with the rapidity of lightning, there they would be suspended motionless; sometimes, crowding together in groups, they would form new galaxy; at others, disappearing all at once, and, to use the expression of Tertullian, reading the curtain of the universe, they would expose to view the abysses of eternity. [30]

---

28   James C. Livingston, *Modern Christian Thought*, 144.

29   François-René Chateaubriand, *The Genius of Christianity; or the Spirit and Beauty of the Christian Religion*, 695.

30   François-René Chateaubriand, *The Genius of Christianity; or the Spirit and Beauty of the Christian Religion*, 140-141.

George MacDonald as Philosopher, Mystic, and Apologist

Note that, for Chateaubriand, poetic style coexists with substance. He makes no metaphysical connections, no abstract reasoning; he merely encourages the reader, in expressive fashion, to ponder the universe and contemplate its obvious order and dependence on a divine coordinator. While there is no evidence of an interaction between this Frenchman and MacDonald, it will be demonstrated that they both had a similar distaste for mere metaphysical argumentation, thus independently reflecting an aspect of the spirit of the times, and both had an imaginative-apologetic style.

Of all of the Christian thinkers, theologians, and apologists in this brief survey of the apologetic landscape in the nineteenth century, Coleridge is the one with the strongest connection to George MacDonald.[31] Not only is he often mentioned in MacDonald's works, but MacDonald calls him a "sage" and is said to have opened Wordsworth's eyes "to such visions"; he even goes so far as to say that "the ecstasy is even loftier in Coleridge than in Wordsworth."[32] Thus it is not an exaggeration to suggest that he held Coleridge's perspective and literary prowess in high regard.

Similarly to other Romantics during this era, Coleridge limited the impact of rationalistic arguments and, instead, focused on the imagination. Coleridge's system of thought was an exemplar of his era. In the age of Coleridge, "reason was quickened, sometimes indeed superseded, by imagination...the knowledge of truth, for the Romantic mind, was a visionary experience, an intuition or immediate beholding. But vision, intuition, is of its very nature subjective proof. External proof is irrelevant, even alien to it."[33]

Coleridge himself explains his disdain for the focus on rationalistic argumentation and evidence: "I more than fear, the prevailing taste for Books of Natural Theology, Physico-theology, Demonstrations of God from Nature, Evidences of Christianity, and the like. *Evidences* of Christianity! I am weary of the Word. Make a man feel the *want* of it; rouse him, if you can, to the self-knowledge of his *need* of it; and you may safely trust it to its own Evidence--remembering only the express declaration of Christ himself: No man cometh to me, unless the Father leadeth him!"[34] As will be explored later, this analogy

---

31   Gisela H. Kreglinger, "Reading Scripture in Crisis: The Victorian Crisis of Faith and MacDonald's Response to Coleridge," 81.

32   George MacDonald, *England's Antiphon*, 307.

33   Bernard M.G. Reardon, *Religious Thought in the Victorian Age*, 7.

34   Samuel Taylor Coleridge, *Aids to Reflection*. (London: Hurst, Chance

of waking, or rousing the lost sleeper sounds profoundly similar to MacDonald's own words: "Let the dead bury their dead, and the dead teach their dead; for me, I will try to wake them."[35]

Unfortunately for Coleridge, similarly to how Chateaubriand was treated above, many proof-text his statements, and conclude that he was completely anti-rationalistic. Note Reardon's assessment: "Current religious discussion, in so far as it ventured upon philosophical problems at all, fastened on the 'evidences' of Christianity, chiefly in an attempt to refuse the skeptic Hume. Coleridge's aim was to break entirely with these arid and unconvincing methods…. For not only was evidence-theology useless – ineffectual for its own end; it was also false in principle. Its procedure was purely rationalistic and made no appeal to religious feeling. To the believer external evidences are unnecessary: he builds his faith on other grounds; whilst the philosophically minded unbeliever they rest on a mistaken premise. The reader Coleridge sought to address was the intelligent doubter, especially if he were among the young, whom the conventional arguments left untouched."[36] Reardon seems to argue that Coleridge was completely anti-rationalistic, and if we were to take the Coleridge passage above and extract it from the rest of his work, it would be easy to arrive at this conclusion, but as we see below, in an excerpt from the same work by Coleridge quoted above, this is not completely the case:

> Do I then utterly exclude the speculative Reason from Theology? No! It is its office and rightful privilege to determine on the *negative* truth of whatever we are required to believe. The doctrine must not *contradict* any universal principle: for this would be a Doctrine that contradicted itself. Or Philosophy? No. It may be and has been the servant and pioneer of Faith by convincing the mind, that a doctrine is cogitable, that the soul can present the *Idea* to itself; and that *if* we determine to contemplate, or *think* of, the subject at all, so and in no other form can this be effected. So far are both Logic and Philosophy to be received and trusted. But the *duty*, and in some cases and for some persons even the *right*, of thinking on subjects beyond the bounds of sensible experience; the grounds of the *Real* truth; the *Life*, the *Substance*, the *Hope*, the *Love*, in one word, the *Faith*; — these

---

& Company, 2nd edition, 1831), 399. *Collected Works of STC* 9 ed. John Beer, 405-6.

35 George MacDonald, *Unspoken Sermons*, "Righteousness," 268.

36 Bernard M.G. Reardon, *Religious Thought in the Victorian Age*, 46-47.

are derivatives from the practical, moral, and spiritual Nature and Being of Man.[37]

Thus, for Coleridge, as for Chateaubriand, logic, philosophy, and even apologetics have their place, but not in the heightened state in which the spirit of the prior age had elevated them. In the same way that MacDonald had been charged with being "anti-science," so have these Romantic writers been charged with "anti-rationalism," when these thinkers seem merely trying to take rationalism and science off of the pedestal on which they have been erected, lowering them to a more humble position of priority. While there is some incongruity among historians on Coleridge's own words, there is no doubt that Coleridge himself "was a man for whom any rationale of faith must be made in essentially personal terms.... It was something which every man must work out for himself."[38]

With Coleridge being the last of the Romantics we will cover in this section, it should be pointed out that the theme of most nineteenth century Romantics, and with MacDonald as well, was to find a more holistic approach to evidence, apologetics, and faith itself. Some may assume that the impact of the nineteenth century apologetic landscape is most notably a rejection of rationalism, but this would be an overstatement: "It would be quite wrong…to envision the Romantic Movement as simply the repudiation of the Age of Reason. Rather, the Romantics strove to enlarge the vision of the eighteenth-century and to return to a wider, more richly diversified tradition."[39] They simply were "unwilling to reduce experience either to an abstract rationalism or a narrow, scientific empiricism. Experience involved much that eluded both analytical reasoning and scientific experiment, including the power of imagination, feeling, and intuition."[40]

John Henry Newman, Anglican priest and theologian, published his *Sermons, Chiefly on the Theory of Religious Belief* in 1844. He also had a disdain for rationalistic evidence. James C. Livingston even argued that Newman found Paley's arguments "repellant," the problem with this style of apologetics being that it attempted "to prove Christianity independently of the grace of faith…religious faith and truth may on occasion be justified by reason, but reason never can produce faith. Religious knowledge arises from moral obedience, out of hunger and

---

37   Samuel Taylor Coleridge, *Aids to Reflection*, 177. *Collected Works* 9, 188.
38   Bernard M.G. Reardon, *Religious Thought in the Victorian Age*, 52.
39   James C. Livingston, *Modern Christian Thought*, 83.
40   Ibid., 84.

thirst after righteousness."[41] Newman did not attempt to make an analysis of the change in apologetic styles over the two centuries, but did allow himself to make this argument,

> I have not here to make any formal comparison of the last century with the present, or to say whether they are nearer the truth, who in these matters advance with the present age, or who loiter behind with the preceding. I will only state what seems to me meant when persons disparage the Evidences, — viz. they consider that, as a general rule, religious minds embrace the Gospel mainly on the great antecedent probability of a revelation, and the suitableness of the Gospel to their needs; on the other hand, that on men of irreligious minds Evidences are thrown away. Further, they perhaps would say, that to insist much on matters which are for the most part so useless for any practical purpose, draw men away from the true view of Christianity, and leads them to think that Faith is mainly the result of argument, that religious Truth is a legitimate matter of disputation, and that they who reject it rather err in judgment than commit sin. They think they see in the study in question a tendency to betray the sacredness and dignity of Religion, when those who profess themselves its champions allow themselves to stand on the same ground as philosophers of the world, admit the same principles, and only aim at drawing different conclusions. For is not this the error, the common and fatal error, of the world, to think itself a judge of Religious Truth without preparation of heart?[42]

As mentioned in chapters two, three, and four, MacDonald realized that without the person being a true person, no argument would shake his already-held belief. In Newman's words, there has to be a "preparation of heart" in order for these evidences to root into one's cognitive soil. Even if there was evidence that would change one's mind, it likely would not end in saving faith: "I do but say that it is antecedent probability that gives meaning to those arguments from fact which are commonly called the Evidences of Revelation; that, whereas mere probability proves nothing, mere facts persuade no one; that probability is to fact, as the soul to the body; that mere presumptions may have no force, but that mere facts have no warmth. A mutilated and defective evidence suffices for persuasion where the

---

41   James C. Livingston, *Modern Christian Thought*, 176.

42   John Henry Newman, *Sermons, Chiefly on the Theory of Religious Belief: Preached Before the University of Oxford* (London: Francis and John Rivington, 1844), 189-190.

heart is alive; but dead evidences, however perfect, can but create a dead faith."⁴³ In Newman's mind, the evidences that might produce belief would only produce mere belief and not saving faith, nor a relationship with the living God.

In the same vein as Chateaubriand, Newman did not completely disregard rationalistic evidences; he found that they could have their place among the laity and Christian scholars alike:

> Yet, serious as these dangers may be, it does not therefore follow that the Evidences may not be of great service to persons in particular frames of mind. Careless persons may be startled by them as they might be startled by a miracle, which is no necessary condition of believing, notwithstanding. Again, they often serve as a test of honesty of mind; their rejection being the condemnation of unbelievers. Again, religious persons sometimes get perplexed and lose their way; are harassed by objections; see difficulties which they cannot surmount; are a prey to subtlety of mind or over-anxiety. Under these circumstances the varied proofs of Christianity will be a stay, a refuge, an encouragement, a rallying point for Faith, a gracious economy; and even in the case of the most established Christian are they a source of gratitude and reverent admiration, and a means of confirming faith and hope.⁴⁴

Thus, Newman saw rational arguments as potential discipleship material, or possibly used as an uplifting devotional; but needless to say, he did not find them useful for evangelistic means.

Charles Hodge was a Presbyterian and Calvinist who taught at Princeton for fifty-eight years and "is the person most associated with and representative of the Princeton Theology."⁴⁵ He published multiple works, but the one with substantial apologetics content was his *Systematic Theology*, first published in 1865. Of the nineteenth-century thinkers mentioned earlier, Hodge would be most aligned with Paley's apologetic approach, and he even suggested Paley's *Natural Theology* to his readers as a good demonstration that God uses the physical world to proclaim his existence and his glory.⁴⁶ Hodge,

---

43 John Henry Newman, *Sermons, Chiefly on the Theory of Religious Belief*, 191-192.

44 Ibid., 191.

45 James C. Livingston, *Modern Christian Thought*, 304.

46 Charles Hodge, *Systematic Theology*, Vol. 1 (New York: Charles Scribers and Company, 1872), 25.

who held his position at Princeton through much of the century, noticed the trend in apologetics to demean the rationalistic arguments and reacted thus: "The arguments are not designed so much to prove the existence of an unknown being, as to demonstrate that the Being who reveals himself to man in the very constitution of his nature must be all that Theism declares him to be. Such writers as Hume, Kant, Coleridge, and the whole school of transcendental philosophers, have more or less expressly denied the validity of the ordinary arguments for the existence of a personal God."[47]

He did not succumb to this cultural pressure, but instead doubled down on the traditional approach. He argued: "The existence of God is an objective fact. It may be shown that it is a fact which cannot be rationally denied. Although all men have feelings and convictions which necessitate the assumption that there is a God; it is, nevertheless, perfectly legitimate to show that there are other facts which necessarily lead to the same conclusion."[48] Hodge did not merely defend Natural Theology but even rationalism itself, and argued the classical arguments for God's existence. Thus, even in the midst of the nineteenth century and the reaction against rationalism from the skeptics and Romantics alike, there were those who still held to traditional, rational apologetics.

Alexander Balmain Bruce (1831-99), who was the professor of Apologetics and New Testament exegesis at Free Church Hall, had a unique view. Reardon argued that "Apologetics was necessary – and Bruce himself was the author of a well-known treatise thereon – but he despaired of any successful defense of traditionalist positions. The apologist's proper task is to present the Christianity of Christ himself, in the assurance that its intrinsic worth must convince any man of good will."[49] In his *Apologetics: or, Christianity Defensively Stated* Bruce wrote:

> When one considers the facts connected with the history of theistic evidence: how few arguments command the general assent even of theists, how much the line of proof adopted depends on the advocate's philosophic viewpoint, and how little respect the rival schools of philosophy pay to all methods of establishing the common faith but their own, he is tempted to think that that faith is without sure foundation, and that

---

47   Ibid., 202.

48   Ibid., 203.

49   Bernard M.G. Reardon, *Religious Thought in the Victorian Age*, 313.

the agnostic is right when he asserts that knowledge of God is unattainable. But there is another way of looking at the matter which deserves serious attention. While differing as to what proofs are valid and valuable, all theists are agreed as to the thing to be proved: that God is, and to a certain extent what God is. This harmony in belief ought to weigh more in our judgment than the variation in evidence. It suggests the thought that the belief in God is antecedent to evidence, and that in our theistic reasonings we formulate proof of a foregone conclusion innate and inevitable. How otherwise can it be explained that men who have demolished what have passed for the strongest arguments for the theistic creed are not content to be done with it, but hold on to the conviction that God is, on grounds which to all others but themselves appear weak and whimsical? Thus a recent writer, after searching in vain the whole universe of matter and of mind for traces of Deity, finds rest at last for his weary spirit in this train of thought: There is such a thing as error, but error is inconceivable unless there be such a thing as truth, and truth is inconceivable unless there be a seat of truth, an infinite all-including Thought or Mind, therefore such a Mind exists. That Mind is God, the "infinite Seer," whose nature it is to think, not to act. "No power it is to be resisted, no plan-maker to be foiled by fallen angels, nothing finite, nothing striving, seeking, losing, altering, growing weary; the All-Enfolder it is, and we know its name. Not Heart, nor Love, though these also are in it and of it; Thought it is, and all things are for Thought, and in it we live and move." How weak the proof here, but how strong the conviction! So it is, more or less, with us all. In our formal argumentation we feebly and blunderingly try to assign reasons for a belief that is rooted in our being. In perusing works by others devoted to the advocacy of theism, we are conscious of disappointment, and possibly even of doubt suggested rather than of faith established, only to recover serene and strong conviction when the book is forgotten. It would seem as if the way of wisdom were to abstain from all attempts at proving the divine existence, and, assuming as a *datum* that God is, to restrict our inquiries to *what* He is.[50]

To those uninitiated in the thought of Bruce, it would likely seem that he was at once supporting and denouncing the apologetic method. Once one understands the limited intention and role he ascribed to apologetics, the argument becomes clear:

---

50   Alexander Balmain Bruce, *Apologetics; or, Christianity Definitely Stated* (New York: Charles Scribner's Sons, 1892), 157-158.

> Apologetic [sic], then, as I conceive it, is a preparer of the way of faith, an aid to faith against doubts whencesoever arising, especially such as are engendered by philosophy and science. Its specific aim is to help men of ingenuous spirit who, while assailed by such doubts, are morally in sympathy with believers. It addresses itself to such as are drawn in two directions, towards and away from Christ, as distinct from such as are confirmed either in unbelief or in faith. Defence presupposes a foe, but the foe is not the dogmatic infidel who has finally made up his mind that Christianity is a delusion, but anti-Christian thought in the believing man's own heart.[51]

Thus, in Bruce's mind, the apologetic arguments can be helpful, and indeed, he made strides to produce his own, but these were not geared to convert the staunch nonbeliever. Apologetics appeals to those who have a "moral sympathy" with Christians, or those men and women who have doubts that arise in their minds. Thus, for Bruce, apologetics was not as much pre-evangelism, even though there is an element of that, but it normatively took a form of defensive discipleship.

For Christian thought and apologetics in the nineteenth century, the conflict between the traditional, rationalistic approach, and the romantic, experiential approach came to a pinnacle. The prior age "was to suppose that the understanding is competent to treat of what belongs to the sphere of reason…[they] had reduced spiritual religion to mere rationalism."[52] Thus, while some stayed firmly planted in this mindset and it is a mistake to over-simplify to the contrary, others found their evidences not in external arguments and scientific facts, but rather an "inner witness of moral feeling and perception."[53] To determine whether this had beneficial or detrimental consequences is not the intention of this section of study, but rather, to demonstrate and survey the current apologetic milieu in which George MacDonald lived, reasoned, and wrote.

Was George MacDonald an Apologist?

MacDonald scholars will likely cringe at the prospect of even designating MacDonald an apologist simply due to the negative

---

51 Alexander Balmain Bruce, *Apologetics; or, Christianity Definitely Stated*, 37.
52 Bernard M.G. Reardon, *Religious Thought in the Victorian Age*, 49.
53 Bernard M.G. Reardon, *Religious Thought in the Victorian Age*, 233.

connotations of the word as well as the 'baggage of rationality' which the word brings along with it. Avery Dulles contends: "In the minds of many Christians today the term 'apologetics' carries unpleasant connotations. The apologist is regarded as an aggressive, opportunistic person who tries, by fair means or foul, to argue people into joining the Church. Numerous charges are laid at the door of apologetics: its neglect of the grace of prayer, and of the life-giving power of the word of God; its tendency to oversimplify and syllogize the approach to faith; its dilution of the scandal of the Christian message; and its implied presupposition that God's word should be judged by the norm of fallible, not to say fallen, human reason."[54]

Before we can continue, we should consider another definition of apologetics: "It is an intellectual discipline that is usually said to serve at least two purposes: (1) to bolster the faith of Christian believers, and (2) to aid in the task of evangelism. Apologists seek to accomplish these goals in two distinct ways. One is by refuting objections to the Christian faith, such as the problem of evil or the charge that key Christian doctrines...are incoherent. This apologetic task can be called negative or defensive apologetics. The second, perhaps complementary, way apologists fulfill their purposes is by offering positive reasons for the Christian faith. The latter, called positive or offensive apologetics, often takes the form of arguments for God's existence or for the resurrection and deity of Christ but are no means limited to these."[55] Many of the particulars within this definition are exemplified in the works of George MacDonald.

Would MacDonald desire to be considered an apologist? It is possible that he would not, but while MacDonald likely did not deliberately set out to make sets of reasonable arguments in his works, he often did. This may seem paradoxical, for, as mentioned earlier in chapter four, he had a disdain for mere intellectual arguments. His contempt was not due to the fact that they employed reason, but rather that the underpinning assumption of those nineteenth century arguments was that the intellect was epistemologically antecedent and superior to the moral will. In MacDonald's position, as argued in section three of chapter four, the moral will, from which subsequent duty flows, is the well-spring of epistemology; everything else, including rationality, follows. To put this succinctly, MacDonald

---

54   Avery Dulles, *A History of Apologetics* (Eugene: Wipf and Stock, 1999), xv.

55   Stephen Cowan, *Five Views on Apologetics*, 8.

states, "All form of persuasion is empty except in vital association with regnant obedience. Talking and not doing is dry rot."[56] Thus, it would be remiss to call MacDonald an apologist in the common usage of the term. As MacDonald modified the terms "pantheism" and "mystic" to suit his intentions, we could do well to modify the common usage of "apologist" to describe the intention and tactics of MacDonald's writings. Thus we will adopt the term "imaginative apologetics" to identify MacDonald's intention and approach, which will be discussed in the next section, in contrast to the twentieth-century apologist, who is usually painted as a strong rationalist and/or evidentialist. While we have adapted the style of apologetics in which MacDonald used, there is no doubt that he, in fact, employed many of the tactics mentioned in the definition of apologetics. MacDonald's unique intentions will be found in the next section, and some of his arguments for God's existence will shortly follow.

As discussed in the second section of chapter four, MacDonald did not dispense with rationality; he merely argued that the role of rationality in the mind of a human was not to initiate faith. His argument against rationality was akin to his argument against scientism. He was not anti-science, but merely wanted to knock science off its epistemic pedestal. There is no doubt, relying on the evidence presented earlier, that he approached rationality the same way. While rationality did not produce faith, it could prompt someone to search for God, and that could lead the way for an inspired searcher to look further. Rationality could never twist arms, but it could direct the mind, and by steps of varying degrees, eventually help change the heart. Again, to repeat, and stress indefinitely, in MacDonald's position, this change could not happen without resolute obedience to the will of the Father: "Obedience alone can convince. To convince without obedience I would take no bootless labour; it would be but a gain for hell. If any man call these things foolishness, his judgement is to me insignificant. If any man say he is open to conviction, I answer him he can have none but on the condition, by the means of obedience."[57]

While this last paragraph presents MacDonald's view with confidence and inflexibility, it must be admitted that our Victorian

---

56 George MacDonald, *Home Again* and *The Elect Lady* (Whitehorn: Johannesen, 2003), 63.

57 George MacDonald, *A Dish of Orts*, "A Sketch of Individual Development," 74.

author was enigmatic on the issue. In his *Paul Faber, Surgeon*, he writes: "Argument, save that of a man with himself, when council is held between heart, will, imagination, conscience, vision, and intellect, is of little avail or worth."[58] Again in another section of the work the narrator states, "Argument should be kept to books; preachers ought to have nothing to do with it — at all events in the pulpit. There let them hold forth light, and let him who will, receive it, and him who will not, forbear. God alone can convince, and till the full time is come for the birth of the truth in a soul, the words of even the Lord Himself are not there potent."[59] Yet then, in the same book, the curate and protagonist Thomas Wingfold mentions this in a discussion with the non-believing Paul Faber: "I fancy you will yourself admit there is some blind driving law behind the phenomenon. But now I will beg the whole question, if you like to say so, for the sake of a bit of purely metaphysical argument: the law of life behind, if it be spontaneously existent, cannot be a blind, deaf, unconscious law; if it be unconscious of itself, it cannot be spontaneous; whatever is of itself must be God, and the source of all non-spontaneous, that is, all other existence."[60] Here, one of MacDonald's most cherished and beloved characters presents a rational argument that posited that the spontaneous generation of life was nonsensical, that laws cannot unexpectedly generate anything, and that only a personal being can create at all. This appears to be an apologetic argument, admitted by the author to be metaphysical in nature. While this argument did not sway Faber, the discussion ended positively, in that both parties were able to explain and clearly distinguish their worldview perspectives. Thus, the author seemed to offer this discussion as a challenging experience for both parties; yet he painted Wingfold as the humble victor,[61] not because he won the debate, but because he had caused Faber to reconsider his own position.

Not only was MacDonald keen on presenting metaphysical argumentation developed by rationalists, but he even posited a few that may have been of his own creation. In *There and Back* we find this discussion concerning MacDonald's "argument from operation":

"...would you allow thought concerned in it? Would you allow that thought must have preceded and occasioned its

---

58 George MacDonald, *Paul Faber-Surgeon*, 97.
59 Ibid., 156.
60 Ibid., 123.
61 George MacDonald, *Paul Faber-Surgeon*, 123-124.

existence? Would you allow that thought therefore must yet be interested in its power to produce thought, and might, if it chose, minister to the continuance or enlargement of the power it had originated?"

"Perhaps I should be compelled to allow that much in regard to a clock even! — Are we coming to the Paley-argument, sir?" said Richard.

"I think not," answered Wingfold. "My argument seems to me one of my own. It is not drawn from design but from operation: where a thing wakes thought and feeling, I say, must not thought and feeling be somewhere concerned in its origin?"

"Might not the thought and feeling come by association, as in the case of the clock suggesting the flight of time?"

"I think our associations can hardly be so multiform, or so delicate, as to have a share in bringing to us half of the thoughts and feelings that nature wakes in us. If they have such a share, they must have reference either to a fore-existence, or to relations hidden in our being, over which we have no control; and equally in such case are the thoughts and feelings waked in us, not by us. I do not want to argue; I am only suggesting that, if the world moves thought and feeling in those that regard it, thought and feeling are somehow concerned in the world. Even to wake old feelings, there must be a likeness to them in what wakes them, else how could it wake them? In a word, feeling must have put itself into the shape that awakes feeling."[62]

MacDonald causes the reader to ask this question: from whence do my thoughts originate? If something has awakened humanity's ability to feel, or even if there awoke therein a specific thought, should not its originator also have this ability to think and feel? This is, in fact, an argument for God's existence, for Wingfold's counterpart suggests that he is leading him to Paley's design argument. The protagonist denies this, but instead, suggests that his argument is his own. This argument is the basis of this section of *Unspoken Sermon*: "Nay, is it not his thinking in which I think? is it not by his consciousness that I am conscious?"[63]

Again, these lines may run paradoxical to what MacDonald

---

62 George MacDonald, *There and Back*, 238-239.

63 George MacDonald, *Unspoken Sermons*, "The Word of Jesus on Prayer," 109.

implied elsewhere, but he firmly believed that "the laws of nature reveal the character of God, not merely as regards to their ends, but as regards their kind, being of necessity fashioned after ideal facts of his own being and will."[64] Thus, the character of God is revealed in nature, as Paul definitively states in Romans 1:20, "For since the creation of the world, God's invisible qualities, his eternal power and divine nature can be clearly seen, being understood from what has been made, so that men are without excuse." While it could be argued that there was a change in MacDonald's mood toward rational thinking with his publication of *Thomas Wingfold* in 1876, it is not the intention of this study to track this change in attitude, or even if said change occurred, but to simply make the case that MacDonald was more of an apologist than modern scholars give him credit. The above case is not the only instance in which MacDonald presented an argument for God in his oeuvre; in fact, his work is riddled with rational argumentation, but, as will be discussed in the next section, MacDonald reasoned in his own unique fashion.

While not an original argument on his part by any means, MacDonald often used a reflection of the aesthetic experience to draw the reader toward the beautiful, then redirects them to the existence of the grand and ultimate artist. MacDonald discusses this in detail in narrative fashion in his *Wilfred Cumbermede:*

> "Suppose I asked you wherein its beauty consisted: would you be satisfied if I said — In the arrangement of the blue and the white, with the sparkles of yellow, and the colours about the scarce visible moon?"
>
> "Certainly not. I should reply that it lay in the gracious peace of the whole — troubled only with the sense of some lovely secret behind, of which itself was but the half-modelled representation, and therefore the reluctant outcome."
>
> "Suppose I rejected the latter half of what you say, admitting the former, but judging it only the fortuitous result of the half-necessary, half-fortuitous concurrences of nature. Suppose I said: — The air which is necessary to our life, happens to be blue; the stars can't help shining through it and making it look deep; and the clouds are just there because they must be somewhere till they fall again; all which is more agreeable to us than fog because we feel more comfortable in weather of the sort, whence, through complacency and habit, we have got to call it beautiful: — suppose I said this, would you accept

---

64   George MacDonald, *The Seaboard Parish*, 621.

Waking the Dead

it?"

"Such a theory would destroy my delight in nature altogether."

"Well, isn't it the truth?"

"It would be easy to show that the sense of beauty does not spring from any amount of comfort; but I do not care to pursue the argument from that starting-point. — I confess when you have once waked the questioning spirit, and I look up at the clouds and the stars with what I may call sharpened eyes — eyes, that is, which assert their seeing, and so render themselves incapable for the time of submitting to impressions, I am as blind as any Sadducee could desire. I see blue, and white, and gold, and, in short, a tent-roof somewhat ornate. I dare say if I were in a miserable mood, having been deceived and disappointed like Hamlet, I should with him see there nothing but a foul and pestilent congregation of vapours. But I know that when I am passive to its powers, I am aware of a presence altogether different — of a something at once soothing and elevating, powerful to move shame — even contrition and the desire of amendment."

"Yes, yes," said Charley hastily. "But let me suppose further — and, perhaps you will allow, better — that this blueness — I take a part for the whole — belongs essentially and of necessity to the atmosphere, itself so essential to our physical life; suppose also that this blue has essential relation to our spiritual nature — taking for the moment our spiritual nature for granted — suppose, in a word, all nature so related, not only to our physical but to our spiritual nature, that it and we form an organic whole full of action and reaction between the parts — would that satisfy you? Would it enable you to look on the sky this night with absolute pleasure? would you want nothing more?"

I thought for a little before I answered.

"No, Charley," I said at last – "it would not satisfy me. For it would indicate that beauty might be, after all, but the projection of my own mind — the name I gave to a harmony between that around me and that within me. There would then be nothing absolute in beauty. There would be no such thing in itself. It would exist only as a phase of me when I was in a certain mood; and when I was earthly-minded, passionate, or troubled, it would be *nowhere*. But in my best moods I feel that in nature lies the form and fashion of a peace and grandeur so much beyond anything in me, that they rouse the sense of poverty and incompleteness and blame in the want of them."

"Do you perceive whither you are leading yourself?"

"I would rather hear you say."

"To this then — that the peace and grandeur of which you speak must be a mere accident, therefore an unreality and pure *appearance*, or the outcome and representation of a peace and grandeur which, not to be found in us, yet exist, and make use of this frame of things to set forth and manifest themselves in order that we may recognize and desire them."

"Granted — heartily."

"In other words — you lead yourself inevitably to a God manifest in nature — not as a powerful being — that is a theme absolutely without interest to me — but as possessed in himself of the original pre-existent beauty, the counterpart of which in us we call art, and who has fashioned us so that we must fall down and worship the image of himself which he has set up."

"That's good, Charley. I'm so glad you've worked that out!"

"It doesn't in the least follow that I believe it. I cannot even say I wish I did: — for what I know, that might be to wish to be deceived. Of all miseries — to believe in a lovely thing and find it not true — that must be the worst."[65]

MacDonald delves into this subject matter in prose style in *A Dish of Orts* where he reasons, "Let us go further; and, looking at beauty, believe that God is the first of artists; that he has put beauty into nature, knowing how it will affect us, and intending that it should so affect us; that he has embodied his own grand thoughts thus that we might see them and be glad. Then, let us go further still, and believe that whatever we feel in the highest moments of truth shining through beauty, whatever comes to our souls as a power of life, is meant to be seen and felt by us, and to be regarded not as the work of his hand, but as the flowing forth of his heart, the flowing forth of his love of us, making us blessed in the union of his heart and ours."[66]

For MacDonald, the signaling of aesthetic experience, and the ability of human nature to indicate and enjoy beauty was a sign of God's existence and his creative handiwork. But MacDonald does not stop there. He also suggests that the ability to find new meaning in a work of art, and a meaning that was not intended by the artist, also signals a divine cause: "The fact that there is always more in a work of

---

65 George MacDonald, *Wilfrid Cumbermede*, 296-298.

66 George MacDonald, *A Dish of Orts*, "Wordsworth's Poetry," 246-7.

art — which is the highest human result of the embodying imagination — than the producer himself perceived while he produced it, seems to us a strong reason for attributing to it a larger origin than the man alone — for saying at the last, that the inspiration of the Almighty shaped its ends."[67] So from where does this new meaning emanate? MacDonald argues that it is divine intervention.

To finish this portion on MacDonald's use of art in apologetic arguments, MacDonald asks his readers: "Who invented music? Some one must have made the delight of it possible! With his own share in its joy he had had nothing to do! Was Chance its grand inventor, its great ingeniuer? Why or how should Chance love loveliness that was not, and make it be, that others might love it? Could it be a deaf God, or a being that did not care and would not listen, that invented music? No; music did not come of itself, neither could the source of it be devoid of music!"[68] Thus, music, just like the teleological argument in reference to the design of the world, could not come about randomly, but was created by God, who himself enjoyed music. Thus, MacDonald used rationality in his oeuvre, with art and beauty as the foundation for some of his apologetic cases.

Let not the focus on these unique arguments lead the reader to deduce that MacDonald did not allude to the traditional arguments for God's existence in his work. In *There and Back* MacDonald suggests the Cosmological Argument in reference to the thinking of the novel's atheist, Mr. Tuke:

> It had not occurred to him that there was a stage in his history antecedent to his consciousness — a stage in which his pleasure with regard to the next could not have been appealed to, or his consent asked — a stage, for any satisfaction concerning which, his resultant consciousness must repose on a creative will, answerable to itself for his existence. A man's patent of manhood is, that he can call upon God — not the God of any theology, right or wrong, but the God out of whose heart he came, and in whose heart he is. This is his highest power — that which constitutes his original likeness to God. Had any one tried to wake this idea in Tuke, he would have mocked at the sound of it, never seeing it. The words that represented it he would have thought he understood, but he would never have laid hold of the idea. He found himself what he found himself,

---

67   George MacDonald, *A Dish of Orts*, "The Imagination: Its Functions and its Culture," 25.

68   George MacDonald, *There and Back*, 450.

and was content with the find; therefore asked no questions as to whence he came — was to himself consequently as if he had come from nowhere — which made it easy for him to imagine that he was going nowhither. He had never reflected that he had not made himself, and that therefore there might be a power somewhere that had called him into being, and had a word to say to him on the matter. The region where he began to be, had never, in speculation or mirage any more than in direct vision, lifted itself above the horizon-line of his consciousness.[69]

MacDonald specifically points out that one cannot come from nowhere. All of humanity, all of creation, could not have spawned from impersonal nothingness. There must be consideration of the question of origins, and from whence we have come, and in so doing, consider and eventually reach the conclusion that there must be a divine source. In the same book a conversation revolves around the same subject matter:

> "I will, then! To love all the creatures and not have a word to say to the God that made them for loving them before-hand — is that reasonable?"
>
> "No, if a God did make them."
>
> "They could not make themselves!"
>
> "No; nothing could make itself."
>
> "Then somebody must have made them!"
>
> "Who?"
>
> "Why, the one that could and did — who else?"[70]

MacDonald understood this argument well and found God to be the necessary condition for the world to have any existence at all: "surely there ought to be somewhere a being to account for me, one to account for himself, and make the round of my existence just; one whose very being accounts and is necessary to account for mine; whose presence in my being is imperative, not merely to supplement it, but to make to myself my existence a good?"[71]

Lastly, it should also be demonstrated that MacDonald's emphasis on duty fostered opportunities to make rational arguments

---

69 George MacDonald, *There and Back*, 70-71.

70 Ibid., 220.

71 George MacDonald, *Unspoken Sermons*, "The Word of Jesus on Prayer," 109.

based on morality. He appeals here to the morality of society in comparison to the firm morality of the Divine: "The man will say, 'That is yielding everything. Let us eat and drink, for to-morrow we die. I am of the dust, for I believe in nothing beyond.' 'No,' I return. 'I recognize another law in myself which seems to me infinitely higher. And I think that law is in you also, although you are at strife with it, and will revive in you to your blessed discontent. By that I will walk, and not by yours – a law which bids me strive after what I am not but may become – a law in me striving against the law of sin and down-dragging decay – a law which is one with my will, and, if true, must of all things make one at last."[72] MacDonald then appeals to a higher authority by which we have this absolute sense of morality: "'However goodness may change its forms, I went on, 'it must still be goodness; only if we are to adore it, we must see something of what it is – of itself. And the goodness we cannot see, the eternal goodness, high above us as the heavens are above the earth, must still be a goodness that includes, absorbs, elevates, purifies all our goodness, not tramples upon it and calls it wickedness. For if not such, then we have nothing in common with God, and what we call goodness is not of God. He has not even ordered it; or, if he has, he has ordered it only to order the contrary afterwards; and there is, in reality, no real goodness – at least in him; and, if not in him, of whom we spring – where then? – and what becomes of ours, poor as it is?'"[73] Thus, MacDonald reasons, if there is no God, or if He is not one of pure goodness, from whence did this morality spawn and on what is it based? While Bonnie Gaarden states that MacDonald "asserts that innate human moral sense of what is 'good' is a far more reliable guide to the divine nature than the deductions of abstract theology,"[74] and this researcher would agree, it should also be added that MacDonald used his "imaginative apologetics," and the deductions therein, to suggest to the reader that morality can only be rooted in the divine nature.

While this section demonstrated MacDonald's intention to use rationalistic arguments on occasion, we must now backtrack to show what sort of intention he had for such argumentation. Also, the phrase "imaginative apologetics" was used in the above passages and will be elucidated below.

---

72 George MacDonald, *Miracles of Our Lord*, 129.

73 George MacDonald, *Wilfrid Cumbermede*, 355.

74 Bonnie Gaarden, *The Christian Goddess*, 8.

George MacDonald as Philosopher, Mystic, and Apologist

An Analysis of MacDonald's Intention and Overall Apologetic Goals

Since our definition of apologetics has been established, and our evidence that MacDonald fits into this category has been proposed, it should be pointed out that "Although apologists agree on the basic definition and goals of apologetics, they can differ significantly on the proper methodology of apologetics. That is, they disagree about how the apologist goes about his task – about the kinds of arguments that can and should be employed and about the way the apologist should engage the unbeliever in apologetic discourse."[75] Referring back to information found in the preceding chapters, it would be easy to demonstrate that MacDonald disagreed with many of his contemporaries' apologetic method. He offers his apologetic in a more unique fashion.

While there has been an abundance of research on the role of imagination in MacDonald's works, the best example being Kerry Dearborn's *Baptized Imagination*, many have not proposed to explain how MacDonald's use of imagination informs the readers' rational thinking, especially on their perception of and relation to God. While there will be some scholars who will react negatively to the placing of MacDonald in the category of "apologist," it can be argued that MacDonald presented an imaginative style of reasoning toward the Christian truths, often explained and defended in narrative form; but even when he wrote in prose, he writes with illumination and not with rote logical formulation.

One of the characteristics of modern apologetics, as well as nineteenth century rationalism, is a forceful arrogance that MacDonald despised. He wrote, "...the false and arrogant notion that it is duty to force the opinion upon the acceptance of others. But it is because such men themselves hold with so poor a grasp the truth underlying their forms that they are, in their self-sufficiency, so ambitious of propagating the forms, making of themselves the worst enemies of the truth of which they fancy themselves the champions... They lay hold but of the non-essential...they proceed to force upon the attention and reception of men, calling that the truth which is at best but the draggled and useless fringe of its earth-made garment."[76] MacDonald was not a proponent of direct and forceful persuasion. In a sermon to a Unitarian Congregation, who would obviously have

---

75 Stephen Cowan, *Five Views on Apologetics*, 8.
76 George MacDonald, *George MacDonald in the Pulpit*, "A Sermon," 41.

extensive disagreement with MacDonald's views, he stated, "I will speak plainly. I come before you neither hiding anything of my belief, nor foolishly imagining I can transfer my opinions into your bosoms. If there is one role I hate, it is that of the proselytizer. But shall I not come to you as a brother to brethren? Shall I not use the privilege of your invitation and of the place in which I stand, nay, must I not myself be obedient to the heavenly vision, in urging you with all the power of my persuasion to set yourselves afresh to walk according to that to which you have attained."[77] Again, here is the seeming paradox of MacDonald, for he states that while he cannot change their minds and will not attempt to do so, then admits that he would use his powers of persuasion. Later in the passage MacDonald states that he would not "endeavor by argument to convince another of this."[78] This sounds like an obvious contradiction, but note that the word "seeming" was intentionally placed before "paradox" in the introduction to the passage above. For if one understands MacDonald's excerpt and the intention behind the sermon, the apparent paradox lifts like a fog. First, note that the word "argument" could mean "formal argument" and as already stated and exemplified above, while MacDonald did use persuasion, he never used formal, propositional argumentation. He was strongly against the use of such tactics. Yet this should not then lead us to conclude that MacDonald did not use strategic tactics at all. But as we move the sermon to the Unitarians to the back burner, let us discover MacDonald's overall apologetic intention.

A succinct wording of MacDonald's intention and overarching goal comes from his *A Dish of Orts*: "The best thing you can do for your fellow, next to rousing his conscience, is—not to give him things to think about, but to wake things up that are in him; or say, to make him think things for himself."[79] On first reading, the reader may interpret "give him things to think about" and "make him think for himself" as similar or even the same sentiment, but MacDonald would fervently disagree. In the first phrase, the person knows one has presented thoughts and questions for them to consider. One has entered their thought process and thrown a wrench in their worldview, and in doing so one may have frustrated them for interfering; but in the second, they feel like they have generated the questions on their own, and are addressing these questions as if on their own quest for

---

77 Ibid., "A Sermon," 50.

78 Ibid., 51.

79 George MacDonald, *A Dish of Orts*, "The Fantastic Imagination," 319.

knowledge. Note then, the beauty and uniqueness of MacDonald's imaginative apologetic: it appeals to the readers' subconscious, and not directly to their conscious, rational mind.

This is no new discovery, for MacDonald scholars have been arguing for decades: "MacDonald's intention was by symbolic suggestion to penetrate eternal reality. Many readers seem to feel he has succeeded, at least to the extent of arousing within them longings after truth and goodness."[80] Often times writers will symbolically use "the heart" for this sort of argumentation: "MacDonald's insights are less directed to the mind than to his heart, and appeal as much to a reader's subconscious as to his conscious realm of thought."[81] While it seems strange to use the heart as the seat of one's subconscious, the point of this quotation is essentially the same: MacDonald is subverting the conscious reasoning faculty and is directing his urgings on a deeper level. Richard Reis agrees: "Fortunately, he hit upon the symbolic way to insinuate the concept into his reader's mind without, perhaps, the reader's ever being quite aware that he was being subtly instructed; and it is in this area that MacDonald's deliberate didacticism was most successful, both intellectually and artistically."[82] MacDonald states succinctly: "let men of science or philosophy say what they will, the rousing of a man's conscience is the greatest event in his existence."[83] Of course, in this case MacDonald is referring to the moral conscience, but this principle still applies. His purpose is not to take the tactic of "direct attack" on his readers or listeners; instead his method is more intuitive and subliminal. But in using those terms the reader of this research may then think that this means his methods were less intentional, but this was not the case.

To state again succinctly, MacDonald proposes the task of the preacher: "the office of preaching is, after all, to wake them up lest their sleep turn to death; next, to make them hungry, and lastly, to supply that hunger".[84] It would seem that modern preachers, and modern apologists as well, have jumped to the last of the three charges. They offer facts, whether spiritual or intellectual, yet have never ignited the spark or stoked the fire, but yet, they expect the

---

80 Rolland Hein, *The Harmony Within*, x.

81 James Patrick Van Eerden, *An Inquiry into the Use of Human Experience as an Apologetic Tool*, 37.

82 Richard H. Reis, *George MacDonald's Fiction*, 126.

83 George MacDonald, *Wilfrid Cumbermede*, 173.

84 George MacDonald, *Thomas Wingfold, Curate*, 73.

fire to burn therein. But this concept does not merely apply to the apologist, but to the seeker as well. Thus, in the following paragraphs, the themes of waking, making hungry, as well as directing toward and supplying food will be explicated by using MacDonald's novel, *Thomas Wingfold*.

Thomas Wingfold, who, while yet a curate, had not fully grasped the faith in which he espoused. Wingfold is initially awoken by Bascombe, an atheist, who confronted the curate and challenged his belief and his choice of profession: "I do not believe that *you* believe more than an atom here and there of what you profess."[85] The challenge and ensuing discussion shook Wingfold to the core: "Was there—could there be a living heart to the universe that did positively hear him—poor, misplaced, dishonest, ignorant Thomas Wingfold, who had presumed to undertake a work he neither could perform nor had the courage to forsake, when out of the misery of the grimy little cellar of his consciousness he cried aloud for light and something to make a man of him? For now that Thomas had begun to doubt like an honest being, every ugly thing within him began to show itself to his awakened probity."[86] MacDonald has been often quoted as saying, "For doubt is the hammer that breaks the windows clouded with human fancies, and lets in the pure light,"[87] and this is an instance where this truth is modeled in one of his own novels. For MacDonald, the pain of doubt and struggle for understanding can shake the foundation of the individual, causing them to take the proper steps toward seeking the truth, and the Author of said truth.

To add to Wingfold's trauma, MacDonald added the shock of being discovered that the curate had been preaching sermons that were not his own. Not merely were Wingfold's spiritual and factual faculties shocked, but also his moral sensibilities. Joseph Polwarth writes to his curate: "I had not listened long to the sermon ere I began to fancy I foresaw what was coming, and in a few minutes more I seemed to recognise it as one of Jeremy Taylor's. When I came home, I found that the best portions of one of his sermons had, in the one you read, been wrought up with other material."[88] Wingfold was stunned. He had been using his uncle's written sermons, and did not realize that his uncle had apparently slipped in information that was not his

---

85 Ibid., 24.

86 Ibid., 54.

87 Greville MacDonald, *George MacDonald and His Wife*, 374.

88 George MacDonald, *Thomas Wingfold, Curate*, 63.

own, and intentionally or not, had not cited these passages. Wingfold had been found out, and was encouraged to visit Polwarth. Wingfold obliged, and it was not long into their meeting that Wingfold was captivated by the man, and found him a source of empathy as well as wisdom. Wingfold considers that this man may lead him to the food he desires. The reader may find it ironic that Polwarth himself uses MacDonald's analogy in his response to Wingfold's situation: "I will come to the point practically: a man, I say, who does not feel in his soul that he has something to tell his people should straightway turn his energy to the providing of such food for them as he finds feed himself. In other words, if he has nothing new in his own treasure, let him bring something old out of another man's. If his own soul is unfed, he can hardly be expected to find food for other people, and has no business in any pulpit, but ought to betake himself to some other employment—whatever he may have been predestined to—I mean, made fit for."[89] Polwarth directs Wingfold toward proper food, as he suggests what food he should be offering his congregation.

Before allowing his imagination and subconscious to become cognizant, Wingfold begins to scratch and scavenge for food before he realizes what the food is for, or which food is healthy. For example, take again the example of Thomas Wingfold who asked his friend:

> "What shall I do? After the avowal you have made, I may well ask you again, How am I to know that there is a God?"
>
> "It were a more pertinent question, sir," returned Polwarth, — "If there be a God, how am I to find him?"[90]

Though a layperson, Polwarth redirects the protagonist to the proper question, and to seek the proper "food." Wingfold is already hungry. Polwarth need not continue to wake Wingfold, for the atheist Bascombe had already instigated that process and Polwarth has merely fanned the flames. But since, pertaining to Wingfold's question, base intellect and knowledge of God is of little value to MacDonald, Polwarth directs the curate to have the proper mindset. To be seeking the path to God is the route toward the spiritual feast. But he had yet to learn what sort of "food" was not merely good, but also worthy of pursuing.

This is not to limit MacDonald's audience only to the spiritually minded and those who are theistic, for he knew that his books could even impact the atheist. MacDonald had received a "curious letter

---

89   Ibid., 73.
90   Ibid., 79.

from an Italian in Calcutta who had been brought, he says, from being an atheist to believe— by my books."[91] But he did not believe that these sorts of spiritual strides were made without development: from awakening, being made hungry, identifying proper food, and often from someone supplying said food.

Most of MacDonald's arguments, including those that likely converted the atheist, were subconscious and subliminal in nature. How so? In MacDonald's narrative work, where most of MacDonald's apologetic is found, the reader is plunged into a narrative. So, for the reader, they experience life, while fictional, through another person's perspective, causing the reader to lower their defenses and imagine how they would react in these spiritually rich situations. MacDonald attempted to reach the reader where they were. How did he do this? By stimulating the sense that exists in every human, the imagination. MacDonald believed that the imagination was the guide by which science and nature, as well as God Himself, could be understood. He writes of Bascombe, the atheist antagonist in *Thomas Wingfold*: "He did not know, apparently, that Imagination had been the guide to all the physical discoveries which he worshipped, therefore could not reason that perhaps she might be able to carry a glimmering light even into the forest of the supersensible."[92] MacDonald contends that "It is God who gives thee thy mirror of imagination, I will come to the point practically: a man, I say, who does not feel in his soul that he has something to tell his people and if thou keep it clean, it will give thee back no shadow but the truth."[93] He believed that the imagination "is the best guide that man or woman can have; for it is not the things we see the most clearly that influence us the most powerfully; undefined, yet vivid visions of something beyond, something which eye has not seen nor ear heard, have far more influence than any logical sequences whereby the same things may be demonstrated to the intellect. It is the nature of the thing, not the clearness of its outline, that determines its operation. We live by faith, and not by sight."[94]

His son agreed with this assessment. Greville realized that some of his father's readers were not rationalists, so many of MacDonald's more imaginative stories appealed to their sensibilities: "many who,

---

91   Greville MacDonald, *George MacDonald and His Wife*, 478.

92   George MacDonald, *Thomas Wingfold, Curate*, 32.

93   George MacDonald, *Paul Faber-Surgeon*, 29.

94   George MacDonald, *A Dish of Orts*, "The Imagination: Its Function and its Culture," 25.

though tossed in stormy doubts, refuse a Socratic anchorage eagerly grappled by other lovers of my father; those, whose spiritual instinct is more alert than their reasoning faculty, will soon and certainly get sight of some beacon of peace that outshines all their fears. His appeals to the imagination are *verbal inspiration* indeed, and in this gift he towers above any writer I know of. In some prophetic epigram or 'celestial wit,' he will reveal the truth suddenly, convincingly, like the drawing of a nebulous veil from the sky-piercing Jungfrau, his appeal a trumpet-call— 'Awake thou that sleepest and rise from the dead!'"[95]

Most scholars often highlight the imagination in MacDonald's system and the rational is usually downgraded. But many fail to note that the rationality can be, and in Wingfold's situation was, the spark that ignited his spiritual voyage. The moral consciousness stoked the flames; the imagination led him onward and fueled the fire. To neglect any of these would be missing part of the necessary conditions that led to Wingfold's, and possibly the reader of MacDonald's, salvation. While it does not pertain directly to the intention of this section, it would be remiss not to mention the culmination of this analogy: "The imagination is an endless help toward faith, but it is no more faith than a dream of food will make us strong for the next day's work.... Faith, in its simplest, truest, mightiest form is— to do his will."[96] Thus, after rationality, the moral conscious, and the imagination do their work, the appropriate result should be a fulfillment of man's duty.

While the rational element of a person's disposition could be appealed to, MacDonald did not believe that it was always necessary; but to dispense with this option would be to ignore a core part of man, and to potentially miss an opportunity to set the alarm clock of that soul's slumber. But to end this chapter addressing the earlier situation, and to segue into the next chapter, we should return to the sermon mentioned above to the Unitarians. Why did MacDonald not use rationality and apologetics to move the Unitarians? Why not simply make the same arguments that Wingfold made in his reasoning toward God?

Rules of Engagement and the Tactful Spirit of the Apologist

To keep from appearing elusive, and to directly answer this

---

95   Greville MacDonald, *George MacDonald and His Wife*, 375-376.
96   Ibid., 495.

question, MacDonald did not have the relationship with the Unitarians in the congregation in order to properly challenge his hearers. As we shall see, a step-by-step process should be followed in order to further a friend on their spiritual path. If one attempts to skip ahead of said steps, the interaction, and possibly the relationship, could unravel. If MacDonald were to stand in front of a Unitarian congregation and state, "You all have it all wrong. Jesus is the only way to the Heavenly Father," he would have immediately lost his hearers, and would likely have no further chance to encourage them along their spiritual path. Thus this section will suggest MacDonald's apologetic and evangelistic tactics.

Preparation of Self and the Development of Relationship

The primary, and possibly the most disregarded modern element of a proper apologetic and evangelistic dialogue is the preparation of the self, and an investment in the relationship of the hearer. It starts with a development of the interior life, the initiation of true manhood. MacDonald implores his readers: "The best thing we can do, infinitely the best, indeed the only thing, that men may receive the truth – is to be ourselves true."[97]

In one of Wingfold's interactions with his atheist antagonist, he realized that it was not his business to "prove to any other man that there is a God, but to find him for myself. If I should find him, then will be time enough to think of showing him."[98] Without Wingfold being a true man, he could not hope to even have an impact on the fierce atheism of Bascombe. Being a true man is the first step. As a brief aside, it should be noted that God can use non-believers to further a future believer's journey, as George Bascombe was the one who roused Wingfold's conscience initially. But to actively and intentionally attempt to help a friend move along in their spiritual journey, the individual themselves need to be a true man or woman.

Secondly, the relationship between the two individuals needs to be positive. The hearer needs to know that you genuinely care about them: "There is no way of helping them but by being good to them, and making them trust me."[99] And of course, MacDonald is famous for stating that "to be trusted is a greater compliment than being

---

97   George MacDonald, *George MacDonald in the Pulpit*, "A Sermon," 57.
98   George MacDonald, *Thomas Wingfold, Curate*, 219.
99   George MacDonald, *Paul Faber-Surgeon*, 259.

loved."[100] Moreover, MacDonald argued that by loving your neighbor, you may possibly be making the strongest argument for the love of Christ possible: "But love is the first comforter, and where love and truth speak, the love will be felt where the truth is never perceived. Love indeed is the highest in all truth; and the pressure of a hand, a kiss, the caress of a child, will do more to save sometimes than the wisest argument, even rightly understood."[101] Thus a foundation of a trusting and loving relationship must precede any pointed interaction.

With that being noted, the apologist has to be living the life that Christ expects of his followers. He must obey the moral and volitional commands of God: "A man who has not the mind of Christ — and no man has the mind of Christ except him who makes it his business to obey him — cannot have correct opinions concerning him; neither, if he could, would they be of any value to him he would be nothing better, he would be worse for having them. Our business is not to think correctly, but to live truly; then first will there be a possibility of our thinking correctly."[102] As was mentioned earlier, no epistemological gains are made, and MacDonald would add spiritual gains, until those on the journey take some steps. Our focus in this section is the preparation of the apologist; thus, the apologist must not be standing with arms folded on this journey, but must be also making his or her steps along God's path. If they are not living truly, we should not expect the listener to listen.

Before continuing, the point must be made that MacDonald believed that any Christian who has themselves gone through the trial of skepticism has the unique ability to empathize and direct an individual struggling with that philosophical trap: "An ordinary mind that has had doubts, and has encountered and overcome them, or verified and found them the porters of the gates of truth, may be profoundly useful to any mind similarly assailed; but no knowledge of books, no amount of logic, no degree of acquaintance with the wisest conclusions of others, can enable a man who has not encountered skepticism in his own mind, to afford any essential help to those caught in the net. For one thing, such a man will be incapable of conceiving the possibility that the net may be the net of The Fisher of Men."[103] MacDonald seemed to know from firsthand experience that the trial

---

100 George MacDonald, *The Marquis of Lossie*, 15.

101 George MacDonald, *Paul Faber-Surgeon*, 259.

102 George MacDonald, *Unspoken Sermons*, "Justice," 236-237.

103 George MacDonald, *Paul Faber-Surgeon*, 131.

of skepticism can be the rouser of one's consciousness, and even the open door to the pathway of life. Only through walking through that door can one help another who is struggling with skepticism.

Empathize and Understand

Once the trusting relationship has been established, and the friend is willing to share some deeper thoughts and feelings of their spiritual journey, or possibly, the questions that are keeping them from starting that voyage, one must take the role of compassionate listener. In current apologetic culture, emphasis is placed on purporting the truth and arguing in air-tight logical syllogisms, but little weight is allocated to understanding the life, background, and beliefs of those whom one is attempting to help. MacDonald lovingly chastises Charley out of the mouth of Wilfrid Cumbermede: "You always seem to shut your eyes to the mental condition of those that differ from you. Instead of trying to understand them first, which gives the sole possible chance of your ever making them understand what you mean, you care only to present your opinions; and that you do in such a fashion that they must appear to them false."[104] This could as easily have been aimed at nineteenth century apologists who had little regard for where their hearer rested in their spiritual journey, and instead, merely browbeat them with the truth. It is a part of our fallen human nature to posit our answers without considering the one receiving the truth, "We do not try enough to know our fellow – men. We are ready enough to judge them; but we do not try enough to understand them – to know what they are, to see what it is at the root that makes them do this or that, that seems to us so strange or unfitting."[105]

Thus, empathy, in its most honorable form, must be present for an apologetic discourse to have even the hope of reaching fruition. In order to do this, one must be aware of their own depravity before empathy can even take root: "He had begun to hope he saw a glimmer somewhere afar at the end of the darksome cave in which he had all at once discovered that he was buried alive, he began also to feel how wretched those must be who were groping on without even a hope in their dark eyes."[106] As a first step, we must connect with our friend to allow us to understand them, and to help turn the truth

---

104 George MacDonald, *Wilfrid Cumbermede*, 357.

105 George MacDonald, *George MacDonald in the Pulpit*, "Growth in Grace and Knowledge," 156.

106 George MacDonald, *Thomas Wingfold, Curate*, 227.

that they already believe into further truth: "Set any one to talk about himself, instead of about other people, and you will have a seam of the precious mental metal opened up to you at once: only ore, most likely, that needs much smelting and refining; or, it may be, not gold at all, but a metal which your mental alchemy may turn into gold. The one thing I learned was, that they and I were one, that our hearts were the same."[107]

This concept appears not merely in MacDonald's works of fiction, but according to his son Greville, in the life of his father as well:

> "He feared no man, yet waited upon what was discoverable in everyone. This made him no less a keen and patient listener than a masterly, even prophetic, talker when any big subject was to the fore. He did not love debate, feeling always afraid lest the apparent need to justify one's own opinion should outbid zeal for truth. Yet his keen sense of logic made him shine in controversy, even if sometimes, in the strength of his convictions, his utterance was rather the inspired advocate's than the dispassionate judge's. He was Luther, not Erasmus."[108]

This is exemplified in an excerpt in *The Vicar's Daughter*, which reads almost as a letter from George to his wife: "I don't exactly know how he has been brought up; and it is quite possible he may have had such evil instruction in Christianity that he attributes to it doctrines which, if I supposed they actually belonged to it, would make me reject it at once as ungodlike and bad. I have found this the case sometimes. I remember once being astonished to hear a certain noble-minded lady utter some indignant words against what I considered a very weighty doctrine of Christianity; but, listening, I soon found that what she supposed the doctrine to contain was something considered vastly unchristian... But we must give him time, wife; as God has borne with us, we must believe that he bears with others, and so learn to wait in hopeful patience until they, too, see as we see."[109]

Discontent and God's Preparation of the Heart

It is clear to MacDonald that a feeling of discontent must overwhelm the person before any change can be made. If the individual is content in their current place, there is little that can be done by

---

107 George MacDonald, *Adela Cathcart* (Whitehorn: Johannesen, 2000), 175.

108 Greville MacDonald, *George MacDonald and His Wife*, 365.

109 George MacDonald, *The Vicar's Daughter*, 11.

way of spiritual development. MacDonald argued: "Words cannot convey the thought of a thinker to a no-thinker; of a largely aspiring and self-discontented soul, to a creature satisfied with his poverty, and counting his meagre faculty the human standard."[110] So, if the person is satisfied, content, and comfortable in their current place, there will be no motivation to change. In an interaction concerning a theological difference between Ian and his mother in *What's Mine's Mine*, MacDonald writes, "I am not going to talk about it. So long as your theory satisfies you, mother, why should I show you mine? When it no longer satisfies you, when it troubles you as it has troubled me, and as I pray God it may trouble you, when you feel it stand between you and the best love you could give God, then I will share my very soul with you — tell you thoughts which seem to sublimate my very being in adoration."[111] Without Ian's mother, on her own accord or by being inspired by her Heavenly Father, becoming troubled by her view, no movement could be made in her theological misunderstanding.

Like the story of Thomas Wingfold, who is chastised and discomforted by the atheist Bascombe, one begins his journey to God by being ill-content. In *Paul Faber*, MacDonald explains, "The true man troubled by intellectual doubt, is so troubled unto further health and growth. Let him be alive and hopeful, above all obedient, and he will be able to wait for the deeper content which must follow with completer insight."[112] To demonstrate the opposite end of the spectrum, MacDonald says: "For the greatest fool and rascal in creation there is yet a worse condition, and that is not to know it, but think himself a respectable man…the man who is honestly ashamed has begun to be clean."[113] So what is to be done with the individual who is absolutely content and considers himself a "rational man?" MacDonald responds: "Ah! The man who is most sure that there is no God and that he can get on pretty well – he won't say first-rate – but pretty well without Him; I think the better way would be just to let him live on and on and on, until he got heartily sick of himself and hated himself, and would gladly yield anything to get out of himself."[114] This comes to the forefront in *Thomas Wingfold*, when

---

110 George MacDonald, *The Hope of the Gospel*, "The Hope of the Universe," 89.

111 George MacDonald, *What's Mine's Mine*, 110-111.

112 George MacDonald, *Paul Faber-Surgeon*, 264-265.

113 George MacDonald, *Thomas Wingfold, Curate*, 281-282.

114 George MacDonald, *George MacDonald in the Pulpit*, "Faith the Proof

Leopold commits a heinous murder and hits the proverbial "rock bottom." Wingfold speaks to Leopold's sister on the matter: "When a man is once overwhelmed in his own deeds, when they have turned into spectres to mock at him, when he loathes himself and turns with sickness from past, present, and future, I know but one choice left, and that is between the death your friend Mr. Bascombe preaches and the life preached by Jesus, the crucified Jew. Into the life I hope your brother will enter."[115] Leopold himself reacts to Wingfold and Polwarth's help: "When a man is going to the bottom as fast as he can and another comes diving after him, it isn't for me to say how he is to take hold of me. No, Helen; when I trust, I trust out and out."[116] While an extreme example, MacDonald represents the concept that only through discontent, and proper reaction to that discontent, can the journey to Christ even be initiated.

MacDonald appeals to this sense directly on occasion: "Do you never feel wretched and sick in your very soul? — disgusted with yourself, and longing to be lifted up out of yourself into a region of higher conditions altogether?"[117] MacDonald even challenges his reader a bit more bluntly in *Unspoken Sermons:*

> But, thou who lookest for the justification of the light, art thou verily prepared for thyself to encounter such exposure as the general unveiling of things must bring? Art thou willing for the truth whatever it be? I nowise mean to ask, Have you a conscience so void of offence, have you a heart so pure and clean, that you fear no fullest exposure of what is in you to the gaze of men and angels? — as to God, he knows it all now! What I mean to ask is, Do you so love the truth and the right, that you welcome, or at least submit willingly to the idea of an exposure of what in you is yet unknown to yourself — an exposure that may redound to the glory of the truth by making you ashamed and humble? It may be, for instance, that you were wrong in regard to those, for the righting of whose wrongs to you, the great judgment of God is now by you waited for with desire: will you welcome any discovery, even if it work for the excuse of others, that will make you more true, by revealing what in you was false? Are you willing to be made glad that you were wrong when you thought others were

---

of the Unseen," 77.

115 George MacDonald, *Thomas Wingfold, Curate,* 286.

116 Ibid., 288.

117 George MacDonald, *Paul Faber-Surgeon,* 256.

wrong? If you can with such submission face the revelation of things hid, then you are of the truth, and need not be afraid; for, whatever comes, it will and can only make you more true and humble and pure.[118]

MacDonald understood the human condition, and realized that self-assurance and vain conceit would be the death of any spiritual progression: "The man or woman who can thus say, *Thy will be done*, with the true heart of giving up, is nearer the secret of things than the geologist and theologian."[119] Thus, until the person is humbled and discontented, no advancement can be made.

PRAXIS: Remove Obstructions, Inspire, and Discovery for One's-self

In this section dealing with practical apologetics, we must begin by remembering that the last two sections must be considered before these practical steps are followed. Even once these have been considered, one must be careful to consider how much information one's friend can handle before progressing forward. MacDonald explains, "If I could get his feelings right in regard to other and more important things, a reform in that matter would soon follow; whereas to make a mountain of a molehill would be to put that very mountain between him and me. Nor would I ask him any questions, lest I should just happen to ask him the wrong one; for this parishioner of mine evidently wanted careful handling, if I would do him any good. And it will not do any man good to fling even the Bible in his face. Nay, a roll of bank-notes, which would be more evidently a good to most men, would carry insult with it if presented in that manner. You cannot expect people to accept before they have had a chance of seeing what the offered gift really is."[120] Note in this specific example, although fictional, the parson treads carefully, knowing that certain tactics may actually cause a rift in their relationship, and thus would obstruct rather than encourage more conversation. This concept is even more succinctly stated in his *David Elginbrod*: "Janet, my woman, gie a body the guid that they can tak,' an' they'll sune tak' the guid that they canna."[121] MacDonald encourages us to give them the good they can handle, and soon enough they will be able to take the good one

---

118 George MacDonald, *Unspoken Sermons*, "The Final Unmasking," 271.
119 George MacDonald, *The Seaboard Parish*, 32-33.
120 George MacDonald, *Annals of a Quiet Neighbourhood*, 50.
121 George MacDonald, *David Elginbrod*, 446.

wants them to understand, but are currently unable.

Where MacDonald's apologetic is unique is that instead of attempting to alter an individual's sloppy theology, he often simply looks to remove obstructions that block the person's relationship with God. If the theology is untenable, yet the person is satisfied, and they believe their relationship with the divine is solid, he finds that it is not effective to intervene: "If any man come to me with theological questions, if I find that they are troubling him, and keeping him from giving himself to God, I do my best to remove any such obstructions as are the result of man's handling of the eternal things: what I count false, I will not spare. But if the man come to me only for the sake of conference on the matter, I will hold none. Let him get what teaching he is capable of receiving from his knowledge of Christ, and the spirit given him. If he is satisfied with the theology he has learned, I should give myself no trouble to alter his opinion."[122] MacDonald's challenge was to obliterate "oppressive theology" from the minds of those who were seeking a relationship with Christ: "Neither will I now enter any theological lists to be the champion for or against mere doctrine. I have no desire to change the opinion of man or woman. Let everyone for me hold what he pleases. But I would do my utmost to disable such as think correct opinion essential to salvation from laying any other burden on the shoulders of true men and women than the yoke of their Master; and such burden, if already oppressing any, I would gladly lift."[123] Again MacDonald explains, "So long as a man will not set himself to obey the word spoken, the word written, the word printed, the word read, of the Lord Christ, I would not take the trouble to convince him concerning the most obnoxious doctrines that they were false as hell. It is those who would fain believe, but who by such doctrines are hindered, whom I would help. Disputation about things but hides the living Christ who alone can teach the truth, who is the truth, and the knowledge of whom is life; I write for the sake of those whom the false teaching that claims before all to be true has driven away from God—as well it might, for the God so taught is not a God worthy to be believed in."[124] For MacDonald, those who desire a relationship with the Father are the individuals where he directs his attention, and to those, he allows himself to prod and prick their faulty theology. While MacDonald empathizes with the atheist, he

---

122 Rolland Hein, *George MacDonald: Victorian Mythmaker*, 496.

123 George MacDonald, *Unspoken Sermons*, "Justice," 236-7.

124 George MacDonald, *Unspoken Sermons*, "The Truth in Jesus," 184.

realizes that something internal needed to take place before their interactions would be fruitful. Take for example the last theological discussion between Wingfold and Bascombe in *Thomas Wingfold:*

> "But if what you find is not true!" cried George, with a burst of semi-grand indignation.
>
> "But if what I find should be true, even though you should never be able to see it!" returned the curate.
>
> And as if disjected by an explosion between them, the two men were ten paces asunder, each hurrying his own way.
>
> "If I can't prove there is a God," said Wingfold to himself, "as little surely can he prove there is none."
>
> But then came the thought, "The fellow will say that, there being no sign of a God, the burden of proof lies with me."[125]

Therewith MacDonald saw how useless it would be to discuss the question with anyone who, not seeing him, had no desire to see him: "I have to do no more than with the deaf dead, who sleep too deep for words to reach them."[126] MacDonald asserted the fact that some are beyond help, without God's intervention and their experience of deep personal discontentment with resulting humility.

Yet if the above criteria have been met, and obstructions have begun to be toppled, what is next to be done? MacDonald starts with a bold fact: "No one can remember what is entirely uninteresting to him."[127] If the person is not interested in a walk with Christ, they will not be interested in learning more about him; thus, MacDonald does not first encourage one to teach, but to inspire. MacDonald gives a fictional narrative in *There and Back*: "There's an undertow bringing us on to each other. It would spoil all if he thought I threw a net for him. I do mean to catch him if I can, but I will not move till the tide brings him into my arms. At least, that is how the thing looks to me at present. I believe enough not to make haste. I don't want to throw salt on any bird's tail, but I do want the birds to come hopping about me, that I may tell them what I know!"[128] This instruction is most specifically encouraged by Thomas Wingfold to Barbara in *There and Back:*

---

125 George MacDonald, *Thomas Wingfold, Curate*, 218.

126 George MacDonald, *A Dish of Orts*, "A Sketch of Individual Development," 48.

127 George MacDonald, *David Elginbrod*, 152.

128 George MacDonald, *There and Back*, 241.

Talk to Richard of the God you love, the beautiful, the strong, the true, the patient, the forgiving, the loving; the one childlike, eternal power and Godhead, who would die himself and kill you rather than have you false and mean and selfish. Let him feel God through your enthusiasm for him. You can't prove to him that there is any God. A God that could be proved, would not be worth proving. Make his thoughts dwell on such a God as he must feel would be worth having. Wake the notion of a God such as will draw him to wish there were such a God. There are many religious people who will tell you there is no such God as I mean; but God will love you for believing that he is as good and true as you can think… Set in Richard's eye a God worth believing in, a God like the son of God, and he will go and look if haply such a God may be found; he will call upon him, and the God who is will hear and answer him.[129]

Thus, for MacDonald, there is no occasion to twist the arm of the listener's rationality. Yes, one's rational faculties can be utilized, especially in the removal of obstacles stage, but at this point in the process, MacDonald encourages the helper to refrain from overstepping one's bounds. In Thomas Wingfold's initial spiritual progression, MacDonald notes Polwarth's restraint: "Here Polwarth was tempted to give him a far more important, because more immediately practical hint, but refrained, from the dread of weakening by presentation, the force of a truth which, in discovery, would have its full effect."[130] MacDonald places a primacy on allowing the listeners to come to their own conclusions. He found that leading a horse to water was much less effective than giving a general direction. MacDonald explains in prose form: "It is a principle of mine never to push anything over the edge. When I am successful in any argument, my one dread is of humiliating my opponent. Indeed I cannot bear it. It humiliates me. And if you want him to think about anything, you must leave him room, and not give him such associations with the question that the very idea of it will be painful and irritating to him. Let him have a hand in the convincing of himself."[131]

Seek and Obey

Lastly, instead of forcing upon them any of his own opinions,

---

129 Ibid., 363-364.
130 George MacDonald, *Thomas Wingfold, Curate*, 145-146.
131 George MacDonald, *Annals of a Quiet Neighbourhood*, 47.

Waking the Dead

MacDonald encouraged his readers to seek and obey. He firmly believed that "an honest mind must, sooner or later, open its doors to every truth."[132] So, if that is the case, then MacDonald was willing to wait patiently for the person to make his own discoveries. Yet he encouraged them to press forward on the path of discovery with a heart of obedience. In fact, he believed that this search was a part of man's nature: "God will not compel the adoration of men: that would be but a pagan worship that will bring him to. he will rouse in men a sense of need, which shall grow at length into a longing; he will make them feel after him, until by their search becoming able to behold him, he may at length reveal to them the glory of their Father.... It would seem that the correlative of creation is search; that as God has *made* us, we must *find* Him."[133] In fact, MacDonald held that if one was not seeking God, he was surely not going to be compelled to find God: "But he is there for them that seek him, not for those who do not look for him. Till they do, all he can do is to make them feel the want of him."[134]

This encouragement to seek is most exquisitely described in narrative in *David Elginbrod* where Euphrasia has started her journey and is seeking her creator, but wants direction from David: "If there be a God; and if you can make me believe that there is a God, I shall not need to be persuaded that he will help me; for I will besiege him with prayers night and day to set me free. And even if I am out of my mind, who can help me but him? Ah! is it not when we are driven to despair, when there is no more help anywhere, that we look around for some power of good that can put right all that is wrong? Tell me, dear sir, what to do. Tell me that there certainly is a God; else I shall die raving."[135] As it happens, at the time that this letter was written, David had already passed away, but our narrator does not hesitate to help us understand what David's response would have been: "David's answer to this letter, would have been something worth having. But I think it would have been all summed up in one word: 'Try and see: call and listen.'"[136] MacDonald concludes: "Our searcher at least holds open the door for the hearing of what voice may come to him from the

---

132 George MacDonald, *There and Back*, 605.
133 George MacDonald, *Miracles of Our Lord*, 23.
134 George MacDonald, *There and Back*, 140.
135 George MacDonald, *David Elginbrod*, 313.
136 Ibid., 313.

region invisible: if there be truth there, he is where it will find him."[137]

Again, I would be remiss not to mention MacDonald's overwhelming focus on obedience in the mind and will of the searcher. Since this theme has been explored elsewhere in detail, this statement should suffice: "Obedience alone places a man in the position in which he can see so as to judge that which is above him.... Help cannot come to one made in the image of God, save in the obedient effort of what life and power are in him, for God is action. In such effort alone is it possible for need to encounter help. It is the upstretched that meets the downstretched hand. He alone who obeys can with confidence pray — to him alone does an answer seem a thing that may come. And should anything spoken by the Son of Man seem to the seeker unreasonable, he feels in the rest such a majesty of duty as compels him to judge with regard to the other, that he has not yet perceived its true nature, or its true relation to life."[138] Thus MacDonald reminds the seeker that the path to understanding is paved with the stones of obedience, and if this is not the case, then understanding the divine is unattainable.

Existential Angst: the Concept of *Sehnsucht* in George MacDonald and C.S. Lewis

As an excursion into the previous "Praxis" subsection, it is a beneficial aside to explore MacDonald and C.S. Lewis' subconscious inspiration that has been traditionally called *Sehnsucht*. While Lewis simply described this term as "longing,"[139] Jedidiah Evans gives more elucidation, explaining that *Sehnsucht* "...is not simply homesickness, nostalgia, or nihilism, but instead, an addiction to the very act of longing. According to the *Deutsches Wörterbuch*, the verb *Sehen* approximates the English 'to long,' or, more strongly, 'to crave,' and Jacob and Wilhelm Grimm use a number of quotations from Romantic poets to gesture toward the insatiable nature of the longing. The noun *Sucht*—which is combined with *Sehen* to produce *Sehnsucht*—implied 'physical illness' in its early usage, but most nearly translates as 'addiction.' *Sucht* entered the English lexicon briefly in the nineteenth century as part of a curious mental disease named *Grübelsucht*, which

---

137 George MacDonald, *A Dish of Orts*, "A Sketch of Individual Development," 70-1.

138 Ibid., "A Sketch of Individual Development," 72.

139 C.S. Lewis, *Surprised By Joy* (New York: Harcourt, Brace, and World, Inc., 1955), 6.

one psychiatrist described as 'metaphysical insanity.' *Sehnsucht*, the composite of these two concepts, is thus virtually untranslatable, but its suggestion of both an infinite and inarticulate yearning, as well as a compulsive addiction to the very experience of longing."[140]

Both C.S. Lewis and MacDonald are touted as employing this concept: "Throughout their fiction, both writers reveal a world haunted by heaven and both relate rapturous human longing after the source of earthly glimpses; both show that the highest function of art is to initiate these visions of heaven; and both describe a heaven that swallows up Earth in an all-embracing finality."[141] Manley continues: "MacDonald was committed to revealing glimpses of heaven to those who do not see heaven in their lives. His writings, and those of Lewis, are true art if they can make their readers taste something unearthly for a moment, something that suggests that 'all shall be well.'"[142] As stated in MacDonald's famous anagram-motto that is recorded on his bookplate, "Corage. God Mend Al.", MacDonald was often focused on the future reinstatement of God's creation. Yet this reinstatement is not merely paradise lost and regained, but for MacDonald, it needed to be more than that:

> "Because of our need and aspiration, the snowdrop gives birth in our hearts to a loftier spiritual and poetic feeling, than the rose most complete in form, colour, and odour. The rose is of Paradise — the snowdrop is of the striving, hoping, longing Earth. Perhaps our highest poetry is the expression of our aspirations in the sympathetic forms of visible nature. Nor is this merely a longing for a restored Paradise; for even in the ordinary history of men, no man or woman that has fallen, can be restored to the position formerly held. Such must rise to a yet higher place, whence they can behold their former standing far beneath their feet. They must be restored by the attainment of something better than they ever possessed before, or not at all."[143]

Thus, the longing of MacDonald's *Sehnsucht* is not merely a nostalgic hope for what once was, but while possibly resembling the past, it is wholly new; the final cause for which nature is created.

As an example of how C.S. Lewis used this concept, take this

---

140 Jedidiah Evans, "C.S. Lewis, Thomas Wolfe, and the Transatlantic Expression of *Sehnsucht*" in *Inklings Forever* 9, 2014.

141 David Manley, "Shadows that Fall," 43.

142 Ibid., 48.

143 George MacDonald, *The Portent and Other Stories*, 274-275.

section from *Surprised by Joy:* "Now step a little way—only two fields and across a lane and up to the top of the bank on the far side—and you will see, looking south with a little east in it, a different world. And having seen it, blame me if you can for being a romantic. For here is the thing itself, utterly irresistible, the way to the world's end, the land of longing, the breaking and blessing of hearts. You are looking across what may be called, in a certain sense, the plain of Down, and seeing beyond it the Mourne Mountains."[144] The reader has no choice but to be subconsciously drawn into the trap of wonder in which Lewis hopes they will fall. Questions could possibly follow: What is it about these Irish mountains that draw the author? What is he hoping to find? Each question that follows simply draws the reader further into Lewis' snare.

While both Lewis and MacDonald use *Sehnsucht* as a tool, some may argue that Lewis directly discusses and intellectualizes it more than MacDonald. Lewis even creates an argument based on the deep longing: "If I find in myself a desire which no experience in this world can satisfy, the most probable explanation is that I was made for another world…I must make it the main object of life to press on to that other country and to help others do the same."[145] He knew that this longing was a part of the human condition and did not mind pointing out this sensation to others while drawing a conclusion based on this hypothetical concept.

While there are exceptions, MacDonald seemed to take a more subliminal and indirect route in his use of *Sehnsucht*: "MacDonald had a Christianized view of *Sehnsucht*. That he would not have intellectualized it as Lewis does leaves unaltered the probability that his fantasies are intended to work on the reader in the way that Lewis describes. The only theoretic obstacle to the success of the method is the reader's own subjectivity (not everyone will respond to a given image of desire): and this MacDonald perhaps circumvents through his use of archetypal rather than the 'algebraic' symbolism…. The images in MacDonald's fantasies may thus work sacramentally, and the reader may have a form of religious experience through them…"[146] Thus MacDonald used these images to inspire a longing for something more, for an unseen home of which we only find glimpses of in this world.

---

144 C.S. Lewis, *Surprised By Joy*, 155.

145 C.S. Lewis, *Mere Christianity* (New York: Macmillan, 1960), 120.

146 Colin Manlove, *Modern Fantasy: Five Studies*, 97.

Waking the Dead

One of the most famous and oft-cited examples of *Sehnsucht* in MacDonald's work comes from the story of Tangle and Mossy in *The Golden Key*: "About the middle of the plain they sat down to rest in the heart of a heap of shadows. After sitting for a while, each, looking up, saw the other in tears: they were each longing after the country whence the shadows fell. 'We MUST find the country from which the shadows come,' said Mossy. 'We must, dear Mossy,' responded Tangle."[147] The story concludes with a potential fruition of their longing: "They knew that they were going up to the country whence the shadows fall. And by this time I think they must have got there."[148] "Homecoming fulfilled" is a common theme in MacDonald's oeuvre. In his *The Wow O' Rivven* MacDonald emotes: "a feeling as if the ghostly old bell hung at the church-door of the invisible world, and ever and anon rung out joyous notes (though they sounded sad in the ears of the living), calling to the children of the unseen to *come home, come home*."[149] Again, similarly to Lewis' statement above, the reader is left to question and wonder what could be meant by what could be in this land from which the shadows fall? What "home" is the gonging of the bell hastening the listeners onward?

MacDonald has his protagonist in *What's Mine's Mine* state directly: "The World never did seem my home; I have never felt quite comfortable in it."[150] If here is not home, what is this home where MacDonald feels pulled and he wishes to draw the reader? A direct discussion on the topic can be found in MacDonald's *Seaboard Parish*:

> Then I began to question myself wherein the idea of this home consisted. I knew that my soul had ever yet felt the discomfort of strangeness, more or less, in the midst of its greatest blessedness. I knew that as the thought of water to the thirsty *soul*, for it is the soul far more than the body that thirsts even for the material water, such is the thought of home to the wanderer in a strange country. As the weary soul pines for sleep, and every heart for the cure of its own bitterness, so my heart and soul had often pined for their home. Did I know, I asked myself, where or what that home was? It could consist in no change of place or of circumstance; no mere absence of care; no accumulation of repose; no blessed communion even with those whom my soul loved; in the midst of it all I should

---

147 George MacDonald, *The Light Princess and Other Fairy Tales*, 195-196.
148 Ibid., 215.
149 George MacDonald, *The Portent and Other Stories*, 250.
150 George MacDonald, *What's Mine's Mine*, 168.

be longing for a homelier home—one into which I might enter with a sense of infinitely more absolute peace than a conscious child could know in the arms, upon the bosom of his mother. In the closest contact of human soul with human soul, when all the atmosphere of thought was rosy with love, again and yet again on the far horizon would the dim, lurid flame of unrest shoot for a moment through the enchanted air, and Psyche would know that not yet had she reached her home. As I thought this I lifted my eyes, and saw those of my wife and Connie fixed on mine, as if they were reproaching me for saying in my soul that I could not be quite at home with them. Then I said in my heart, "Come home with me, beloved—there is but one home for us all. When we find—in proportion as each of us finds—that home, shall we be gardens of delight to each other—little chambers of rest—galleries of pictures—wells of water.

Again, what was this home? God himself. His thoughts, his will, his love, his judgment, are man's home. To think his thoughts, to choose his will, to love his loves, to judge his judgments, and thus to know that he is in us, with us, is to be at home. And to pass through the valley of the shadow of death is the way home, but only thus, that as all changes have hitherto led us nearer to this home, the knowledge of God, so this greatest of all outward changes—for it is but an outward change—will surely usher us into a region where there will be fresh possibilities of drawing nigh in heart, soul, and mind to the Father of us.[151]

While Lewis focuses on our heavenly home, as well as John the apostle who writes in John 14:2-3, "There are many dwelling places in my Father's house. Otherwise, I would have told you, because I am going away to make ready a place for you. And if I go and make ready a place for you, I will come again and take you to be with me, so that where I am you may be too." MacDonald does not suggest that mere heaven is the home for which we seek. 'Home' is not simply an eternal dwelling place, it is the face and will of God; he is our home: "She knew that the goal of all life is the face of God. Perhaps she had to learn yet higher lesson: that our one free home is the Heart, the eternal lovely Will of God…this Will is our Salvation."[152] Again in *Castle Warlock*: "When we have God, all is holy, and we are at

---

151 George MacDonald, *The Seaboard Parish*, 605-6.
152 George MacDonald, *Alec Forbes of Howglen*, 378.

home."[153] Thus for MacDonald, heaven is, in fact, our home, but not merely because it is our eternal dwelling place, but because it is where God's face can be fully beheld and his will unequivocally known. And while this is true, there can be a step in the progression to this final home, by seeking and doing God's will here on earth. In the same way that many scholars reflect on Jesus' teaching on the Kingdom of God as "already/not yet," the will and face of God can be known, but not so clearly as in our next life. Paul's metaphor in 1 Corinthians 13:12 resonates here: "For now we see in a mirror indirectly, but then we will see face to face. Now I know in part, but then I will know fully, just as I have been fully known."

Unfortunately, many in this world feel the painful longing for something more, but have not yet understood that this longing has an object: "It is the formless idea of something at hand that keeps men and women striving to tear from the bosom of the world the secret of their own hopes. How little they know what they look for in reality is their God! This is that for which their heart and their flesh cry out."[154] MacDonald felt it was his directive to make known the divine object of this longing: "Strange as it may sound to those who have never thought of such things save in connection with Sundays and Bibles and churches and sermons, that which was now working in Falconer's mind was the first dull and faint movement of the greatest need that the human heart possesses — the need of the God-Man."[155]

MacDonald and Lewis' calculated appeal to the human condition and natural, inner *Sehnsucht* was an apologetic tactic, geared to propel the reader into the next step in their spiritual progression. The infinite and inarticulate yearning of *Sehnsucht* is utilized by Lewis and MacDonald to inspire and awaken the reader, just as they themselves had been awakened in the past. Lewis in "Christianity and Culture," writes, "I am quite ready to describe *Sehnsucht* as 'spilled religion,' provided it is not forgotten that the spilled drops may be full of blessing to the unconverted man who licks them up, and therefore begins to search for the cup whence they were spilled."[156] Thus, MacDonald and Lewis were intentional about their purpose to

---

153 George MacDonald, *Castle Warlock*, translated by David Jack (North Charleston: Createspace, 2017), 11.

154 George MacDonald, *Alec Forbes of Howglen*, 433.

155 George MacDonald, *Robert Falconer*, 154.

156 C.S. Lewis, "Christianity and Culture" in *Theology* Vol 40: Issue 237, 1940, 177.

fuel the flame of this longing, and hope that their audience would seek the home from which the sense of homelessness springs. Succinctly, they hoped to take their audience from the position of "longing for home" to a realization that "God is our home," to a lifelong seeker of that home.

To conclude in a similar fashion as the previous sections, MacDonald held that for those who noticed their inner *Sehnsucht*, the force that propelled them along this path was, as in all of MacDonald's praxis, obedience: "The sole wisdom for man or boy who is haunted with the hovering of unseen wings, with the scent of unseen roses, and the subtle enticements of 'melodies unheard,' is work. If he follow any of those, they will vanish. But if he work, they will come unsought, and, while they come, he will believe that there is a fairy-land, where poets find their dreams, and prophets are laid hold of by their visions. The idle beat their heads against its walls, or mistake the entrance, and go down into the dark places of the earth."[157]

---

157 George MacDonald, *Alec Forbes of Howglen*, 148.

Waking the Dead

CONCLUSION

George MacDonald was an unprofessed philosopher, hesitant theologian, unique mystic, and an unconventional apologist. His enigmatic beliefs and eccentric style often leave casual readers and even scholars scratching their heads in bewilderment; regularly resulting in the asking of more questions than getting answers. Was George MacDonald a Universalist, a Platonist, and did he hold the Neo-Platonic belief in emanationism? Was George MacDonald a pantheist or a mystic? Did he wholesale dispense with rationality in the style of the Romantics? Was he an apologist, and if so, what was his apologetic method and purpose, especially in his works of fiction? Since the original question above remained intentionally unanswered due to the abundance of research on MacDonald's theology and universalism[1], the focus of this study was to clarify his positions as a philosopher, mystic, and apologist. Below is a summary of our findings.

MacDonald as Philosopher

While he never claimed to be two of the three designations above, it has been demonstrated that he did have philosophical moorings that grounded his theology, mysticism, and thus his entire oeuvre. His lack of discussion on specific philosophical systems was preventative; he did not want to cause more factions in the church and wanted to focus on the gospel, or for those who were already Christians, on doing the will of their Heavenly Father. While his discourses in these areas are limited, there is no doubt he had philosophical moorings since he applauded the philosophical positions of Shakespeare and Henry More, and he recognized that the truth of God himself must be philosophically sound.[2]

Since Plato is the most frequently-named philosopher mentioned by MacDonald, many scholars categorize him as a Platonist, or even more commonly, a Neo-Platonist. The information above reveals that this is not the case. There are stark differences between MacDonald's and Plato's philosophies, especially in the realm of metaphysics.

---

[1] For more information on this topic see Michael Phillips' *George MacDonald & Late Great Hell Debate* and David L. Neuhouser's lecture "George MacDonald on Universalism: The Extent of God's Love"

[2] George MacDonald, *Thomas Wingfold, Curate*, 424.

Plato was an uncompromising idealist; he believed that this world was a world of shadows; it was fundamentally illusory and that its reality was only found in the ideals that the physical world reflected. MacDonald was a metaphysical realist in that he believed that the physical world and the ideal world were both creations of God that were true reality. While these facts created a gulf between the metaphysic of MacDonald and Plato, there is no doubt that our subject operated under Plato's shadow. They both recognized physical objects as symbols of something other: "The heavens and the earth are around us that it may be possible for us to speak of the unseen by the seen; for the outermost husk of creation has correspondence with the deepest things of the Creator."[3] Yet as discussed in the second section of chapter three, MacDonald did not merely see these correspondences and physical signs as unreal shadows pointing toward ideals or forms, but rather, as two realities that are in extrinsically and metaphysically linked.

The second piece of evidence that caused many readers to consider MacDonald a Neo-Platonist was his insistence that God created the world *Ex Deo*, which, at first glance, seems to align with Origen's, and possibly Plotinus' theories. The inquiries above found that beyond similar terminology in some cases, MacDonald's theory of creation was extremely different from those two Neo-Platonists. MacDonald believed that creation was not a mere accident or happenstance, but rather, that we originated from the creative imagination of God: "It is better to keep the word *creation* for that calling out of nothing which is the imagination of God."[4] We were not created as mere artistic pieces, but rather "'we are his offspring'; not the work of his hand, but the children that came forth from his heart."[5] MacDonald desired that his readers would understand that we were created out of God's heart and imagination, although those words can only be used analogically. He wanted to emphasize our intimate connection to our creator.

While the question concerning emanationism was answered, MacDonald's response could lead one to conclude that he leant toward a pantheistic philosophy. If we were truly offspring of the divine, are

---

3   George MacDonald, *Unspoken* Sermons, "The Knowing of the Son," 201.

4   George MacDonald, *A Dish of Orts*, "The Imagination: Its Function and its Culture," 3.

5   Ibid., "Wordsworth's Poetry," 246.

we not then divine? While he often used pantheistic terminology, even going so far as causing one of his characters to use the term and claim it, MacDonald was not a pantheist in the traditional sense of the term. He held to the individuality and uniqueness of each human. While he often referenced the "oneness" of God and man, he also admitted that for there to be harmonic oneness, at least two unique individuals must be involved. Also, his concept of oneness is not metaphysical, it is volitional:[6] oneness can only occur when one chooses the will of their Heavenly Father. Thus, MacDonald's Christian pantheism is not the traditional pantheism of the east: "This Christian pantheism, this belief that God is in everything, and showing himself in everything...."[7]

To finish our summary of MacDonald's philosophical moorings, significant progress was made in the research to record MacDonald's position on epistemology. While there is no question among scholars that MacDonald rebelled against the primacy of empiricism and rationalism of his day, to suggest that he rejected those fields outright would be unfounded. He merely contended that the "man of science" who did not understand that God was the creator and designer of the universe was embarking on a journey without destination or atlas. Science can lead one on a ruthless and selfish quest for knowledge that could only help but distract the scientist from finding the true Living One: "Their sagacity labours in earthly things, and so fills their minds with their own questions and conclusions, that they cannot see the eternal foundations God has laid in man."[8] MacDonald's condemnation of scientific endeavors only focused on the man of "mere science," one who embarked on this journey from a naturalistic perspective. For MacDonald, a Godly scientist was possible, and it is even likely, because of MacDonald's own scientific training in chemistry and medicine as well as his discussions with his son Greville, that MacDonald himself fit into that category.

MacDonald's outlook on rationality was somewhat similar. While he sought to knock both science and rationality off their epistemic footstool and found that neither directly produced faith, both lines of epistemic persuasion could be utilized as helpful prompts which could cause an inward conviction of the hearer. As will be summarized below in the section on apologetics, neither empiricism

---

6   George MacDonald, *Unspoken Sermons*, "The Creation in Christ," 194.

7   George MacDonald, *A Dish of Orts*, "Wordsworth's Poetry," 246.

8   George MacDonald, *The Hope of the Gospel*, "The Yoke of Jesus," 68-9.

nor rationality should be used to attempt to forcibly change another's mind, but to dispense with these tools completely would be to reject how humans have been created as rational and sensory creatures: "the same thing that the intellect does with Euclid, the whole mind, heart, intellect, imagination, conscience, and will does with regard to God when a man sees God and knows Him."[9] God has created his creatures with curiosity, the senses and the intellect, and these can be used in our attainment of knowledge of our Creator, but are not to be used for aggressive persuasion.

MacDonald as Mystic

There are no known modern scholars who argue that MacDonald was not a mystic, for he intentionally stated, "If anyone accuses me here of mysticism, I plead guilty with gladness: I only hope it may be of that true mysticism which, inasmuch as he makes constant use of it, St. Paul would understand at once."[10] Thus, the significance of the research above was not focused on designating MacDonald as a mystic, for scholars such as Carl McColman listed him firmly as a visionary mystic,[11] but rather, when MacDonald wished that his readers to become "mystical,"[12] what did he mean? How was that to be done? He wanted to his reader to "find himself in such conscious as well as vital relation with the source of his being, with a Will by which his own will exists, with a Consciousness by and through which he is conscious."[13] What were the steps or at least the avenues toward the mystical experience, or "the way" to the Father?

Like traditional mystics, MacDonald did believe that there could be direct insight from God. While we have little explanation from him concerning what this looked like in his own life, there were signs that MacDonald did, in fact, have this experience. In a less esoteric fashion, MacDonald also believed that through symbols and correspondences as well as dreams and visions, we could connect with God, but these could not come to fruition without an understanding of these correspondences and an openness to the Divine's interaction

---

9   George MacDonald, *George MacDonald in the Pulpit*, "Faith the Proof of the Unseen," 75.

10   George MacDonald, *The Seaboard Parish*, 140.

11   Carl McColman, *Christian Mystics: 108 Seers, Saints, and Sages*, 8.

12   George MacDonald, *The Seaboard Parish*, 141.

13   George MacDonald, *A Dish of Orts*, "A Sketch of Individual Development," 69.

through mental phenomena. Yet even more importantly, absolutely none of these experiences would take place, and no potential for mystical encounters would ensue, without the individual striving for the will of God, and in MacDonald's words, becoming "true." This obedience and action under the category of "duty" was one of MacDonald's most common themes in his oeuvre, and he felt it crucial to any progress on an individual's mystical and spiritual path.

To summarize, MacDonald believed that the individual who was true and who was doing his duty on the path which had laid before them, could commune with God. Whether through symbols and correspondences noticed in the physical world, through dreams and visions in that psychological world, or even through direct mystical insights from the divine, MacDonald did not shy away from these possibilities; in fact, he hoped that each of his readers would seek them wholeheartedly.[14]

MacDonald as Apologist

Twenty-first century apologetics lean heavily on rational argumentation; MacDonald would shun such an approach. To consider him an apologist under the conventional definition would be simply untenable. In the same way we had to qualify the terms "mystic", "philosopher", and "pantheist" to get to the root of MacDonald's beliefs, it also seemed appropriate to qualify his apologetic endeavors as "imaginative apologetics" to distinguish his methodology from current approaches of the discipline. The main delineation was that MacDonald did not hold the belief that the intellect was epistemologically antecedent and superior to the moral will. Duty comes first, then rationality and the intellect trail behind.

This ordering of the epistemic hierarchy did not demonstrate that MacDonald had cast aside rationality; for as seen above in the section on MacDonald's epistemology, he did value the rational and sensory faculties. Often times, especially out of the mouth of Thomas Wingfold, MacDonald presented metaphysical, rational argumentation; even occasionally, some of the argumentation appeared to be original to MacDonald. While MacDonald did, in fact, devalue rationality and place it subsequent to the volitional duty of man, he did on occasion use it to make an argument and in an attempt to persuade his audience.

Since it has been established that MacDonald does fall under

---

14   Ibid., "A Sketch of Individual Development," 69.

the category of apologist, albeit an unconventional one, we should then ask: "How could his approach affect the realm of our current apologetic landscape?" Even more specifically, "How would George MacDonald, if he were alive today, suggest a change of course for modern apologists?" It should be noted that while the suggestions below can be derived from the information provided above, the actuality of such suggestions coming from the mind of MacDonald are, admittedly, conjecture. He could not have comprehended the worldview shift that has occurred in western society in the twentieth and which continued on into the twenty-first century. As James Patrick Van Eerden laments, "It remains clear that there has been a dramatic shift in the religious consensus that undergirds Western culture, and especially American society. The predominant world-and-life view was once Judeo-Christian, but it is now clearly humanistic."[15] MacDonald could not have known that in this twenty-first century that almost twenty three percent of Americans would consider themselves "unaffiliated" with any religion,[16] nor that there would be a resurgence of the Classical and Evidential apologetic models that were notorious in his own age. With these caveats presented, these three proposals could be directed to current apologists:

1) Rationality disengaged from relationship is meaningless.

There is a tendency in modern apologetics, similar to MacDonald's day, to present evidences, whether in written or spoken form, without the speaker or the hearer having much, if any, relational import. The assumption is that the force of the rational arguments trumps the necessity of the relational element. In today's religious culture, and specifically the apologetic scene, there are few popular apologists who are employed on a national level to step into conferences across North America and speak to the adults and youth who attend. While there are obvious exceptions, apologetics is seldom happening on a relational level. Friends give struggling friends a book, or take them to hear a speaker, but few are engaging in their own apologetic pursuits. It would do the community a much better service if we were training

---

15 James Patrick Van Eerden, *An Inquiry into the Use of Human Experience as an Apologetic Tool*, 14.

16 Pew Forum on Religion & Public Life, *U.S. Religious Landscape Survey* (Washington, D.C.: Pew Research Center), 2008). Available at http://www.pewforum.org/religious-landscape-study/

apologists, whether in youth groups or even adult small groups, to learn to become relationally involved with those who could use a spiritual and apologetic guide.

2) Awaken, before any argument.

To springboard from the prior point, this age's tendency to elevate the role of rationality tends to cause modern apologists to "quick-draw" the weapon of logical argumentation. There is even an element of using argumentation to strong-arm your opponent to force them in a logical corner, without recognizing whether the individual has been roused from his spiritually dead state. One of MacDonald's most unique, and potentially useful, elements in his apologetic was his tactic of "awakening the imagination and getting readers to think for themselves."[17] In today's apologetic landscape, there is little use for creativity and the imagination. Due to this generation's aversion to absolute truth as well as the fixation on relativism, as well as exhibiting an antipathy toward logical argumentation, it would seem that a subliminal and subversive imaginative apologetic could be successful. As an example, Lewis' and MacDonald's use of *Sehnsucht* quite possibly could be implemented in this current age simply due to the fact that over half of the "nones" mentioned in the Pew research poll have a high "frequency of feeling wonder about the universe."[18] Could this wonder be a sign of existential longing? Is it possible this longing be cultivated by a modern-imaginative apologetic?

3) Discipleship and Doubt

MacDonald's attitude toward discipleship and doubt could vastly change the way modern apologists operate. First, his reaction to doubt is not overwhelmingly negative as many modern pastors would imply: "A man may be haunted with doubts, and only grow thereby in faith. Doubts are the messengers of the Living One to rouse the honest. They are the first knock at our door of things that are not yet, but have to be, understood."[19] To MacDonald, as noted earlier, doubt was a tool to further a believer's faith, and curious questions, introspection, and doubt of one's own secular worldview could initiate

---

17 Rebecca Langworthy, "Crossing that Great Frontier" in *Northwind* Vol. 36, 2017, 91.

18 Ibid., n All its spt Library, (getics Studentsing bush Pew Forum on Religion & Public Life, *U.S. Religious Landscape Survey*.

19 George MacDonald, *Unspoken Sermons*, "The Voice of Job," 164.

a non-believer's discipleship.

That leads to MacDonald's second area of focus: discipleship. If today's apologists had a slogan it would be something akin to: "If you've got questions, we've got answers"; but MacDonald would likely suggest a wordier motto: "Let's walk this path of life, and discuss your questions as you seek the answers." To use the analogy of navigation and a sojourner, the modern apologist would hand them a map and tell them where to go. MacDonald would rather walk alongside the sojourner, encourage him on his journey, discuss the various paths that could be taken, and occasionally point out the potential pitfalls on the way. Modern apologists try to make the journey easy by showing the steps that logically need to be made, but MacDonald realized the value in letting the sojourner take the steps for themselves, even when some of the steps could lead down a treacherous path. It is often only through sorrow, confusion, and the pitfalls of life that one can find the correct path to our Heavenly Father.

With these three humble suggestions for implementation by current apologists, the apologetics landscape could drastically change, and most importantly, could become much more effective. The changing of minds and hearts cannot happen in a vacuum; they occur in relationships, in community. The role of the imagination in apologetics needs to be raised to a more prominent position and the attitudes toward doubt and the methodology of discipleship should be altered for maximum effectiveness. These suggestions, based on MacDonald's own apologetic methodology, have the potential to positively change the world of modern apologetics.

George MacDonald as Philosopher, Mystic, and Apologist

Waking the Dead

BIBLIOGRAPHY

Amell, Barbara. "George MacDonald on the Logic of Faith" in *Inklings Forever* Vol. 2 (1999), 82-87.

Anonymous, "Dr. MacDonald's Testimony" in *Wingfold: Celebrating the Works of George MacDonald*. Vol. 87, 30-33. Originally published in *Christian World*, July 20, 1882.

_____. "Visit of Dr. George MacDonald" in *Wingfold: Celebrating the Works of George MacDonald*. Vol. 88, 43-45. Originally published in *Banffshire Journal*, September 23, 1873.

Auden, W. H. *The Visionary Novels: Lilith and Phantastes*. Ed. Anne Fremantle. New York: Noonday Press, 1962.

Augustine of Hippo. *On Christian Doctrine*. Nicene and Post-Nicene Fathers, First Series, Vol. 2. Edited by Philip Schaff. Translated by James Shaw. Buffalo, NY: Christian Literature Publishing, 1887.

Ballard James. "Dreams, Reality, the Soul and the Supernatural in George MacDonald's 'The History of Photogen and Nycteris: A Day and Night Märchen'" [Unpublished manuscript], 2008.

Barnard, Justin D. "Cartesian Epistemology and Religious Belief" in *Journal of the Union Faculty Forum*. Vol. 35 (2015), 21-27.

Beinecke Collection. The George MacDonald Collection at the Beinecke Rare Book and Manuscript Library, (1830-1890).

The Bible. *NET Bible* (New English Translation). Biblical Studies Press, 1996-2007. https://netbible.com/.

Bruce, Alexander Balmain. *Apologetics; or, Christianity Definitely Stated*. New York: Charles Scribner's Sons, 1892.

Carpenter, Humphrey and Mari Prichard. *The Oxford Companion to Children's Literature*. Oxford: Oxford University Press, 1999.

Chambers, Oswald. *Christian Disciplines: Building Strong Christian Character.* Grand Rapids: Discovery House, 1995.

Chateaubriand, François-René. *The Genius of Christianity; or the Spirit and Beauty of the Christian Religion.* Translated by Charles I. White. Philadelphia: John Murphy & Co., 1884.

Chesterton, G.K. "George MacDonald" in *The Daily News*, 23 September, 1905. https://www.wheaton.edu/media/migrated-images-amp-files/media/files/centers-and-institutes/wade-center/vii/vii20online20articles/Gabelman-GKConGM-Vol28.pdf. Accessed May 23, 2019.

_____. Introduction to *George MacDonald and His Wife* by Greville MacDonald, Whitehorn: Johannesen, 9-15, 2005.

Cheyne, Alec. "The Bible and Change in the Nineteenth Century" in *The Bible in Scottish Life and Literature*. Ed. David Wright. Edinburgh: The Saint Andrews Press, 1988, 192-207.

Colenso, John William. *The Pentateuch and the Book of Joshua Critically Examined.* London: Longman's, Green, & Co., 1894.

Coleridge, Samuel Taylor. *Aids to Reflection.* London: Hurst, Chance & Company, 2nd edition, 1831. http://www.gutenberg.org/ebooks/44795. Accessed May 23, 2019.

_____. *Confessions of an Inquiring Spirit.* London: Edward Moxon, 1853. http://www.gutenberg.org/files/2575/2575-h/2575-h.htm. Accessed May 23, 2019.

Collins, B.G. "George MacDonald" in *The Baptist Quarterly* 1.4 (1951), 61-74. https://biblicalstudies.org.uk/pdf/bq/14-2_061.pdf. Accessed May 23, 2019.

Cooper, John W. *Panentheism: The Other God of the Philosophers.* Grand Rapids: Baker Academic, 2006.

Copleston, Frederick. *A History of Philosophy* Vol. I: *Greece and Rome.* New York: Image Books, 1993.

Cowan, Stephen. *Five Views on Apologetics.* Ed. Stephen Cowan. Grand Rapids: Zondervan, 2000.

Creegan, Nicola Hoggard. "Schleiermacher as apologist: Reclaiming the Father of Modern Theology" in *Christian Apologetics in the Postmodern World.* ed. Timothy R. Phillips & Dennis L. Okholm. Downers Grove: InterVarsity Press, 1995, 59-74.

Dearborn, Kerry. *Baptized Imagination: The Theology of George MacDonald.* Farnham: Ashgate Publishing, 2006.

_____. "Bridge over the River Why: The Imagination as a Way to Meaning" in *North Wind* Vol. 16 (1997), 29-40.

Dulles, Avery. *A History of Apologetics.* Eugene: Wipf and Stock, 1999.

Evans, Jedidiah. "C.S. Lewis, Thomas Wolfe, and the Transatlantic Expression of *Sehnsucht*" in *Inklings Forever* 9 (2014). https://pillars.taylor.edu/cgi/viewcontent.cgi?article=1234 &context=inklings_forever. Accessed May 23, 2019.

Frei, Hans W. "Apologetics, Criticism, and the Loss of Narrative Interpretation" in *Why Narrative? : Readings in Narrative Theology.* Ed. Stanley Hauerwas and L. Gregory Jones. Grand Rapids: Eerdmans, 1989, 45-64.

Gaarden, Bonnie. *The Christian Goddess.* Lanham: Fairleigh Dickinson University Press, 2011.

Geisler, Norman. *Baker Encyclopedia of Christian Apologetics.* Grand Rapids: Baker Books, 1999.

Geisler, Norman and Winfried Corduan. *Philosophy of Religion* Eugene, OR: Wipf and Stock, 2003.

Greene, Dana. "The Mystic and the Church" in *Mysticism, Christian Reflection: A Series in Faith and Ethics*, Vol. 17 (2005). Waco: The Center for Christian Ethics at Baylor University, 70-76.

Gregs, Favour James. *William Wordsworth.* London: Forgotten Books, 290-1, 2013.

Grierson, H.J.C. "George MacDonald" in *Aberdeen University Review*, Vol. XII: No. 34 (1924).

Hein, Rolland. *George MacDonald: Victorian Mythmaker*. Whitehorn: Johannesen, 1999. 1st Printing.

_____. *The Harmony Within: the Spiritual Vision of George MacDonald*. Eureka: Sunrise Books, 1989.

Hindmarsh, Douglas Bruce. *The Faith of George MacDonald: A Biographical and Critical Examination of the Theology Represented in his Sermons and Letters*. Master's Thesis. Regent University, 1990.

_____."George MacDonald and the Forgotten Father" in *North Wind* Vol. 9 (1991), 55-79.

Hodge, Charles. *Systematic Theology*, Vol. 1. New York: Charles Scribers and Company, 1872.

Holmes, Urban T. *A History of Christian Spirituality*. San Francisco: Harper & Row, 1980.

Houghton, Walter E. *The Victorian Frame of Mind*. New Haven: Yale University Press, 1957.

Ingham, Tanya. "George MacDonald: An Original Thinker" in *Knowing and Doing: A Teaching Quarterly for Discipleship of Heart and Mind*. Fall 2009, 1 & 8-14. http://www.cslewisinstitute.org/webfm_send/509. Accessed May 23, 2019.

Johnson, Kirstin Jeffrey. "Rooted Deep: Relational inklings of the Mythopoetic Maker, George MacDonald" in *Informing the Inklings: George MacDonald and the Victorian Roots of Modern Fantasy*. Ed. Michael Partridge and Kirstin Jeffrey Johnson,

_____. *Rooted in All its Story, More is Meant than Meets the Ear*. Ph.D. diss., University of Saint Andrews, 2011. https://research-repository.st-andrews.ac.uk/handle/10023/1887. Accessed May 23, 2019.

Hamden, CT: Winged Lion Press, 2018, 31-56.

Kegler, Adelheid. "Some Aspects of the Oeuvre of George MacDonald in a Curriculum of Philosophy Courses and in the Production of a Play at a German Gymnasium" in *North Wind* Vol. 22 (2003), 14-20.

Kreglinger, Gisela H. "Poets, Dreamers, and Mediators" in *George MacDonald: Literary Heritage and Heirs*. Wayne: Zossima Press, 25-43, 2008.

_____."Reading Scripture in Crisis: The Victorian Crisis of Faith and MacDonald's Response to Coleridge" in *Northwind* Vol. 27 (2008), 79-103.

_____. *Storied Revelations: Parables, Imagination and George MacDonald's Christian Fiction*. Cambridge: Lutterworth, 2014.

Langworthy, Rebecca. "Crossing that Great Frontier" in *Northwind* Vol. 36 (2017), 87-95.

Lewis, C.S. "Christianity and Culture" in *Theology* Vol 40: Issue 237 (1940), 166-179.

_____. *Mere Christianity*. New York: Macmillan, 1960.

_____. Introduction to *George MacDonald: An Anthology*. New York: Macmillan, 1947.

_____. *Surprised By Joy*. New York: Harcourt, Brace, and World, Inc, 1955.

_____. "They Asked For A Paper" in *Is Theology Poetry?* London: Geoffrey Bless (1962), 164-165.

Livingston, James C. *Modern Christian Thought* Vol. 1: The Enlightenment and the Nineteenth Century. Upper Saddle River, NJ: Prentice Hall, 1997.

MacDonald, George. *Adela Cathcart*. Whitehorn: Johannesen, 2000, 2nd Printing.

_____. *Alec Forbes of Howglen*. Whitehorn: Johannesen, 2003, 2nd Printing.

_____. *Annals of a Quiet Neighbourhood*. Whitehorn: Johannesen, 2004, 2nd Printing.

_____. *At the Back of the North Wind*. Whitehorn: Johannesen, 2002, 3rd Printing.

_____. *Castle Warlock*. Translated by David Jack. North Charleston: Createspace, 2017.

_____. *David Elginbrod*. Whitehorn: Johannesen, 1995, 1st Printing.

_____. *A Dish of Orts, Chiefly Papers on the Imagination, and on Shakespeare*. London: Sampson Low Marston & Co., 1895.

_____. *Donal Grant*. New York: John W. Lovell, 1990.

_____. *England's Antiphon*. Whitehorn: Johannesen, 1996, 1st Printing.

_____. *The Flight of the Shadow*. Whitehorn: Johannesen, 2001, 2nd Printing.

_____. *George MacDonald in the Pulpit*. Whitehorn: Johannesen, 2009, 3rd Printing.

_____. *Home Again* and *The Elect Lady*. Whitehorn: Johannesen, 2003, 2nd Printing.

_____. *The Hope of the Gospel*. Las Vegas: International Alliance, 2012.

_____. "A Letter to American Boys" in *St. Nicholas Magazine for Boys and Girls*, Vol. 5: No. 3 (1878), 202-205. Available at George MacDonald Society, http://www.george-macdonald.com/etexts/letter_american_boys.html. Accessed May 23, 2019.

_____. *The Light Princess and Other Fairy Tales*. Whitehorn: Johannesen, 2009, 4th Printing.

_____. *Lilith*. Whitehorn: Johannesen, 2009, 3rd Printing.

_____. *Malcolm*. Whitehorn: Johannesen, 2004, 2nd Printing.

_____. *The Marquis of Lossie*. Whitehorn: Johannesen, 2004, 2nd Printing.

_____. *Miracles of Our Lord*. Ed. Rolland Hein. Wheaton: Harold Shaw, 1980.

_____. *Paul Faber-Surgeon*. Whitehorn: Johannesen, 2009, 3rd Printing.

_____. *Phantastes*. Whitehorn: Johannesen, 2009, 3rd Printing.

_____. *The Portent and Other Stories.* Whitehorn: Johannesen, 1999, 2nd Printing.

_____. *The Princess and Curdie.* New York: Puffin Books/Penguin Group, 1966.

_____. *Ranald Bannerman's Boyhood.* Whitehorn: Johannesen, 1999, 2nd Printing.

_____. *Robert Falconer.* Whitehorn: Johannesen, 2005, 2nd Printing.

_____. *Salted With Fire.* Whitehorn: Johannesen, 2009, 2nd Printing.

_____. *The Seaboard Parish.* Whitehorn: Johannesen, 2004, 2nd Printing.

_____. *Sir Gibbie.* Whitehorn: Johannesen, 2000, 3rd Printing.

_____. *There and Back.* Philadelphia: David McKay, 1891.

_____. *Thomas Wingfold, Curate.* Whitehorn: Johannesen, 2002, 2nd Printing.

_____. *The Tragedie of Hamlet, Prince of Denmarke; a study with the text of the folio of 1623.* London: Longmans, Green, and Co., 1885.

_____. *Unspoken Sermons.* Memphis: Bottom of the Hill Publishing, 2012.

_____. *The Vicar's Daughter.* Whitehorn:Johannesen, 1998, 2nd Printing.

_____. *Warlock o' Glenwarlock: A homely romance.* Boston, Lothrop, Lee & Shepard Co., 1881.

_____. *Weighed and Wanting.* Boston, D. Lothrop and Company, 1882.

_____. *What's Mine's Mine.* Whitehorn: Johannesen, 2000, 3rd Printing.

_____. *Wilfrid Cumbermede.* Whitehorn: Johannesen, 2009, 2nd Printing.

_____. *The Wise Woman/Gutta Percha Willie.* Whitehorn: Johannesen, 1998, 2nd Printing.

MacDonald, Greville. *George MacDonald and His Wife.* Whitehorn: Johannesen, 2005.

MacDonald, Ronald. *From a Northern Window: A Personal Reminiscence of George*

MacDonald by His Son. Ed. Michael Philips. Eureka: Sunrise Books, 1989.

Manley, David. "Shadows that Fall: The Immanence of Heaven in the Fiction of C.S. Lewis and George MacDonald" in *Northwind* Vol. 17 (1998), 43-49.

Manlove, Colin N. *Christian Fantasy.* Notre Dame: University of Notre Dame Press, 1992.

_____. "MacDonald and Kingsley: A Victorian Contrast" in *The Gold Thread: Essays on George MacDonald.* Ed, William Raeper. Edinburgh: Edinburgh UP, 1990, 140-162.

_____. *Modern Fantasy: Five Studies.* New York: Cambridge University, 1978.

_____. "Parent or Associate? George MacDonald and the Inklings" in *George MacDonald: Literary Heritage and Heirs.* Wayne: Zossima Press, 2008, 227-238.

_____. "The Princess and the Goblin and The Princess and Curdie" in *Northwind* Vol. 27 (2007), 1-36.

Maurice, F.D. *The Claims of the Bible and of Science: A Correspondence between a layman and the Rev. F.D. Maurice on some questions arising out of the controversy respecting the Pentateuch.* London: MacMillan & Co., 1863.

McColman, Carl. *Christian Mystics: 108 Seers, Saints, and Sages.* Charlottesville: Hampton Roads, 2016.

McGillis, Roderick. "Fantasy as Miracle" in *George MacDonald: Literary Heritage and Heirs* Zossima Press, 2008, 201-215.

McInnis, Jeff. *Shadows and* Chivalry. Hamden, CT: Winged Lion Press, 2012.

Mendelson, Michael. "The Fairy Tales of George MacDonald and the Evolution of a Genre" in *For the Childlike: George MacDonald's Fantasies for Children*. Ed. Roderick McGillis. Metuchen, NJ: Scarecrow Press, 1992, 31-50.

Nelson, Dale J. "MacDonald and Jacob Boehme" in *North Wind* Vol. 8 (1989), 24-36.

Neuhouser, David L. "Mathematics, Science, and George MacDonald" in *Journal of the Association of Christians in the Mathematical Sciences*. Vol. 1 (2003), 46-58.

Newell, J. Philip. *A.J. Scott and his Circle*. Dissertation. The University of Edinburgh, 1981.

Newman, John Henry. *Sermons, Chiefly on the Theory of Religious Belief: Preached Before the University of Oxford*. London: Francis and John Rivington, 1844.

Novalis (Georg Philipp Friedrich Freiherr von Hardenberg). *The Novices of Sais*. Vol. 4, The

German Classics, ed. Kuno Francke. Albany, NY: German Publications Society, 1913.

Nystoyl, Narve Kragset. *Worldviews in George MacDonald's Phantastes and C.S. Lewis' The Chronicles of Narnia*. Master's Thesis. The University of Oslo, 2013.

Origen. *Commentary on the Gospel of John*. From Ante-Nicene Fathers, Vol. 9. Ed. by Allan Menzies. Buffalo, NY: Christian Literature Publishing Co., 1896.

_____. *De Principiis*. From Ante-Nicene Fathers, Vol. 4. Ed. by Alexander Roberts, James Donaldson, and A. Cleveland Coxe. Buffalo, NY: Christian Literature Publishing Co., 1885.

Paley, William. *Natural Theology and Tracts*. New York: S. King, 1824.

Pew Forum on Religion & Public Life. *U.S. Religious Landscape Survey*. Washington, D.C.: Pew Research Center, 2008. http://www.pewforum.org/religious-landscape-study/. Accessed March 11, 2014.

Phillips, Michael R. *George MacDonald: Scotland's Beloved Storyteller*. Minneapolis: Bethany House, 1987.

Plato. *The Dialogues of Plato*. Chicago: William Benton, 1952.

Plotinus. *Enneads*. Chicago: Encyclopedia Britannica, 1952.

Prickett, Stephen. "The Two Worlds of George MacDonald" in *North Wind* Vol. 2 (1983), 14-23.

_____. *Victorian Fantasy*. Waco: Baylor University Press, 2005.

Raeper, William. *George MacDonald*. Batavia: Lion Publishing, 1987.

Ramm, Bernard. *Varieties of Christian Apologetics*. Grand Rapids: Baker Book House, 1961.

Reardon, Bernard M.G. *Religious Thought in the Victorian Age: A Survey from Coleridge to Gore*. New York: Longman, 1995.

Reis, Richard H. *George MacDonald's Fiction: A Twentieth Century View*. Eureka: Sunrise Books, 1989.

Riddle, John M. *A History of the Middle Ages, 300-1500*. Plymouth: Rowman & Littlefield, 2008.

Riga, Frank. "The Platonic Imagery of George MacDonald and C.S. Lewis" in *For the Childlike: George MacDonald's Fantasies for Children*. Ed. Roderick McGillis. Metuchen, NJ: Children's Literature Association, 1992, 111-132.

Robb, David S. *George MacDonald*. Edinburgh: Scottish Academic Press, 1987.

Sadler, Glenn Edward. *An Expression of Character: the Letters of George MacDonald*. Grand Rapids: Eerdmans, 1994.

Salvey, Courtney. "Riddled with Evil: Fantasy as Theodicy in George MacDonald's *Phantastes and Lilith*" in *North Wind* Vol. 27 (2008), 16-24.

Schaeffer, Francis A. *He is There and He is not Silent*. Wheaton, Illinois: Tyndale, 2001.

Scott, Alexander J. *Discourses*. London and Cambridge: MacMillan and Co, 1866.

Slepyan, Jocelyne. "'With all sorts of doubts I am familiar': George MacDonald's Literary Response to John Ruskin's Struggles with Epistemology" in in *Rethinking*

George MacDonald. Glasgow: Scottish Literature International, 2013, 36-51

Soto, Fernando. "Mirrors in MacDonald's *Phantastes*: A Reflexive Structure" in *North Wind: A Journal of George MacDonald Studies*. Vol. 23 (2004), 27-47.

Swedenborg, Emanuel . *Heaven and Hell: the Portable New Century Translation*. Trans. By George F. Dole. West Chester, Swedenborg Foundation, 2010.

——————. *Sacred Scripture /White Horse: the Portable New Century Translation* Trans. By George F. Dole. West Chester, Swedenborg Foundation, 2015.

Trexler, Robert. "George MacDonald: Merging Myth and Method" in *CSL: The Bulletin of the New York C.S. Lewis Society* Vol. 34 (2003), No. 4. http://citeseerx.ist.psu.edu/ viewdoc/download?doi=10.1.1.353.4916&rep=rep1&type=pdf. Accessed January 16, 2014.

——————. "George MacDonald Society Post." Facebook.com. October 22 2014. Web. Accessed October 25, 2014.

Troup, Edward. "George MacDonald's Boyhood in Huntly" reprinted in *North Wind* Vol. 1 (1982), 4-9.

Underhill, Evelyn. *Mysticism*. New York: Mcridian Books, 1957.

——————. *Practical Mysticism*. Columbus: Ariel Press, 1942.

Van Eerden, James Patrick. *An Inquiry into the Use of Human Experience as an Apologetic Tool: Illustrations from the Writings of George MacDonald, G.K. Chesterton and C.S. Lewis*. Master's Thesis. Grove City College, 1995.

Waddle, Keith. "George MacDonald and the Homiletics of Religious Imagination." *North Wind* Vol. 18 (1999), 1-11.

Wade Center. "George MacDonald Family Library." https://www.wheaton.edu/media/wade-center/files/collections/author-library-listings/MacDonald_Family_Library _20181114.pdf. Accessed January 16, 2014.

Wild, Robert. *The Tumbler of God: Chesterton as Mystic.* Kettering: Angelico Press, 2013.

Wiles, Maurice. *Documents in Early Christian Thought.* Cambridge: Cambridge University Press, 2001.

Williams, Thomas. "Augustine and the Platonists." A Lecture given to the Freshman Program of Christ College, the Honors College of Valparaiso University, October 23, 2003. http://shell.cas.usf.edu/~thomasw/aug&plat.pdf. Accessed November 11, 2014.

Withrow, Josh. "In the Service of Freedom: Postmodernism in the Writing of George MacDonald." *The Wise Imagination*, February 23, 2015, http://thewiseimagination.com/2015/02/23/in-the-service-of-freedom-postmodernism-in-the-writing-of-george-macdonald-1-of-3/. Accessed March 3, 2015.

Wolffe, John. *God and Greater Britain: Religion and National Life in Britain and Ireland.* New York: Routledge, 1994.

Zimmerman, Brandon. *Sight Becomes Seeing: Plotinian Emanation as a Dynamic of Procession and Return.* Master's Thesis. Catholic University of America, 2009.

ABOUT THE AUTHOR

Dean Hardy is the Christian Philosophy and Apologetics teacher at Charlotte Christian School in North Carolina. His resume includes working with Youth for Christ, a Master's degree under the tutelage of Norman Geisler at Southern Evangelical Seminary, and a Doctorate in Theology from UNISA. He is also the director of the Youth Apologetics Conference, a conference dedicated to helping students understand and defend the Christian faith.

Waking the Dead

INDEX

A

Allegory: 63

Apologetics: viii, 3, 135-141, 147-149, 150-154, 162-163, 169, 176, 191, 193-196.

Arguments for God: 17, 75, 83-85, 88, 89, 91, 138-140, 145-154, 160-163, 168-169, 194.

Aristotle: 31.

Art: 31, 63, 159-160, 182.

Atheism: 28, 78, 81-82, 141, 160, 166-168, 170, 174, 177.

Augustine: 31, 34, 43, 62-66, 69, 72.

B

Bacon, Francis: 13.

Bible (Scripture) [See also Gospel]: 14, 21, 44, 63-68, 72, 75, 84, 98-106, 109-112, 119, 125, 176, 186.

Jacob Boehme (Behemen): 15, 17, 21, 43, 116, 124.

Robert Browning: 16-17, 23, 65, 86.

Bruce, Alexander Balmain 150-152.

C

Calvin, John (and Calvinism): 7, 9, 25, 27-28, 53, 100, 113, 141, 149.

Catholic: 7, 8, 114, 141.

Chambers, Oswald : 1, 185.

Chateaubriand, François-René: 141-149.

Chesterton, G.K.: 1-2, 113, 115-117.

Church: 7-9, 12 (kirk), 18, 20, 26-27, 40, 42, 71, 80, 100, 103, 107, 125, 153, 186, 189.

Church of Scotland: 8.

Coleridge, Samuel Taylor: 16, 21, 57, 98-106, 111, 142, 145-147, 150.

Correspondences: 14, 19, 32-33, 58, 62-63, 66-72, 83, 92-93, 102, 110, 122-124, 133, 190, 192-193.

D

Dante: 17-18, 20, 80.

Darwin: 81, 98, 141.

Dearborn, Kerry: 16, 20, 33, 51-52, 58-61, 133, 163.

Doctrine of Becoming: 121, 133.

Duty: 60-61, 93-94, 96, 122, 127-129, 133, 146, 153, 161-163, 169, 181, 193.

E

Emanationism: 41-43, 47, 56, 190-189.

Empiricism: 75-77, 98, 147, 191.

Evangelicals: 75.

Fantasy: 31, 64, 66.

Fairy: 72, 187.

Faith: 12, 19, 23, 29-30, 51, 59, 75-78, 83, 85-87, 90-99, 108-109, 113, 141-142, 146-153, 166, 168-169, 191, 195.

F

Fichte: 17.

G

Gaarden, Bonnie: 54-55, 76-77, 83, 91, 162.

Gospel(s): 26-27, 40-41, 44-45, 53, 78-79, 107, 109, 129, 148, 189.

H

Hein, Rolland: 7-8, 11-12, 20-21, 27-28, 43-44, 50, 55, 60, 81, 93, 96, 99, 118, 120, 121-122, 126, 130, 165, 174, 177.

Hindmarsh, Douglas Bruce: 25, 62, 78, 82, 91, 95.

I

Imagination: 15, 45-46, 53, 56, 58-61, 88-89, 91, 119, 123, 141-143, 145, 147, 155, 160, 163, 167-169, 190, 192, 195-196.

Imaginative apologetics: 145, 154, 162-165, 193, 195.

Inerrancy (Inerrant): 98-103, 105-106, 110.

Inspiration: 100, 109-110, 119, 160, 169, 181.

J

Johnson, Kirstin Jeffrey: 14, 18, 55, 99, 103, 105, 202.

Immanuel Kant: 17, 137, 150.

K

King's College, Aberdeen: 13, 15-16.

Kingsley, Charles: 18, 77, 118.

Klopstock: 14, 18.

Knox, John: 7.

Kreglinger, Gisela: 47, 84, 98-99, 105, 111, 145.

L

Lewis, C.S.: 1-2, 39, 83, 96, 138, 181-186, 195.

M

MacDonald, George

Adela Cathcart: 107.

Alec Forbes of Howglen : 9, 185-187.

Annals of a Quiet Neighbourhood : 16-17, 82, 84, 111, 120-121, 176, 179.

At the Back of the North Wind :126, 128.

Castle Warlock : 185.

David Elginbrod :18, 84, 96, 134, 176, 178, 180.

A Dish of Orts, Chiefly papers on the Imagination, and on Shakespeare : 16-17, 23, 31, 44-46, 49, 51, 64-65, 69, 71, 78, 81, 86-87, 89, 119, 154, 159-160, 164, 168, 178, 180, 190-192.

Donal Grant : 88.

England's Antiphon : 16, 30, 32, 39, 123-124, 145.

The Flight of the Shadow : 69.

George MacDonald in the Pulpit :45, 47, 77, 82, 85, 87, 89, 93, 106, 113, 155, 163, 170, 172, 174, 192.

Home Again and *The Elect Lady* :154.

The Hope of the Gospel :10, 13, 26-27, 44-45, 53, 78-79, 84, 94, 98, 174, 191.

"A Letter to American Boys" : 34, 128-129.

The Light Princess and Other Fairy Tales : 36, 184.

Lilith : 15, 34-38, 61, 117, 123, 126-127.

Malcolm : 66, 130.

The Marquis of Lossie : 17, 119, 170.

Miracles of Our Lord : 93, 131, 133, 162, 180.

Paul Faber-Surgeon : 26, 90, 125, 127, 132, 155, 168, 170-171, 174-175.

Phantastes : 17, 34, 37-39, 123, 126, 133.

The Portent and Other Stories : 44, 55, 182, 184.

Ranald Bannerman's Boyhood : 5, 14.

Robert Falconer : 19, 28, 45, 94, 125, 186.

Salted With Fire : 89, 95, 107, 114.

The Seaboard Parish : 18, 83-84, 87-88, 91-92, 120, 122, 157, 176, 184-185, 192.

Sir Gibbie : 61, 118-119.

There and Back : 45, 85, 155-156, 160-161, 178, 180.

Thomas Wingfold, Curate: 82, 132, 155, 157, 166-168, 174, 178-179, 193.

The Tragedie of Hamlet, Prince of Denmarke : 30.

Unspoken Sermons : 19, 25, 27, 29, 33, 37, 44, 47, 49, 52-54, 58-61, 63, 66, 69-72, 77, 80, 87, 91-94, 98, 105, 107, 110-111, 117, 120, 122-125, 127, 129, 135, 146, 156, 161, 171, 175-177, 190-191, 195.

The Vicar's Daughter : 107, 109, 173.

Warlock o' Glenwarlock : 51.

Weighed and Wanting 26, 117-118, 141.

What's Mine's Mine : 48-49, 51, 130-133, 174, 184.

Wilfrid Cumbermede : 30-31, 130, 157, 159, 162, 165, 172.

The Wise Woman/Gutta Percha Willie : 84, 128.

MacDonald, Greville : 2, 7-8, 11-12, 14-16, 18-21, 27-28, 49-52, 61, 69-70, 75, 81, 84, 86, 99, 106, 109-110, 117, 124-125, 166, 168-169, 173, 191.

Magic : 15, 121.

Manlove, Colin: 32, 34, 59, 70-71, 77, 83, 97, 118, 183.

McGillis, Roderick: 32, 39, 127.

McInnis, Jeff: 75-76, 84.

Maurice, F.D.: 2, 19-21, 41,

57, 98-99, 102-106.

Metaphysics (Metaphysical): 25, 30, 33-34, 37-39, 53-54, 56, 69-70, 77, 79, 85, 93, 111, 113, 143-145, 155, 181, 189-191, 193.

Milton: 14, 16-18, 60.

Henry More : 17, 30, 39, 189.

Mysticism: 2-3, 21, 23, 66, 69, 71, 110, 112-116, 119-124, 133, 189, 192.

N

Newman, John Henry: 2, 137, 148-149.

Novalis: 15, 23, 34, 126.

Nystoyl, Narve Kragset: 34, 39.

O

Obedience (Obey): 26, 93-95, 96-98, 127, 129, 147, 154, 171, 177, 179-181, 187, 193.

Origen : 18, 40-43, 47, 190.

P

Paley, William: 17, 75, 86, 88, 137, 140, 147, 149, 156.

Pantheism: 42, 48, 50-52, 54-55, 130, 154, 191.

Panentheism: 54-55.

Philosophy: 12-13, 16, 23, 25-26, 28-32, 39, 42, 56, 62, 66, 79, 91, 101, 112-113, 115, 120-122, 137, 141, 146-147, 150, 152, 165, 190.

Plato (Platonism): 13, 16-18, 21, 31-41, 56, 116, 189-190.

Plotinus : 21, 31, 40-43, 47, 190.

Poet (poetry): 16-18, 30, 44-45, 46, 49, 51, 80-84, 96, 101, 121, 123, 143, 145, 181-182, 187.

Prickett, Stephen: 31-33, 35-36, 39, 62-63.

R

Raeper, William: 8-10, 12, 14-17, 19-21, 27, 40, 50, 77, 81, 105, 107, 110, 122-124.

Rationalism : 75-76, 85, 98, 139, 147, 150, 152, 163, 191.

Reis, Richard: 8, 13-14, 18, 31, 106, 110, 119-120, 122, 124, 165.

Relativism (relative): 57, 59, 116, 195.

Religion: 27-28, 30, 42, 50, 71, 77, 79, 81-82,

95-96, 115, 137, 140-144, 148, 152, 186, 194-195.

Revelation: 20-21, 33, 45, 47, 59, 65, 68, 71, 75, 77, 80, 99, 102-105, 110-111, 125, 141, 143, 148, 175.

Romanticism (romantics): 16, 18, 52, 76-77, 139, 145, 147, 150, 152, 181-183, 189.

Ruskin, John: 19, 75, 81, 92.

S

Sacramentalism: 39, 55-56, 72, 122, 125, 130, 133, 183.

Science: 29-30, 75-89, 99-102, 111, 131, 139-142, 147, 152, 154-155, 164-165, 168, 170, 175, 191-192.

Schelling: 17.

Schlegels: 17.

Schleiermacher: 17, 31, 139-140.

Scott, A.J.: 19-20, 55, 75, 98-99, 103-106.

Sehnsucht: 181-187, 195.

Slepyan, Jocelyne: 75-76, 88, 92, 98.

Soul: 13, 18, 23, 28, 30, 33, 37, 41, 43, 47, 50, 55, 59-60, 63, 65-66, 72, 82, 85, 90, 93-94, 96, 104, 110, 117-118, 122-123, 126, 130, 143-144, 146, 148, 155, 159, 167-169, 174-175, 184-185.

Spirituality: 2-3.

Swedenborg, Emanuel: 15-17, 21, 62, 66-72, 92-93, 124, 126.

Symbolism: 14-15, 32, 39, 45-46, 49, 55-56, 58, 62-64, 66-73, 86, 93, 105, 122-124, 128, 130, 133, 139, 165, 183, 190, 192-193.

T

Tolkien, J.R.R.: 1.

Theology: 2, 12-20, 25-29, 33, 40, 50, 54, 56, 61-62, 64, 71, 75, 79, 109, 112-113, 119, 120, 122, 137, 139, 145, 146, 149-150, 160, 162, 177, 189.

Trexler, Robert: V, 2, 39, 55.

U

Underhill, Evelyn: 114-115, 119.

V

Volition (See also "The Will"): 53, 171, 191, 193.

W

Wade Center at Wheaton College: 14.

The Will (see also "Volition"): 26, 53-54, 85, 94, 128, 154, 186, 189, 191, 193.

OTHER BOOKS OF INTEREST

***Phantastes* by George MacDonald: Annotated Edition**
John Pennington and Roderick McGillis, Editors

Phantastes was a groundbreaking book in 1858 and continues to be a seminal example of great fantasy literature. Its elusive meaning is both alluring and perplexing, inviting readers to experience a range of deep feelings and a sense of profound truth. This annotated edition, by two renowned MacDonald scholars, provides a wealth of information to better understand and enjoy this masterpiece. In addition to the text, there are 184 pages containing an authoritative introduction, life chronology, textual notes, book reviews, and comparative source materials. With 354 footnotes to explain obscure words and literary references, this enhanced edition will benefit any reader and provide a solid foundation for future scholarship.

> A good critical edition of George MacDonald's *Phantastes* has long been needed, and now we have it. This fine, comprehensive edition provides an accessible and illuminating introduction to this profound work.
>
> —Colin Manlove, author of *Scotland's Forgotten Treasure: The Visionary Novels of George MacDonald*

C. S. LEWIS

C. S. Lewis: Views From Wake Forest - Essays on C. S. Lewis
Michael Travers, editor

Contains sixteen scholarly presentations from the international C. S. Lewis convention in Wake Forest, NC. Walter Hooper shares his important essay "Editing C. S. Lewis," a chronicle of publishing decisions after Lewis' death in 1963.

"Scholars from a variety of disciplines address a wide range of issues. The happy result is a fresh and expansive view of an author who well deserves this kind of thoughtful attention."
  Diana Pavlac Glyer, author of *The Company They Keep*

The Hidden Story of Narnia:
A Book-By-Book Guide to Lewis' Spiritual Themes
Will Vaus

A book of insightful commentary equally suited for teens or adults – Will Vaus points out connections between the *Narnia* books and spiritual/biblical themes, as well as between ideas in the *Narnia* books and C. S. Lewis' other books. Learn what Lewis himself said about the overarching and unifying thematic structure of the Narnia books. That is what this book explores; what C. S. Lewis called "the hidden story" of Narnia. Each chapter includes questions for individual use or small group discussion.

Why I Believe in Narnia:
33 Reviews and Essays on the Life and Work of C. S. Lewis
James Como

Chapters range from reviews of critical books, documentaries and movies to evaluations of Lewis' books to biographical analysis.
"A valuable, wide-ranging collection of essays by one of the best informed and most accute commentators on Lewis' work and ideas."
  Peter Schakel, author of *Imagination & the Arts in C. S. Lewis*

C. S. Lewis: His Literary Achievement
Colin Manlove

"This is a positively brilliant book, written with splendor, elegance, profundity and evidencing an enormous amount of learning. This is probably not a book to give a first-time reader of Lewis. But for those who are more broadly read in the Lewis corpus this book is an absolute gold mine of information. The author gives us a magnificent overview of Lewis' many writings, tracing for us thoughts and ideas which recur throughout, and at the same time telling us how each book differs from the others. I think it is not extravagant to call C. S. Lewis: His Literary Achievement a tour de force."
  Robert Merchant, *St. Austin Review*, Book Review Editor

In the Footsteps of C. S. Lewis: A Photographic Pilgrimage to the British Isles
Will Vaus

Over the course of thirty years, Will Vaus has journeyed to the British Isles many times to walk in the footsteps of C. S. Lewis. His private photographs of the significant places in Lewis' life have captured the imagination of audiences in the US and UK to whom he has lectured on the Oxford don and his work. This, in turn, prompted the idea of this collection of 78 full-color photographs, interwoven with details about Lewis' life and work. The combination of words and pictures make this a wonderful addition to the library of all Lewis scholars and readers.

Speaking of Jack: A C. S. Lewis Discussion Guide
Will Vaus

C. S. Lewis Societies have been forming around the world since the first one started in New York City in 1969. Will Vaus has started and led three groups himself. *Speaking of Jack* is the result of Vaus' experience in leading those Lewis Societies. Included here are introductions to most of Lewis' books as well as questions designed to stimulate discussion about Lewis' life and work. These materials have been "road-tested" with real groups made up of young and old, some very familiar with Lewis and some newcomers. *Speaking of Jack* may be used in an existing book discussion group, to start a C. S. Lewis Society, or as a guide to your own exploration of Lewis' books.

Light: C. S. Lewis's First and Final Short Story
Charlie W. Starr
Foreword by Walter Hooper

Charlie Starr explores the questions surrounding the "Light" manuscript, a later version of story titled "A Man Born Blind." The insights into this story provide a na ew key to understanding some of Lewis's most profound ideas.

"*As literary journalism, both investigative and critical, it is top shelf*"
    James Como, author of *Remembering C. S. Lewis*

"*Starr shines a new and illuminating light on one of Lewis's most intriguing stories*"
    Michael Ward, author of *Planet Narnia*

C. S. Lewis & Philosophy as a Way of Life: His Philosophical Thoughts
Adam Barkman

C. S. Lewis is rarely thought of as a "philosopher" per se despite having both studied and taught philosophy for several years at Oxford. Lewis's long journey to Christianity was essentially philosophical – passing through seven different stages. This 624 page book is an invaluable reference for C. S. Lewis scholars and fans alike

WWW.WINGEDLIONPRESS.COM

C. S. Lewis' Top Ten: Influential Books and Authors, Volume One
Will Vaus

Based on his books, marginal notes, and personal letters, Will Vaus explores Lewis' reading of the ten books he said shaped his vocational attitude and philosophy of life. Volume One covers the first three authors/books: George MacDonald: *Phantastes*, G.K. Chesterton: *The Everlasting Man*, and Virgil: *The Aneid*. Vaus offers a brief biography of each author with a helpful summary of their books.

"Thorough, comprehensive, and illuminating"
    Rolland Hein, Author of *George MacDonald: Victorian Mythmaker*

C. S. Lewis' Top Ten: Influential Books and Authors, Volume Two
Will Vaus

Volume Two covers the following authors/books: George Herbert: *The Temple*, William Wordsworth: *The Prelude*, Rudopf Otto, *The Idea of the Holy*.

C. S. Lewis' Top Ten: Influential Books and Authors, Volume Three
Will Vaus

Volume Three covers the following authors/books: Boethius: *The Consolation of Philosophy*, James Boswell, *The Life of Samuel Johnson*, Charles Williams: *Descent into Hell*, A.J. Balfour: *Thiesm and Humanism*.

C. S. Lewis Goes to Heaven:
A Reader's Guide to The Great Divorce
David G. Clark

This is the first book devoted solely to this often neglected book and the first to reveal several important secrets Lewis concealed within the story. Lewis felt his imaginary trip to Hell and Heaven was far better than his book *The Screwtape Letters*, which has become a classic. Readers will discover the many literary and biblical influences Lewis utilized in writing his brilliant novel.

C. S. Lewis Goes to Hell
A Companion and Study Guide to The Screwtape Letters
William O'Flaherty

The creator and host of "All About Jack" (a podcast feature of EssentialCSLewis.com) has written a guide to *The Screwtape Letters* suitable for groups or individuals. Features include a topic index of major and minor themes, summaries of each letter, questions for reflection, and over a half-dozen appendices of useful information.

Informing the Inklings: George MacDonald & the Roots of Modern Fantasy
Michael Partridge and Kirstin Jeffrey Johnson, Editors
Preface by Stephen Prickett

In the summer of 2014, the George MacDonald Society held a conference at Magdalen, C.S. Lewis' old college in Oxford. Twelve papers from the conference were selected for publication by established and new scholars mining the depths of the rich correlations between fantasy writers of the 19th and 20th centuries.

Joy and Poetic Imagination: Understanding C. S. Lewis's "Great War" with Owen Barfield and its Significance for Lewis's Conversion and Writings
Stephen Thorson

Author Stephen Thorson began writing this book over 30 years ago and published parts of it in articles during Barfield's lifetime. Barfield wrote to Thorson in 1983 saying, ""*...you have surveyed the divergence between Lewis and myself very fairly, and truly 'in depth...*'". This book explains the "Great War" between these two friends.

Exploring the Eternal Goodness: Selected Writings of David L. Neuhouser
Joe Ricke and Lisa Ritchie, Editors

In 1997, due to David's perseverance, the Brown Collection of books by and about C. S. Lewis and related authors came to Taylor University and the Lewis and Friends Colloquium began. This book of selected writings reflects his scholarship in math and literature, as well as his musings on beauty and the imagination. The twenty-one tributes are an indication of the many lives he has influenced. This book is meant to acknowledge David L. Neuhouser for his contributions to scholarship and to honor his life of friendship, encouragement, and genuine goodness.

Inklings Forever, Volume X: Proceedings from the 10th Francis White Ewbank Colloquiunm on C. S. Lewis & Friends
Joe Ricke and Rick Hill, Editors

In June 2016, the 10th biennial Frances Ewbank Colloquium on C. S. Lewis and Friends convened at Taylor University with the special theme of "friendship." Many of the essays and creative pieces collected in this book explore the important relationships of Inklings-related authors, as well as the relationships between those authors and other, sometimes rather surprising, "friends." The year 2016 marked the 90th anniversary of the first meeting of C.S. Lewis and J.R.R. Tolkien – a creative friendship of epic proportions

> *What a feast! It is rare that a book of proceedings captures the energy and spirit of the conference itself: this one does. I recommend it.*
>
> Diana Pavlac Glyer, Professor of English at Azusa Pacific University and author of *The Company They Keep* and *Bandersnatch: C. S. Lewis, J. R. R. Tolkien, and the Creative Collaboration of the Inklings*

Mythopoeic Narnia: Memory, Metaphor, and Metamorphoses in C. S. Lewis's The Chronicles of Narnia
Salwa Khoddam

Dr. Khoddam offers a fresh approach to the *Narnia* books based on an inquiry into Lewis' readings and use of classical and Christian symbols. She explores the literary and intellectual contexts of these stories, the traditional myths and motifs, and places them in the company of the greatest Christian mythopoeic works of Western Literature.

CHRISTIAN LIVING

Keys to Growth: Meditations on the Acts of the Apostles
Will Vaus

Every living thing or person requires certain ingredients in order to grow, and if a thing or person is not growing, it is dying. *The Acts of the Apostles* is a book that is all about growth. Will Vaus has been meditating and preaching on *Acts* for the past 30 years. In this volume, he offers the reader forty-one keys from the entire book of Acts to unlock spiritual growth in everyday life.

Open Before Christmas: Devotional Thoughts For The Holiday Season
Will Vaus

Author Will Vaus seeks to deepen the reader's knowledge of Advent and Christmas leading up to Epiphany. Readers are provided with devotional thoughts for each day that help them to experience this part of the Church Year perhaps in a more spiritually enriching way than ever before.

"Seasoned with inspiring, touching, and sometimes humorous illustrations .... I found his writing immediately engaging and, the more I read, the more I liked it. God has touched my heart by reading Open Before Christmas, and I believe he will touch your heart too."
    The Rev. David Beckmann, The C.S. Lewis Society of Chattanooga

God's Love Letter: Reflections on I John
Will Vaus

Various words for "love" appear thirty-five times in the five brief chapters of I John. This book invites you on a journey of reading and reflection: reading this book in the New Testament and reflecting on God's love for us, our love for God, and our love for one another.

Jogging with G.K. Chsterton: 65 Earthshaking Expeditions
Robert Moore-Jumonville

Jogging with G.K. Chesterton is a showcase for the merry mind of Chesterton. But Chesterton's lighthearted wit always runs side-by-side with his weighty wisdom. These 65 "earthshaking expeditions" will keep you smiling and thinking from start to finish. You'll be entertained, challenged, and spiritually uplifted as you take time to breath in the fresh morning air and contemplate the wonders of the world.

"This is a delightfully improbable book in which Chesterton puts us through our spiritual and intellectual exercises."
    Joseph Pearce, author of *Wisdom and Innocence: A Life of G.K. Chesterton*

GEORGE MACDONALD

Diary of an Old Soul & The White Page Poems
George MacDonald and Betty Aberlin

The first edition of George MacDonald's book of daily poems included a blank page opposite each page of poems. Readers were invited to write their own reflections on the "white page." MacDonald wrote: "Let your white page be ground, my print be seed, growing to golden ears, that faith and hope may feed." Betty Aberlin responded to MacDonald's invitation with daily poems of her own.

> *Betty Aberlin's close readings of George MacDonald's verses and her thoughtful responses to them speak clearly of her poetic gifts and spiritual intelligence.*
> Luci Shaw, poet

George MacDonald: Literary Heritage and Heirs
Roderick McGillis, editor

This latest collection of 14 essays sets a new standard that will influence MacDonald studies for many more years. George MacDonald experts are increasingly evaluating his entire corpus within the nineteenth century context.

> *This comprehensive collection represents the best of contemporary scholarship on George MacDonald.*
> Rolland Hein, author of *George MacDonald: Victorian Mythmaker*

In the Near Loss of Everything: George MacDonald's Son in America
Dale Wayne Slusser

In the summer of 1887, George MacDonald's son Ronald, newly engaged to artist Louise Blandy, sailed from England to America to teach school. The next summer he returned to England to marry Louise and bring her back to America. On August 27, 1890, Louise died leaving him with an infant daughter. Ronald once described losing a beloved spouse as "the near loss of everything". Dale Wayne Slusser unfolds this poignant story with unpublished letters and photos that give readers a glimpse into the close-knit MacDonald family. Also included is Ronald's essay about his father, *George MacDonald: A Personal Note*, plus a selection from Ronald's 1922 fable, *The Laughing Elf*, about the necessity of both sorrow and joy in life.

A Novel Pulpit: Sermons From George MacDonald's Fiction
David L. Neuhouser

Each of the sermons has an introduction giving some explanation of the setting of the sermon or of the plot, if that is necessary for understanding the sermon. "MacDonald's novels are both stimulating and thought-provoking. This collection of sermons from ten novels serve to bring out the 'freshness and brilliance' of MacDonald's message." *from the author's introduction*

Behind the Back of the North Wind: Essays on George MacDonald's Classic Book
Edited and with Introduction by John Pennington and Roderick McGillis

The unique blend of fairy tale atmosphere and social realism in this novel laid the groundwork for modern fantasy literature. Sixteen essays by various authors are accompanied by an instructive introduction, extensive index, and beautiful illustrations.

Through the Year with George MacDonald: 366 Daily Readings
Rolland Hein, editor

These page-length excerpts from sermons, novels and letters are given an appropriate theme/heading and a complementary Scripture passage for daily reading. An inspiring introduction to the artistic soul and Christian vision of George MacDonald.

Shadows and Chivalry:
C. S. Lewis and George MacDonald on Suffering, Evil, and Death
Jeff McInnis

Shadows and Chivalry studies the influence of George MacDonald, a nineteenth-century Scottish novelist and fantasy writer, upon one of the most influential writers of modern times, C. S. Lewis—the creator of Narnia, literary critic, and best-selling apologist. This study attempts to trace the overall affect of MacDonald's work on Lewis's thought and imagination. Without ever ceasing to be a story of one man's influence upon another, the study also serves as an exploration of each writer's thought on, and literary visions of, good and evil.

Crossing a Great Frontier: Essays on George MacDonald's Phantastest
John Pennington, Editor

"This is the first collection of scholarly essays on George MacDonald's seminal romance Phantastes. Appropriately to the age of its hero Anodos, here we have twenty-one of the best essays written on Phantastes from 1972 onwards, in which straightforward literary analysis works together with contextual, psychological, metaphysical, alchemical and scientific approaches to the elucidation of this moving and elusive work."

    Colin Manlove, author of *Scotland's Forgotten Treasure: The Visionary Novels of George MacDonald*

The Downstretched Hand:
Individual Development in MacDonald's Major Fantasies for Children
Lesley Willis Smith

Smith demonstrates that MacDonald is fully aware of the need to integrate the unconscious into the conscious in order to achieve mature individuation. However, for MacDonald, true maturity and fulfillment can only be gained through a relationship with God. By exploring MacDonald's major biblical themes into his own myth, Smith reveals his literary genius and profound understanding of the human psyche. Smith interacts with other leading scholarship and in the context of other works by MacDonald, especially those written during the same time period.

Pop Culture

To Love Another Person: A Spiritual Journey Through Les Miserables
John Morrison

The powerful story of Jean Valjean's redemption is beloved by readers and theater goers everywhere. In this companion and guide to Victor Hugo's masterpiece, author John Morrison unfolds the spiritual depth and breadth of this classic novel and broadway musical.

Through Common Things: Philosophical Reflections on Popular Culture
Adam Barkman

"Barkman presents us with an amazingly wide-ranging collection of philosophical reflections grounded in the everyday things of popular culture – past and present, eastern and western, factual and fictional. Throughout his encounters with often surprising subject-matter (the value of darkness?), he writes clearly and concisely, moving seamlessly between Aristotle and anime, Lord Buddha and Lord Voldemort.... This is an informative and entertaining book to read!"
     Doug Bloomberg, Professor of Philosophy, Institute for Christian Studies

The Many Faces of Katniss Everdeen: Exploring the Heroine of The Hunger Games
Valerie Estelle Frankel

Katniss is the heroine who's changed the world. Like Harry Potter, she explodes across genres: She is a dystopian heroine, a warrior woman, a reality TV star, a rebellious adolescent. She's surrounded by the figures of Roman history, from Caesar and Cato to Cinna and Coriolanus Snow. She's also traveling the classic heroine's journey. As a child soldier, she faces trauma; as a growing teen, she battles through love triangles and the struggle to be good in a harsh world. This book explores all this and more, while taking a look at the series' symbolism, from food to storytelling, to show how Katniss becomes the greatest power of Panem, the girl on fire.

Myths and Motifs of The Mortal Instruments
Valerie Estelle Frankel

With vampires, fairies, angels, romance, steampunk, and modern New York all in one series of books, Cassandra Clare is exploding onto the scene. This book explores the deeper world of the Shadowhunters. There's something for everyone, as this book reveals unseen lore within the bestselling series.

Virtuous Worlds: The Video Gamer's Guide to Spiritual Truth
John Stanifer

Popular titles like *Halo 3* and *The Legend of Zelda: Twilight Princess* fly off shelves at a mind-blowing rate. John Stanifer, an avid gamer, shows readers specific parallels between Christian faith and the content of their favorite games. Written with wry humor (including a heckler who frequently pokes fun at the author) this book will appeal to gamers and non-gamers alike. Those unfamiliar with video games may be pleasantly surprised to find that many elements in those "virtual worlds" also qualify them as "virtuous worlds."

BIOGRAPHY

Sheldon Vanauken: The Man Who Received "A Severe Mercy"
Will Vaus

In this biography we discover: Vanauken the struggling student, the bon-vivant lover, the sailor who witnessed the bombing of Pearl Harbor, the seeker who returned to faith through C. S. Lewis, the beloved professor of English literature and history, the feminist and anti-war activist who participated in the March on the Pentagon, the bestselling author, and Vanauken the convert to Catholicism. What emerges is the portrait of a man relentlessly in search of beauty, love, and truth, a man who believed that, in the end, he found all three.

"*This is a charming biography about a doubly charming man who wrote a triply charming book. It is a great way to meet the man behind A Severe Mercy.*"

Peter Kreeft, author of *Jacob's Ladder: 10 Steps to Truth*

Remembering Roy Campbell: The Memoirs of his Daughters, Anna and Tess
Introduction by Judith Lütge Coullie, Editor
Preface by Joseph Pearce

Anna and Teresa Campbell were the daughters of the handsome young South African poet and writer, Roy Campbell (1901-1957), and his beautiful English wife, Mary Garman. In their frank and moving memoirs, Anna and Tess recall the extraordinary, and often very difficult, lives they shared with their exceptional parents. Over 50 photos, 344 footnotes, timeline of Campbell's life, and complete index.

Harry Potter

The Order of Harry Potter: The Literary Skill of the Hogwarts Epic
Colin Manlove

Colin Manlove, a popular conference speaker and author of over a dozen books, has earned an international reputation as an expert on fantasy and children's literature. His book, *From Alice to Harry Potter*, is a survey of 400 English fantasy books. In *The Order of Harry Potter*, he compares and contrasts *Harry Potter* with works by "Inklings" writers J.R.R. Tolkien, C. S. Lewis and Charles Williams; he also examines Rowling's treatment of the topic of imagination; her skill in organization and the use of language; and the book's underlying motifs and themes.

Harry Potter & Imagination: The Way Between Two Worlds
Travis Prinzi

Imaginative literature places a reader between two worlds: the story world and the world of daily life, and challenges the reader to imagine and to act for a better world. Starting with discussion of Harry Potter's more important themes, *Harry Potter & Imagination* takes readers on a journey through the transformative power of those themes for both the individual and for culture by placing Rowling's series in its literary, historical, and cultural contexts.

Hog's Head Conversations: Essays on Harry Potter
Travis Prinzi, Editor

Ten fascinating essays on Harry Potter by popular Potter writers and speakers including John Granger, James W. Thomas, Colin Manlove, and Travis Prinzi.

Repotting Harry Potter: A Professor's Guide for the Serious Re-Reader
Rowling Revisited: Return Trips to Harry, Fantastic Beasts, Quidditch, & Beedle the Bard
Dr. James W. Thomas

In *Repotting Harry Potter* and his sequel book *Rowling Revisited*, Dr. James W. Thomas points out the humor, puns, foreshadowing and literary parallels in the Potter books. In *Rowling Revisted*, readers will especially find useful three extensive appendixes – "Fantastic Beasts and the Pages Where You'll Find Them," "Quidditch Through the Pages," and "The Books in the Potter Books." Dr. Thomas makes re-reading the Potter books even more rewarding and enjoyable.

Sociology and Harry Potter: 22 Enchanting Essays on the Wizarding World
Jenn Simms, Editor

Modeled on an Introduction to Sociology textbook, this book is not simply about the series, but also uses the series to facilitate the reader's understanding of the discipline of sociology and a develops a sociological approach to viewing social reality. It is a case of high quality academic scholarship written in a form and on a topic accessible to non-academics. As such, it is written to appeal to Harry Potter fans and the general reading public. Contributors include professional sociologists from eight countries.

Harry Potter, Still Recruiting: An Inner Look at Harry Potter Fandom
Valerie Frankel

The Harry Potter phenomenon has created a new world: one of Quidditch in the park, lightning earrings, endless parodies, a new genre of music, and fan conferences of epic proportions. This book attempts to document everything - exploring costuming, crafting, gaming, and more, with essays and interviews straight from the multitude of creators. From children to adults, fans are delighting the world with an explosion of captivating activities and experiences, all based on Rowling's delightful series.

POETS AND POETRY

In the Eye of the Beholder: How to See the World Like a Romantic Poet
Louis Markos

Born out of the French Revolution and its radical faith that a nation could be shaped and altered by the dreams and visions of its people, British Romantic Poetry was founded on a belief that the objects and realities of our world, whether natural or human, are not fixed in stone but can be molded and transformed by the visionary eye of the poet. A separate bibliographical essay is provided for readers listing accessible biographies of each poet and critical studies of their work.

The Cat on the Catamaran: A Christmas Tale
John Martin

Here is a modern-day parable of a modern-day cat with modern-day attitudes. Riverboat Dan is a "cool" cat on a perpetual vacation from responsibility. He's *The Cat on the Catamaran* – sailing down the river of life. Dan keeps his guilty conscience from interfering with his fun until he runs into trouble. But will he have the courage to believe that it's never too late to change course? (For ages 10 to adult)

www.ingramcontent.com/pod-product-compliance
Lightning Source LLC
Chambersburg PA
CBHW030322100526
44592CB00010B/530